THE GREAT WORK OF PROVIDENCE

The Great Work of Providence

Jonathan Edwards for Life Today

 RACHEL S. STAHLE

CASCADE *Books* • Eugene, Oregon

THE GREAT WORK OF PROVIDENCE
Jonathan Edwards for Life Today

Copyright © 2010 Rachel S. Stahle. All rights reserved. Except for brief quotations in critical publications or reviews, no part of this book may be reproduced in any manner without prior written permission from the publisher. Write: Permissions, Wipf and Stock Publishers, 199 W. 8th Ave., Suite 3, Eugene, OR 97401.

Cascade Books
An Imprint of Wipf and Stock Publishers
199 W. 8th Ave., Suite 3
Eugene, OR 97401

www.wipfandstock.com

ISBN 13: 978-1-60608-482-3

Cataloguing-in-Publication data:

Stahle, Rachel S.

    The great work of providence: Jonathan Edwards for life today / Rachel S. Stahle.

    xvi + 196 p. ; 23 cm. Includes bibliographical references and index.

    ISBN 13: 978-1-60608-482-3

    1. Edwards, Jonathan, 1703–1758. I. Title.

BX 7260 .E3 S73 2010

Manufactured in the U.S.A.

For Jessica, Gavin, and Aidan

With love, prayers, and hopes
For the woman you are and
For the kind of men you'll soon be

*Even youths grow tired and weary,
and young men stumble and fall;
but those who hope in the LORD
will renew their strength.
They will soar on wings like eagles;
they will run and not grow weary,
they will walk and not be faint.*
Isaiah 40:30–31 (NIV)

Contents

Acknowledgments | *ix*
Abbreviations | *x*

1 The Trinitarian God, through Edwards's Eyes | 1
2 The Trinity Revealed through Creation | 24
3 God's Solution to the Problem of Sin | 49
4 Personal Experience of God | 77
5 The Religious Experience of Christ's Church | 104
6 Spiritual Renewal of the Church | 130
7 The End of the World, and Beyond | 148
8 Sinners in the Hands of an Angry God? | 171

Bibliography | *193*
Index | *197*

✺ Acknowledgments

This project has been in the works off and on for about twenty years. Over that extended time I have been greatly blessed to have people in my life who have encouraged me and sustained me in a variety of ways. The fact that this book is being published is a testimony to them and, above all, to the Lord God. So with gratitude I mention Drs. Wayne Christopherson, Chuck Cline, Howard Friday, Andy Hoffecker, Edith Humphrey, Rick Lints, Richard Lovelace, Michael McGonigal, Ken Minkema, Bob Neville, Garth Rosell, Joel Scandrett, Sharon Taylor, David Wells, and Wesley Wildman. Others who have graciously come alongside are Rev. Rod and Christy Bakker, Pam Bowman, Dr. Rob and Meredith Joss, Nancy, Dave, Connor, and Kyle Kooyers, Patti Picardi Law, Rev. Dan and Beth Merry, Sarina Odden Meyer, Rev. Eric and Holly Nelson, Barb Ostrowski, and Rev. Jim Tinnemeyer. Wipf & Stock Editors Jim Tedrick and Charlie Collier and Editorial Assistant Christian Amondson have been gracious delights to work with. And last but not least, I mention my mother, Susan, who has been an inspiring example of perseverance and courage and a loving friend. In great and small ways each of you has contributed to this book through your kindnesses to me. Thank you.

Abbreviations

Volumes

BT 2 — *The Works of Jonathan Edwards*. Vol. 2. Edinburgh: Banner of Truth Trust, 1974.

WJE 1 — *The Works of Jonathan Edwards*, vol. 1: *Freedom of the Will*. Edited by Paul Ramsey. New Haven: Yale University Press, 1957.

WJE 2 — *The Works of Jonathan Edwards*, vol. 2: *Religious Affections*. Edited by John E. Smith. New Haven: Yale University Press, 1959.

WJE 3 — *The Works of Jonathan Edwards*, vol. 3: *Original Sin*. Edited by Clyde A. Holbrook. New Haven: Yale University Press, 1970.

WJE 4 — *The Works of Jonathan Edwards*, vol. 4: *The Great Awakening*. Edited by C. C. Goen. New Haven: Yale University Press, 1972.

WJE 5 — *The Works of Jonathan Edwards*, vol. 5: *Apocalyptic Writings*. Edited by Stephen J. Stein. New Haven: Yale University Press, 1977.

WJE 6 — *The Works of Jonathan Edwards*, vol. 6: *Scientific and Philosophical Writings*. Edited by Wallace E. Anderson. New Haven: Yale University Press, 1980.

WJE 7 — *The Works of Jonathan Edwards*, vol. 7: *The Life of David Brainerd*. Edited by Norman Pettit. New Haven: Yale University Press, 1985.

WJE 8 — *The Works of Jonathan Edwards*, vol. 8: *Ethical Writings*. Edited by Paul Ramsey. New Haven: Yale University Press, 1989.

WJE 9	*The Works of Jonathan Edwards*, vol. 9: *A History of the Work of Redemption*. Edited by John F. Wilson. New Haven: Yale University Press, 1989.
WJE 10	*The Works of Jonathan Edwards*, vol. 10: *Sermons and Discourses 1720–1723*. Edited by Wilson H. Kimnach. New Haven: Yale University Press, 1992.
WJE 11	*The Works of Jonathan Edwards*, vol. 11: *Typological Writings*. Edited by Wallace E. Anderson and Mason I. Lowance Jr., with David Watters. New Haven: Yale University Press, 1993.
WJE 12	*The Works of Jonathan Edwards*, vol. 12: *Ecclesiastical Writings*. Edited by David D. Hall. New Haven: Yale University Press, 1994.
WJE 13	*The Works of Jonathan Edwards*, vol. 13: *The "Miscellanies," Entry Nos. a–z, aa–zz, 1–500*. Edited by Thomas A. Schafer. New Haven: Yale University Press, 1994.
WJE 14	*The Works of Jonathan Edwards*, vol. 14: *Sermons and Discourses 1723–1729*. Edited by Kenneth P. Minkema. New Haven: Yale University Press, 1997.
WJE 15	*The Works of Jonathan Edwards*, vol. 15: *Notes on Scripture*. Edited by Stephen J. Stein. New Haven: Yale University Press, 1998.
WJE 16	*The Works of Jonathan Edwards*, vol. 16: *Letters and Personal Writings*. Edited by George S. Claghorn. New Haven: Yale University Press, 1998.
WJE 17	*The Works of Jonathan Edwards*, vol. 17: *Sermons and Discourses, 1730–1733*. Edited by Mark Valeri. New Haven: Yale University Press, 1999.
WJE 18	*The Works of Jonathan Edwards*, vol. 18: *The "Miscellanies," Entry Nos. 501–832*. Edited by Ava Chamberlain. New Haven: Yale University Press, 2000.
WJE 19	*The Works of Jonathan Edwards*, vol. 19: *Sermons and Discourses, 1734–1738*. Edited by M. X. Lesser. New Haven: Yale University Press, 2001.
WJE 20	*The Works of Jonathan Edwards*, vol. 20: *The "Miscellanies," Entry Nos. 833–1152*. Edited by Amy Plantinga Pauw. New Haven: Yale University Press, 2002.

WJE 21 *The Works of Jonathan Edwards*, vol. 21: *Writings on the Trinity, Grace, and Faith*. Edited by Sang Hyun Lee. New Haven: Yale University Press, 2003.

WJE 22 *The Works of Jonathan Edwards*, vol. 22: *Sermons and Discourses, 1739–1742*. Edited by Harry S. Stout et al. New Haven: Yale University Press, 2003.

WJE 23 *The Works of Jonathan Edwards*, vol. 23: *The "Miscellanies" Entry Nos. 1153–1360*. Edited by Douglas A. Sweeney. New Haven: Yale University Press, 2004.

WJE 24 *The Works of Jonathan Edwards*, vol. 24: *Pts. 1 & 2: The "Blank Bible."* Edited by Stephen J. Stein. New Haven: Yale University Press, 2006.

WJE 25 *The Works of Jonathan Edwards*, vol. 25: *Sermons and Discourses, 1743–1758*. Edited by Wilson H. Kimnach. New Haven: Yale University Press, 2006.

Documents

"Apocalypse" "Notes on the Apocalypse," *WJE 5*
"Atoms" "Of Atoms," *WJE 6*
"Attempt" "An Humble Attempt to Promote Explicit Agreement and Visible Union of God's People in Extraordinary Prayer for the Revival of Religion and the Advancement of Christ's Kingdom on Earth," *WJE 5*
"Being" "Of Being," *WJE 6*
"Beauty" "Beauty of the World," *WJE 6*
"Calamity" "Sin and Wickedness Bring Calamity and Misery on a People," *WJE 14*
"Charity" "Charity and Its Fruits," *WJE 8*
"Christ" "The Excellency of Christ," *WJE 19*
"Colman" "To the Reverend Benjamin Colman, May 30, 1735," *WJE 16*
"Consideration" "The Sole Consideration, That God Is God, Sufficient to Still All Objections to His Sovereignty," *BT 2*
"Controversy" "Narrative of Communion Controversy," *WJE 12*
"Corrected" "Misrepresentations Corrected," *WJE 12*
"Dedication" "Dedication to God," *WJE 10*

"Denied"	"A Spiritual Understanding of Divine Things Denied to the Unregenerate," *WJE 14*
"Dependence"	"God Glorified in Man's Dependence," *WJE 17*
"Discourse"	"Discourse on the Trinity," *WJE 21*
"Divine"	"A Divine and Supernatural Light," *WJE 17*
"Dudley"	"To Judge Paul Dudley, October 31, 1723," *WJE 16*
"Duty"	"The Duty of Hearkening to God's Voice," *WJE 10*
"End"	"Concerning the End for Which God Created the World," *WJE 8*
"Equality"	"On the Equality of the Persons of the Trinity," *WJE 21*
"Erskine A"	"To the Reverend John Erskine, November 15, 1750," *WJE 16*
"Erskine B"	"To the Reverend John Erskine, July 25, 1757," *WJE 16*
"Erskine C"	"Letter to John Erskine, August 3, 1757," *WJE 1*
"Excellencies"	"God's Excellencies," *WJE 10*
"Faithful"	"A Faithful Narrative of the Surprising Work of God," *WJE 4*
"Feast"	"The Spiritual Blessings of the Gospel Represented by a Feast," *WJE 14*
"Future"	"The Importance of a Future State," *WJE 10*
"Gillespie A"	"To the Reverend Thomas Gillespie, September 4, 1747," *WJE 16*
"Gillespie B"	"To the Reverend Thomas Gillespie of Carnock, Scotland," *WJE 4*
"Glorying"	"Glorying in the Savior," *WJE 14*
"Grace"	"Treatise on Grace," *WJE 21*
"Hearers"	"Profitable Hearers of the Word," *WJE 14*
"Heaven"	"Heaven Is a World of Love," *WJE 8*
"Holiness"	"The Way of Holiness," *WJE 10*
"Images"	"Images of Divine Things," *WJE 11*
"Impending"	"Impending Judgments Averted Only by Reformation," *WJE 14*
"Inquiry"	"An Humble Inquiry into the Rules of the Word of God, Concerning the Qualifications Requisite to a Complete Standing and Full Communion in the Visible Christian Church," *WJE 12*
"Job"	"The Nakedness of Job," *WJE 10*
"Judgment"	"The Day of Judgment," *WJE 14*

"Justification"	"Justification by Faith Alone," *WJE 19*
"Life"	"Life through Christ Alone," *WJE 10*
"Light"	"Christ, the Light of the World," *WJE 10*
"Living"	"Living to Christ *and* Dying to Gain," *WJE 10*
"Marks"	"The Distinguishing Marks of a Work of the Spirit of God," *WJE 4*
"McCulloch A"	"To the Rev. William McCulloch of Cambuslang, Scotland, May 12, 1743," *WJE 16*
"McCulloch B"	"To the Reverend William McCulloch, March 5, 1744," *WJE 16*
"McCulloch C"	"To the Reverend William McCulloch, January 21, 1747," *WJE 16*
"Messiah"	"Types of the Messiah," *WJE 11*
"Mind"	"The Mind," *WJE 6*
"Most High"	"The Most High God a Prayer-Hearing God," *BT 2*
"Nobleness"	"True Nobleness of Mind," *WJE 14*
"None Saved"	"None Are Saved by Their Own Righteousness," *WJE 14*
"Nothing"	"Nothing upon Earth Can Represent the Glories of Heaven," *WJE 14*
"Peaceably"	"Living Peaceably One with Another," *WJE 14*
"Pepperrell"	"To Lady Mary Pepperrell, November 28, 1751," *WJE 16*
"Personal"	"Personal Narrative," *WJE 16*
"Pleasantness"	"The Pleasantness of Religion," *WJE 14*
"Preface"	"Preface to *True Religion*," *WJE 4*
"Reasonable"	"All God's Methods Are Most Reasonable," *WJE 14*
"Scotland"	"To a Correspondent in Scotland, November, 1745," *WJE 5*
"Self-Exam"	"The Duty of Self-Examination," *WJE 10*
"Sinners"	"Sinners in the Hands of an Angry God," *WJE 22*
"Sufficiency"	"God's All-Sufficiency for the Supply of Our Wants," *WJE 14*
"Things"	"Things to Be Considered an[d] Written Fully About," *WJE 6*
"Thoughts"	"Some Thoughts Concerning the Present Revival of Religion in New England," *WJE 4*
"Threefold"	"The Threefold Work of the Holy Ghost," *WJE 14*

"Torments"	"The Torments of Hell Are Exceeding Great," *WJE 14*
"True Love"	"True Love to God," *WJE 10*
"Trustees"	"To the Trustees of the College of New Jersey, October 19, 1757," *WJE 16*
"Types"	"Types," *WJE 11*
"Unconverted"	"Living Unconverted under an Eminent Means of Grace," *WJE 14*
"Unknown"	"To an Unknown Correspondent, after March 13, 1746," *WJE 16*
"Value"	"The Value of Salvation," *WJE 10*
"Virtue"	"The Nature of True Virtue," *WJE 8*
"Warnings"	"Warnings of Future Punishment Don't Seem Real to the Wicked," *WJE 14*
"Wicked"	"Wicked Men Useful in Their Destruction Only," *BT 2*

1

The Trinitarian God, through Edwards's Eyes

First Things First: Why Jonathan Edwards?

RECENTLY I PREACHED AT a local church in place of a vacationing pastor and afterward was treated to lunch by two elders at a delightful mom-and-pop restaurant. I did not know them very well, so we spent a good amount of time asking and answering basic "get-to-know-you" questions. These ladies were generally aware of my background, but were curious about the topic of my doctoral dissertation. "Why did you pick Jonathan Edwards?" Good question.

I came to faith in Jesus Christ as a college sophomore and immediately had questions about . . . well, everything related to God, the Bible, and my conversion experience, which I quickly learned had been unusual. One of my college professors, Dr. Andy Hoffecker, suggested that I read Edwards's writings about conversion and revival—and the rest, as the cliché goes, is history.[1] I did not spend every waking moment reading Edwards, but kept returning to him from time to time on various topics as they arose during my maturation in faith. While I certainly studied other pastors and theologians, Edwards spoke to me in a way no one else did. My interest in his thoughts about revival was further piqued as my college joined others in experiencing widespread spiritual renewal. That interest in turn yielded my seminary master's thesis about Edwards's revival theology.

---

1. Rev. Dr. W. Andrew Hoffecker Jr., is now Professor of Church History at Reformed Theological Seminary in Jackson, Mississippi.

So doing a dissertation about Edwards may seem to some a quirky choice for a late twentieth-century female Presbyterian. But the ladies I enjoyed lunch with that Sunday came to see that this work has never been merely an intellectual curiosity, but a deeply personal venture to understand God and myself. Contrary to what many assume, what Edwards believed and had to say is profoundly relevant to Christians today—and that is why I revised and updated my doctoral dissertation to present this book to you. My hope is not just that you understand what Edwards believed and appreciate his brilliance. My desire is not just that you are moved by his intentionally biblical portrait of God, a grand God who is utterly lovely and beautiful. My hope above all is that this work will either stir you to new faith in Jesus Christ, or bring greater depth to the faith you have already been blessed with. Whatever the case, I know you will be challenged to evaluate what you believe, and why.

But really—how relevant can an eighteenth-century pastor-theologian, and a male WASP no less, possibly be for us today? I have had numerous friends tell me that they have tried to study Edwards and other Christian thinkers of his ilk. Their earnest attempts quickly turned to frustration and perplexity when they picked up the Puritan's writings only to find that they are penned in archaic language comprising marathon sentences, and marathon paragraphs, with marathon lists of supporting Scripture passages . . . and it's sometimes too much for even the most sincere student of religion or seeker of Truth.[2]

So what I have endeavored to do is to eliminate for you the foreignness of Jonathan Edwards's language and writing style while bringing you to the heart of his ideas. For me his ideas, and indeed his entire theological system, have their own beauty—yes, ideas and theology can be beautiful in their symmetry, their faithfulness to Scripture, how well they honor God, and essentially how close they come to bringing us all to Truth. You may not agree with or understand everything you are about to read. But I assure you that in the end, you will have had an astounding new world opened for you—a world that is held gently and loved by God, all seen through Jonathan Edwards's eyes.

---

2. Throughout this work, I mention from time to time key Bible verses Edwards uses to support his theology. Those I note are a tiny sampling of the passages referenced in his writings.

"The Contemplation of Supreme Things"

On October 31, 1723, Jonathan Edwards composed a letter to Judge Paul Dudley that captured his reflections on "the wondrous and curious works of the spider."[3] Later dubbed the "Spider Letter," it eventually became one of Edwards's more famous writings chiefly because it demonstrates his ability to make meticulous observations about the world around him and derive from them principles about nature's laws. In his comments we see the keen intellect of a thoughtful young scholar who at the age of twenty-three still possessed a child-like wonder at the most minuscule of life's matters. We see the patience of an amateur scientist who must have spent hours watching his subjects being blown from limb to branch, spinning their webs "with that wonderful liquor with which their bottle tail is filled, that may so easily be drawn out so exceeding fine."[4] We may even muse at his being "very conversant" with these flying spiders, "these wondrous animals" many of us would rather avoid or squish than spend our time considering.[5]

Above all, we observe that in the "Spider Letter" Edwards is an avid seeker of God. He saw in all of history and nature the wisdom and goodness of the Creator in providing "for all the necessities, but also for the pleasure and recreation of all sorts of creatures, even the insects."[6] Edwards's God is one who is intimately involved in every conceivable detail of existence down to the function and particles of the atoms, and who has designed and purposed all of reality for his own glory through the manifestation of his loving character.[7]

So the value of the "Spider Letter" for our purposes goes beyond its descriptions of biology, and even further beyond Edwards's impressions of the work of God in the natural realm. This brief letter captures for us the theologian's fundamental assumptions about God and about the dependence of reality and its creatures upon God. For Edwards, there is no sharp dichotomy between material and spiritual reality because their purposes and existence are intertwined as part of God's grand design for

---

3. "Dudley," 42. Judge Paul Dudley (1675–1751) was an ardent Puritan and highly respected judge from a prominent Massachusetts family.

4. "Dudley," 45.

5. "Dudley," 43.

6. "Dudley," 45.

7. Throughout this work, male pronouns will be used in reference to God to be consistent with Edwards's own use of them.

creation and, ultimately, redemption. According to Edwards, the God of the Scriptures is not only the God of biblical history, but also of every other historical moment, down to the smallest fraction of a second. As we will see later, every moment is a new creation by the all-sustaining, sovereign God. For Edwards, the activity of this powerful, foreordaining God can and should be earnestly appreciated by humans, who are made in God's image. God desires that they enjoy him by seeing and celebrating his handiwork in creation and in the events of providence.

Humanity's enjoyment of the natural world's beauty is merely a stepping stone to the opportunity for spiritually fulfilling enjoyment of the sublime beauty of God. God offers such joyous pleasure to humanity as a result of the redemption from sin earned by Jesus Christ and through the life-enriching ministry of the Holy Spirit. With both the Scriptures and God's revelation of himself through nature, humans have ample evidence that not only does God communicate with us, but he does so in a meaningful fashion with eternal ramifications: either heavenly glorification or hellish damnation. Thus Edwards's view of God, revelation, history, salvation, and eternity are complexly interfused, and must be described and analyzed as scrupulously and painstakingly as Edwards did those wind-blown spiders.

Scientific writings such as the "Spider Letter" of 1723 also provide us with evidence of Jonathan Edwards's unbridled curiosity, capacity for intellectual insight, and underlying intentions in appreciating the dynamics and functions of natural phenomena. In the workings of creation Edwards certainly saw precision and order that ensure that matter and time progress in a predictable fashion according to laws. He saw as well the interrelatedness of animals, insects, and plants, assigning a role to each creature as part of a vast system of complicated, interdependent life cycles. He saw human history as a significant fraction of a universal history, weaving together myriad life forms in time and space. And he saw knowledge, defined as the workings of intelligent minds, to be a priceless key to understanding physical reality.

Though a faithful amateur scientist, Edwards would never allow his observations and insights about matter and time to cloud his more profound, undergirding assumption that a real spiritual dimension permeates all that can be seen and touched by humanity. That spiritual dimension provides and validates physical reality's purpose. Indeed, apart from the spiritual dimension, the physical is meaningless. For Edwards, the bedrock of the spiritual dimension, and thus the physical dimension, is God. So the proper starting point for any treatment Edwards's theology must be his perspective about who God is, and what God is like.

Exploring the matter of who God is was not for Edwards a merely intellectual or theoretical enterprise, but a doxological responsibility inherent to being human—simply because we exist, God deserves our heartfelt gratitude and praise. "[S]o has God dignified us, that he has made [us] for this very end: to think and be astonished [at] his glorious perfections."[8] In fact, no inquiry, theological or otherwise, should be pursued simply for its own sake, but rightly should have as its goal and passion a true knowledge of God that duly bears fruit in soulful worship. Understanding God "is the very foundation of all religion, both doctrinal and practical; it is to no purpose to worship God, except we know [whom] we worship."[9] These right notions about the nature of God, including the doctrine of the Trinity and the content of God's decrees, "are glorious inlets into the knowledge and view of the spiritual world, and the contemplation of supreme things" which contribute to "the betterment of the heart."[10]

But Edwards was also well aware of the limitations of even the most gifted humans as they study who God is and explore the divine mysteries, including the nature of the Trinity, which is "the greatest and the most glorious of all mysteries."[11] Humans cannot even fathom the depths of their own souls much less plunge into the depths of God's being, which cannot be described "according to exact metaphysical truth."[12] Nevertheless, to accommodate finite human understanding, God has revealed himself in the Scriptures and ultimately in the Person and redemptive work of Jesus Christ.[13] The revelation God has made of

---

8. "Excellencies," 417.
9. "Excellencies," 416.
10. *WJE 13*, 328.
11. *WJE 13*, 393.
12. *WJE 1*, 376. In "Discourse," Edwards states, "I am far from pretending to explaining the Trinity so as to render it no longer a mystery. I think it to be the highest and deepest of all divine mysteries still, notwithstanding anything that I have said or conceived about it. I don't pretend to explain the Trinity, but in time, with reason, may [be] led to say something further of it than has been wont to be said, though there are still left many things pertaining to it incomprehensible" (134).
13. *WJE 13*, 410. Divine revelation in the Scriptures will be discussed in more detail in chapter 3.

himself through the Bible is not exhaustive because no human mind can comprehend God's mind, and no temporal means can adequately capture his eternal essence. Still, biblical revelation is sufficient for human knowledge and salvation, and completely authoritative because of its divine origin. We do understand from the Bible that God is Triune, and God is Spirit. Even with Jesus Christ as fully God and fully human, God essentially remains Spirit. Moreover, we understand that each Person of the Trinity plays a special role in relation to creation, particularly in the redemption of sinners. Through the Scriptures, God "has made us capable of understanding so much of him here as is necessary in order to our acceptable worshipping and praising him."[14]

The Holy Being of God

Suppose that someone judges the *scriptural* evidence for God's existence and nature to be insufficient or irrelevant. Edwards alternatively proposes a *logical* study about God to supplement his scripturally informed reasoning. In this line of thought, an approach to understanding the Trinity begins with the foundational being and essence of God, the core of God's identity. As with any knowledge, pursuing the knowledge of God depends on the "invariable disposition" of our minds to assume that all things have a cause, and accordingly that all reality has a supreme, first Cause.[15] "For we have no way to prove anything else, but by arguing from effects to causes."[16]

For Edwards, with God as the first Cause everything that exists and happens as a result of his activity is not contingent or uncertain, but planned, ordered, and sure.[17] So the fact of our limited, temporary existence as humans provides a logical proof for God's existence, since God (by definition) is self-sufficient in his own being, not depending on anyone or anything. In other words, all reality must have come from one powerful Source, a Source whose creativity and love engendered a flow of things and events that have brought us to this state of life as we know

---

14. "Excellencies," 417.

15. "Mind," 370. A cause is "any antecedent, either natural or moral, positive or negative, on which an event . . . so depends, that it is the ground and reason, either in whole, or in part, why it is" (*WJE* 1, 180).

16. *WJE* 1, 182.

17. *WJE* 1, 420.

it. In contrast to positing God as this Source, the alternative of contingency leads to chaos, "for contingency is blind, and does not pick and choose for a particular sort of events. . . . [It] causes no existence, [and] can't cause the existence which comes to pass, to be of one particular sort only, distinguished from all others."[18] Michael Jinkins explains, "The choice for Edwards seemed relatively clear: either all of life coheres on the basis of causation, or all of life is purely at the mercy of chance."[19]

Implicit in divine causation, then, is the notion that God himself *must be bound* to act *out of necessity* in order to implement his choices in creation. One therefore could object that this kind of God is not totally free and does not possess absolute liberty to act as he would choose. So God consequently either acts immorally by contradicting the freedom of his own nature, or is not in fact God, the ultimate Being. To counter this line of reasoning Edwards defines "necessity" as that which *absolutely must be* and relates it to God's moral nature, the height of which is his holiness. For God, necessity not only involves a sense of causation, but a moral dimension that endows necessity with great value. For example, "the reason why it is not dishonorable, to be necessarily *most* holy, is, because holiness in itself is an excellent and honorable thing," as is divine wisdom.[20] God's acting *with necessity* does not diminish his holiness and praiseworthiness, but actually adds to it because he is *bound* to act supremely morally and utterly consistently with his own character. "There is the greatest and most absolute necessity imaginable, that God should always will good and never evil."[21]

For Edwards, God does many things with necessity that he also does freely. In fact, God *necessarily* acts *freely* in the greatest way possible because he is "in the highest possible respect an agent, and active in the exercise of his infinite holiness."[22] The liberty of God then is expressed perfectly through Edwards's requirements of moral agency: understanding the difference between moral good and evil; discerning moral worthiness; and exercising a capacity for choice guided by moral

---

18. *WJE* 1, 184.
19. Jinkins, "Being of Beings," 162.
20. *WJE* 1, 381, original italics.
21. *WJE* 13, 217.
22. *WJE* 1, 364.

understanding. As the perfect moral agent, God, the ultimate Cause, is the "source of all moral ability and agency" for humanity.[23]

Edwards has deduced for us that God is the first Cause and supreme moral agent. But further explanation is needed about why God is moral as opposed to immoral, and how he fulfills the three criteria for moral agency mentioned above. As we examine Edwards's arguments, it is important to keep in mind that the discussion in this chapter focuses largely upon God apart from creation, in his eternal existence. Prior to creation, "God's acts were only towards himself, for then there was no other being but he."[24]

Given that before creation there was only God, and nothing and no one else, Edwards asserts that God *had to be*. There can never be any such thing as absolutely nothing, which is a "state of absolute contradiction."[25] Of logical necessity, at least one being *must* exist and *must* be infinite and omnipresent. Even when speaking of a being who is spirit, something or someone *must* be eternally everywhere, even if the "where" is a reality much different than the reality we humans perceive. Thus God is the *ens entium*, the Source and Purpose of all existence. However he acts, his essence is necessarily present because nothing is capable of excluding it.[26] So even before creation, there was a kind of "spiritual" space, which was dynamic and pure Being—in other words, God.[27] God is without beginning and is fundamentally the only Being, for all things are from him and dependent upon him.[28] With or without creation as we know

---

23. *WJE* 1, 166. God's capacities for moral agency provide the structure for the image of God in humans, as we will see in chapter 2.

24. *WJE* 15, 388.

25. "Being," 202. God's Spirit is qualitatively much like a human soul, "enlarged infinitely . . . only without our imperfections" (*WJE* 13, 295).

26. "Atoms," 215.

27. "Being," 203. Edwards's equation of God with space will be explored in detail in chapter 2. The nature of this pre-creation space *must* have been of a spiritual nature. Contrary to British philosopher Thomas Hobbes's (1588–1679) conviction that only matter is substance, "no matter is substance but only God, who is a spirit" and is actually more substantial than matter (*WJE* 13, 166). Robert W. Jenson elaborates that spiritual being does not for Edwards mean something invisible, but rather that which is personal and communal, bearing relation to itself or another being (*America's Theologian*, 17).

28. "Torments," 305; see Rom 11:36. Edwards contends, "An infinite being therefore must be an all comprehending Being. . . . That there should be another being underived and independent . . . will argue him not to be infinite, because then there is something more" (*WJE* 18, 94).

it, God's being "is as it were the sum and comprehension of all existence and excellence."[29]

Divine Excellency

Because God "is the infinite, universal and all comprehending existence," he necessarily must demonstrate excellency, which is comprised of both greatness and beauty.[30] Because he is self-sufficient and eternal as the first Cause, God cannot be limited in his being or any of his attributes.[31] Therefore, God *of necessity* exhibits excellence in an unbounded fashion, so that his perfect love of himself substantiates his supreme holiness and the perfect moral agency that flows from it.[32] God justifiably loves himself and his holiness utterly, because he is utterly worthy. What's more, he *enjoys* loving himself and delighting in his perfection.[33] And why is God a loving God of holy goodness, and not a tyrant? Because, in addition to the fact that excellence requires the beauty of love, the alternative is unthinkable. Without holiness, "God himself (if that were possible to be) would be an infinite evil: without which, we ourselves had better never have been; and without which there had better have been no being."[34]

A little confused? Just in case you are, Edwards makes this point another way. Because God is excellent, and consequently because he is the perfect moral agent, he is in fact supremely holy, morally pure, and infinitely good rather than infinitely evil. God's holiness comprehends both facets of excellency (greatness and beauty) and is expressed through both moral and natural attributes. For Edwards, moral attributes are those "which God exercises as a moral agent, or whereby the heart and will of God are good, right, and infinitely becoming, and lovely; such as

---

29. "Virtue," 551. "The essence of God and his nature, is most wonderfully expressed in this, I AM; his excellency, in this, THAT I AM," referring to Exod 3:14 (*WJE* 13, 256).

30. "Mind," 381. For a concise explanation of British philosopher John Locke's (1632–1704) influence on Edwards's view of excellency, see Anderson, "Editor's Introduction," *WJE* 6, 90–94.

31. "Consideration," 107.

32. "Discourse," 113–14.

33. *WJE* 1, 409.

34. *WJE* 2, 274.

his righteousness, truth, faithfulness, and goodness; or, in one word, his holiness."[35] Natural attributes, meanwhile, are those

> wherein, according to our way of conceiving of God, consists, not the holiness or moral goodness of God, but his greatness; such as his power, his knowledge whereby he knows all things, and his being eternal, from everlasting to everlasting, his omnipresence, and his awful and terrible majesty.[36]

Just as God enjoys loving himself and his perfections, he also enjoys and esteems his holy attributes and their exercise.[37] When compared with God's many pure attributes, his holiness is the premier one which subsumes all others, and is the loveliest and most beautiful of all.[38] Prior to creation, God's attributes were expressed and enjoyed only by himself. But their manifestation towards creatures now makes them even more excellent because their perfection exhibits evidence of God's "infinite power, wisdom, righteousness, goodness, etc."[39]

When we speak of the *glory* of God, then, Edwards asserts that it is "the view or knowledge of God's excellency." "Glory is a shining forth, an effulgence; so the glory of God is the shining forth or effulgence of his perfections, or the communication of his perfections, for effulgence is the communication of light."[40] God enjoys his own glory and enjoys communicating it to other beings because it is a trait of "excellency, or great valueableness, dignity, or worthiness of regard."[41] Edwards distinguishes between two manifestations of glory depending upon the receiver of its communication. *Internal* glory resides in God's understanding

---

35. *WJE* 2, 255.
36. *WJE* 2, 255.
37. "End," 430.
38. "Personal," 799.
39. "End," 428.
40. *WJE* 13, 361. In "End," Edwards explains why light is a common comparison in Scripture for the glory of God. "Light is the external expression, exhibition and manifestation of the excellency of the luminary, of the sun for instance. . . . 'Tis by this that all nature is quickened and receives life, comfort and joy. Light is abundantly used in Scripture to represent and signify these three things, knowledge, holiness and happiness" (530). In "Light," Edwards expounds based on John 1:18 that "God the Father is an infinite fountain of light, but Jesus Christ is the communication of this light. . . . God is an infinitely bright and glorious being, but Jesus Christ is that brightness of his glory by which he is revealed to us" (535).
41. "End," 513.

and will, and is expressed and celebrated only among the Persons of the Trinity. The fullness of all of God's attributes is summarized by the three components of internal glory: "his infinite knowledge; his infinite virtue or holiness, and his infinite joy and happiness."[42] *External* glory radiates God's internal glory throughout the created realm and grateful humans return that glory to him in earnest praise, a process Edwards coins "remanation" (for re-emanation).[43] At their root, both manifestations of glory are completely intertwined emanations of God's perfect love, wholly excellent and thoroughly holy.

The Persons of the Trinity

Our discussion so far has assumed that God joyfully manifests his glory both within the Godhead and to us, and enjoys doing so. Implicit to this assumption is that God's emotional enjoyment has an intellectual dimension with infinite knowledge. But of what does this knowledge consist? For example, we can presume that God thinks about his attribute of holiness, but can we know beyond that what the thought of God entails? Edwards has already instructed us that God desires to manifest his goodness and glory, and did so even within the Godhead prior to creation. God has a "communicative disposition in general, or a disposition in the fullness of the divinity to flow out and diffuse itself."[44] In his self-communication, his "thoughts" do not proceed from one to another in a series, the manner in which we think.[45] Edwards contends that according to reason and Scripture, and because God is omniscient, "all God's works, all that he has ever to do, the whole scheme and series of his operations, are from the beginning perfectly in his view."[46] God exists and thinks in a state of ever-presence, having "perfect ideas of all things at once" so that "all things are self-evident to God."[47] In other words, God is never surprised by anything because he is always thinking about all things simultaneously.

42. "End," 528.
43. "End," 531.
44. "End," 435.
45. *WJE 1*, 266–68.
46. *WJE 1*, 254.
47. "Mind," 342.

From Edwards's perspective, the "perfect idea" is the key to understanding the complexity of God's thoughts, as we presume to describe them. This "perfect idea" is God's knowledge of himself: God thinks about himself, and therefore repeats himself in idea (or thought) form, so that there "is God and the idea of God."[48] In his perpetual activity of self-glorification, "'tis by God's idea that His Glory shines forth and appears to Himself."[49] Put another way, when God thinks about himself, his thought is an exact copy or image of himself.

If you are confused, please hang in there! You'll see soon why this discussion of God's thought is so crucial.

The self-reflective image that is a product of God's thought is also a perfect Being, because "it" is an impeccable representation, an exact copy, of his perfect Being.[50] "This representation of the divine nature and essence is the divine nature and essence again. So that by God's thinking of the Deity, [the Deity] must certainly be generated."[51] In short, the Son of God is this impeccable idea, the eternally begotten One, the "necessary, perfect, substantial and personal idea which God hath of Himself."[52]

So we observe that for Edwards, God the Father is the Fountain of the Godhead, the Head of all godly affairs.[53] Though God the Father is also the essence of the Godhead expressed in power, the Father is not superior to the Son because they equally, wholly share a common essence.[54] "There is dependence [between them] without inferiority of deity; because in the Son the deity, the whole deity and glory of the Father, is as it were repeated or duplicated."[55]

As the perfect Idea, the *Logos* or Word of revelation, and the Wisdom of God, God the Son is the "perfect pattern and example of goodness" and is from all eternity named by God the Father to be the "head of the moral world, and . . . the chief of God's servants, appointed

---

48. "Discourse," 114.

49. "Discourse," 119.

50. "Discourse," 114.

51. *WJE* 13, 354.

52. "Discourse," 116. Edwards biblically supports this statement with 2 Cor 4:4; Phil 2:6; Col 1:15; and Heb 1:3. On 118, he follows with John 12:45; 14:7–9; and 15: 22–24. On 119, he adds 1 Cor 1:24; Luke 11:49; Matt 23:34; and Proverbs 8.

53. *WJE* 20, 433–36.

54. *WJE* 13, 262.

55. *WJE* 20, 430.

to be the head of his saints and angels."⁵⁶ The Son eternally and continuously promises to do the Father's will, a pledge growing from the dynamic love within the Godhead.⁵⁷ And because the Son is perfect, just like the Father from whom he is eternally generated, he certainly and of necessity loves the Father and fulfills this promise of faithfulness.

Let's pause for a moment. If you are not totally clear about how the Son of God is eternally begotten from the Father according to Edwards, I encourage you to take a moment to reread the section titled "The Persons of the Trinity" up to this point. What is most important to comprehend is that the Son of God is the Father's perfect thought about himself, and is also a distinct, perfect Person.

For Edwards the binding love between the Father and Son is not merely a nice feeling or a theory within God, but is actually divine power, utterly real and dynamic. This love is the divine vital principle and is denoted as the Person of the Holy Spirit. "'Tis that Spirit that is the very life of God, and so is divine and infinitely perfect life, and act, and energy; for which cause partly the Spirit of God is called 'water of life' (Rev 22:1), because divine life is the very matter of this water."⁵⁸ As the "eternal and essential act and energy of God,"⁵⁹ the Spirit not only demonstrates but also actually *is* the fundamental "disposition, inclination or temper of mind" of the Godhead.⁶⁰ It is the Holy Spirit who implements the plans and activities of the Godhead. In the mutual glorification between the Father and the Son,

> [t]he Deity becomes all act; the Divine essence itself flows out and is as it were breathed forth in love and joy. So that the Godhead therein stands forth in yet another manner of subsistence, and there proceeds the third person in the Trinity, the Holy Spirit, viz. the Deity in act. . . .⁶¹

---

56. "End," 474. "*Logos*" is from the Greek New Testament, is usually translated "word," and is featured in John 1.

57. *WJE* 1, 287.

58. *WJE* 15, 209.

59. "Discourse," 123.

60. "Discourse," 122. See also *WJE* 13, 461–62, which discusses the meaning of the Greek word *pneuma*, or "spirit," in the New Testament.

61. "Discourse," 121.

So Edwards concludes that God's perpetual, vibrant love between the Father and the Son *is* the Holy Spirit.[62] We must ask, though, why this divine energy between the Father and the Son must be a distinct Person and not simply a common love—after all, when two people love each other, another person is not immediately generated (although the tie to human marriage and procreation is unmistakable).[63] Edwards responds to the question by clarifying that this Person *must* be distinct, just as

> the delight and energy that is begotten in us by an idea is distinct from the idea. So it cannot be confounded in God, either with God begetting or [with] his idea and image, or Son. It is distinct from each of the other two, and yet it is God; for the pure and perfect act of God is God.[64]

Therefore, while God the Son is eternally begotten as the impeccable image or idea of God the Father, the Holy Spirit is the eternally dynamic, perfect, and ultimate loving Act of God. In addition to scriptural evidence that describes the Holy Spirit in divine and personal terms, the Spirit is logically an eternal Person because the Father and Son have from all eternity relished mutual delight through an *act* of love. So we see how the Holy Spirit proceeds eternally from both the Father and the Son, while none is inferior to the others in "degrees of dignity or excellency."[65]

But why is this Spirit denoted specially as Holy and as Spirit, if all of the Persons share equally in a holy and spiritual essence? Though God's holiness consists in his infinite love to himself, implying that both the Father and the Son are holy, the Spirit is is distinguished as holy because as the temperament of the Godhead the Spirit is the Person in whom

---

62. *WJE* 13, 300, based on 1 John 4:12–13. For additional Scripture passages used by Edwards to support this point, see *WJE* 13, 390. As Patricia Wilson-Kastner observes, "The Holy Spirit is the love of God personified, and any other actions about the Spirit must all spring from and return to this. . . . Love is no mere abstraction or theological generalization, Edwards maintains, but the person of the Holy Spirit, who proceeds from the Father and the Son" (*Coherence*, 28).

63. In "Discourse," Edwards defines "personhood" as having understanding and will (134).

64. *WJE* 13, 260. A common but deeply grievous mistake many people make today is to use terms such as "it" or "that" to refer to the Holy Spirit. Christian language needs to reflect the reality that the Holy Spirit is not an "it," but a Person.

65. "Threefold," 379; also, "Equality," 145–48.

the locus of holiness resides.[66] Holiness is the Spirit's proper nature and character, "his peculiar [or unique] beauty and glory," since holiness is inherent to his being the expressed love between the Father and the Son.[67] Because the Spirit is utterly holy, he is celebrated by the Father and Son as their "infinite joy and delight,"[68] the "harmony and excellency and beauty of the Deity,"[69] and the "sum of all spiritual blessings."[70] And because the Spirit is holy and thus profoundly beautiful, he is the premier expression of the mutual, relational consent among the Persons of the Godhead.

To sum up, Edwards has described for us a God who is the Cause, the only truly self-sufficient Being upon whom all else is dependent for its existence and sustenance. God's holiness and flawless moral agency are manifest through ceaseless glory that he communicates both within himself and beyond. Such communication originates within the plurality of the Trinity, so that Christ the Son of God reflects the Father's image back to him. The Holy Spirit, then, is the personal bond who unites the Father and Son in love, therein serving as the vital Act of the Godhead. All the Persons dwell in unadulterated, endless harmony, a harmony that is then conveyed and replicated in all they do as one God.

Trinitarian Consent

While Christ is a distinct Person based on his being the Idea of the Father, and the Holy Spirit is a Person based on his being the Act of both the Father and Son, Edwards supplies another way to understand the plurality of Persons within the Godhead: consent to being. In a sense, it is a very simple argument. First, love is the perfection and happiness of any spirit-being. Because God is the matchless, perfect Spirit, and so is supremely loving, he must have another being to whom to manifest and bestow that love meaningfully. Sharing such love requires an "other," and having a relationship with the "other" requires consent, or agreement in unity, with the "other." So for God to love and to be love, as the

---

66. "Discourse," 122–23.
67. "Unknown," 202.
68. *WJE* 13, 342.
69. *WJE* 13, 384.
70. "Attempt," 347.

Scriptures teach, there has to be a plurality of Persons who consent to each other in the most excellent, holy manner, while sharing a unified, common essence.[71] "The happiness of the Deity, as all other true happiness, consists in love and society."[72]

For the theologian, God's happiness and excellency go hand in hand. Edwards defines "excellency" not only as greatness and beauty, as we saw above, but also as the similarity of one being to another, or the "consent of being to being. . . . The more the consent is, and the more extensive, the greater is the excellency."[73] And the greater the excellency of God, the greater the happiness and love of God, even within the Trinity—the Trinity is never static, for the living God's wonderful attributes are always increasing. Edwards summarizes,

> As to God's excellence, it is evident it consists in the love of himself. For he was as excellent before he created the universe as he is now. But if the excellence of spirits consists in their disposition and action, God could be excellent no other way at that time, for all the exertions of himself were towards himself. But he exerts himself towards himself no other way than in infinitely loving and delighting in himself, in the mutual love of the Father and the Son. This makes the third, the personal Holy Spirit or the holiness of God, which is his infinite beauty, and this is God's infinite consent to being.[74]

Edwards has brought us full circle, having started with the first and premier Being who is God, proceeded through the Persons who comprise the Trinitarian Godhead, and shown the delightful and loving interplay of those Persons. But we have to remember that discussing the

---

71. *WJE* 13, 282–83; see 1 John 4:8, 16. Edwards explains why there are no more than three Persons. According to reason, "If God has an idea of himself, there is really a duplicity; because [if] there is no duplicity, it will follow that Jehovah thinks of himself no more than a stone. And if God loves himself and delights in himself, there is really a triplicity, three that cannot be confounded, each of which [is] the Deity substantially. And this is the only distinction that can be found or thought of in God" (262).

72. "Grace," 187. In *Philosophy* Stephen Daniel explains that God does not *do* consent, but in fact *is* consent—the Persons of the Trinity do not simply choose to consent, but *are* utter consent in their common, living essence. To the extent that "signifier and signified are thought of as independent units, they are unintelligible and unimaginable, just as the persons of the Trinity cannot be conceived apart from their relations to one another" (183).

73. "Mind," 336.

74. "Mind," 364.

particular Persons as we have is a somewhat artificial way of investigating their characteristics, because it arbitrarily removes them from the inextricable bonds of relations within the Trinity. Doing so nevertheless provides us with a means to appreciate the dynamic interpenetration the Persons have as they overflow with love one to another. In their continuous consent to being, they have a "mutual free agreement," and are in "an ineffable and inconceivable manner one in another; so that one hath another, and they have communion in one another, and are as it were predicable one of another."[75]

The Father, Son, and Holy Spirit are the ultimate holy and blissful community, since the "eternal and immutable happiness of the Deity himself is represented in Scripture as a kind of social happiness, in the society of the persons of the Trinity."[76] Edwards possessed a vivid mental picture of God's internal community, partially derived from Ezekiel's vision of the windstorm with lightning and fire in Ezek 1:4 and the Israelites' sight of the *Shekinah* glory in Exod 13:21–22.[77] In the Exodus passage, Edwards saw the pillars of cloud and of fire to be manifestations of the divine spiritual essence constantly unfolding itself as the Persons express and share love. In this divine community's dynamics, the "flames of divine love are received and enfolded into the bosom of the deity," and then unfurl and overflow again.[78]

Divine Love in Creation and Redemption

Mutual glorification among the Persons of the Trinity unfolds timelessly in God's ever-present state.[79] But it is the *time-bound* manifestation of this mutual glorification that will be the underlying theme of the rest of this project. God's self-glorifying activity in his timeless condition serves

---

75. "Discourse," 133.

76. "Pepperrell," 415. Daughter of a wealthy Boston merchant and granddaughter of noted Judge Samuel Sewall, Mary Pepperrell (1685–1766) became the widow of Sir William Pepperrell, military leader and prosperous businessman, in 1759. Her mansion, built the next year, still stands in Kittery Point, Maine.

77. "*Shekinah*" is the English transliteration of a Hebrew word that refers to the holy presence or dwelling place of God, particularly in Old Testament passages about Israel's Exodus out of Egypt (Exod 13:21–22) or the temple in Jerusalem (Exod 25:30; 33:7–23, e.g.).

78. WJE 15, 387.

79. WJE 23, 167–68.

as the foundation of creation and time, and consequently the redemption of sinful humanity. Though Edwards teaches us that all things are ever-present to God, from our finite perspective we conclude that this plan for redemption from sin was designed *before* the foundation of the world. Though this is difficult for us to comprehend, from all eternity "the Persons of the Trinity were . . . confederated in a design and a covenant of redemption, in which covenant the Father appointed the Son and the Son had undertaken their work, and all things to be accomplished in their work were stipulated and agreed."[80]

In this covenant, the glorification of each Person is the goal, a goal that is sure to be attained due to God's sovereignty and all-powerful intentions for history. In other words, in God's eternal existence there was never *not* a plan of redemption because it is as much a part of the dynamic being of God as his holiness, self-love, and excellent Trinitarian unity. The fulfillment of the divine design for redemption expresses the Godhead's glory in the realm of creation, allowing humanity to know, love, and praise God as his blessed creatures. "In all this God designed to accomplish the glory of the blessed Trinity in an exceeding degree. God had a design of glorifying himself from eternity, to glorify each person in the Godhead."[81]

Logically speaking (for the sake of our understanding), Edwards asserts that the plan of redemption originates with the Father, because "'tis his majesty and authority as supreme rector, legislator and judge that is con[d]emned [rejected]" by the Fall of humanity into sinful corruption.[82] The Father chooses the Son to be the Redeemer, grants him authority to act as mediator between God and humanity, and designates him "to rule in his name and as his viceregent."[83] The Spirit proceeds from the Father and the Son to effect the practical application of divine desires. Therefore, we determine that although all of the Persons are equally divine and thoroughly share their spiritual essence, with respect to the plan of creation and redemption each Person has a distinct mission.[84]

80. *WJE* 9, 118.
81. *WJE* 9, 125.
82. *WJE* 20, 433.
83. *WJE* 20, 439.
84. *WJE* 20, 431.

But if, as we have noted, Christ the Image of God was already obedient to his Father based upon his inherent divine nature and joyful consent, why was a covenant between the Father and the Son called for? The covenant was deemed necessary by the Father because he asked his Son to act below his divine character, setting aside his glory to enter our broken world. The Son's place in the holy, eternal covenant implies a humiliation not due to being incarnate, but "in his new subjection and obedience to the Father."[85] By willingly subjecting himself to the Father in this plan, Christ not only invested the Father with the right to prescribe to him the events of the plan, but also granted to the Father headship reflected through Christ's creaturely servanthood.[86] In this arrangement, it is not Christ's consent or obedience *within the Trinity* that is to be meritorious in winning salvation for humanity, but only his obedience *as a man* according to the plan of redemption. Jesus Christ had to be both completely God and completely human. Had he been only God, he would not have been "capable . . . of that obedience or suffering that was needful. The divine nature is not capable of suffering, for it is impassable and infinitely above all suffering; neither is it capable of obedience to that law that was given to man."[87] And if Jesus Christ had been only human, he would have been subject to the same sin and judgment to which all other people are subject under God's law.

If the covenant is only between the Father and Son, what is the concern of the Holy Spirit in it? Edwards supposes that though the plan of redemption was likely "concerted among all the persons, and determined by the perfect consent of all," the Spirit was not chosen by the Father to be a direct party in the covenant.[88] The Spirit *was* chosen by the Father, though, to be an invaluable, indirect party. The Holy Spirit's ministry of loving action was given by the Father to the Son as a gift, an eternal inheritance for the redeemed people whom Christ would obtain through completing his work of salvation. Thus, the Spirit is subjected to the Son for the purposes of the covenant of redemption. The God-Man will always be the Head of the Church, and "the vital good that this vital head will eternally communicate to his church will be the Holy Spirit."[89]

85. *WJE 20*, 442.
86. *WJE 20*, 438.
87. *WJE 9*, 295.
88. *WJE 20*, 442.
89. *WJE 20*, 440.

Nevertheless, within the Godhead the Spirit still proceeds from both the Father and the Son equally, and "is sent by both into the world to influence the hearts of the children of men to their salvation."[90]

Lest we think that the Spirit's role in the covenant of redemption is a lesser role than those of the Father and the Son, we need to remind ourselves that in all creative activity, the Holy Spirit "is the divine essence flowing out, or breathed forth, in infinite love and delight."[91] Without the work of the Spirit in creation and more especially in the plan of redemption, humans would have no knowledge whatsoever of God and no means of knowing how to secure eternal salvation through the Gospel. The eternal covenant between the Father and the Son paves the way for redemption, but the Spirit is he who acts as Christ's messenger and applies Christ's redemptive accomplishments to all creation, especially to human hearts.[92] Edwards elaborates:

> If it be said that more glory belongs to the Father and the Son because they manifested a more wonderful love, the Father in giving his Son infinitely dear to him, the Son in laying down his life; yet let it be considered, that the Holy Ghost *is* that wonderful love. Just so much as the two first persons glorify themselves, by showing the astonishing greatness of their love and grace, just so much they glorify that love and grace, who is the Holy Ghost. God's giving his dear Son, and the Son's suffering so much, glorifies the Holy Ghost, as it shows the worth of the Holy Ghost, that the Father should give his Son, and the Son pay so great a price that the Holy Spirit might be purchased.[93]

As that purchased inheritance, the Holy Spirit is the guarantee that those who have faith in Jesus Christ will persevere to eternal salvation in heaven.[94] "[B]elievers are united to Christ, and in a sense are partakers of his nature, in that they are partakers of his Spirit. Christ is therefore said to be in them."[95] And Christ is in them through the Spirit "not in any extraordinary gifts, but in his vital indwelling in the heart, exert-

---

90. "Threefold," 379.

91. *WJE* 13, 468.

92. "Threefold," 378. "What Christ does immediately is not upon men's souls, but for them. . . . Whatsoever in the work of redemption is done immediately in or upon men's souls is the work of the Spirit" (378).

93. *WJE* 13, 467.

94. "Charity," 354.

95. "Threefold," 403, based on Rom 8:9–10 and 2 Pet 1:4.

ing and communicating himself there, in his own proper, holy or divine nature."[96] While the Holy Spirit communicates mutual love between the Father and the Son in the Godhead, his communications within Christians as he indwells them yield God-like virtues and holiness of thought, word, and deed. The Spirit makes "the soul a partaker in God's beauty and Christ's joy, so that the saint has truly fellowship with the Father, and with his Son Jesus Christ, in thus having the communion or participation of the Holy Ghost."[97] As Patricia Wilson-Kastner observes, "The Holy Spirit is the Father's agent in history, to work his saving will in the world, spreading through history the saving work of the Son, particularly in the souls of the elect."[98]

The general understanding of the Trinity we have surveyed so far lays the proper foundation for comprehending the scope, consistency, and complexity of the remainder of Edwards's thought. God the Father, expressed and manifest by the ministry of the Holy Spirit of Christ, creates, shapes, upholds, and directs creation while endowing all of its facets with meaning.[99] An investigation of the most prominent of these facets will occupy the remainder of this project, beginning in the next chapter with a consideration of the nature, purpose, and moral government of the universe.

For Further Thought

1. In what ways does nature most reveal God to you? From these, what do you conclude about what God is like?

---

96. *WJE* 2, 236.

97. *WJE* 2, 201. Edwards also notes that regarding the Persons, "The benefits and blessedness of redemption are wholly and entirely from each of them: it is wholly originally from the Father; the Son is the medium of it all; the Holy Ghost immediately possesses us of it all, or rather is the sum of it all—he possesses us of it by coming and dwelling in us himself. Thus 'of him, and through him, and to him' (or in him) 'are all things,' Rom 11:36" (*WJE* 13, 467).

98. Wilson-Kastner, *Coherence in a Fragmented World*, 30.

99. To McClymond, "The fact that God is the canonical instance of being and truth and goodness and beauty carries the epistemological implication that all reality must be interpreted in light of the divine reality. Nothing in the world can be comprehended unless it has been related back to God. Edwards's theologizing is a many-sided effort to bring all reality into explicit relation to God as the measure of all things" (*Encounters*, 29).

2. Do you agree with Edwards's high valuation of the Bible? Do you agree with him regarding what we can know about God and the world from it? Why?

3. Do you think Edwards's logical argument that God is the first Cause is convincing? Why? How does his view compare with contemporary scientific perspectives about the origins of the universe and of humankind? How does his view compare with yours?

4. List the words Edwards uses to describe God's being and nature. Which of these are most personally meaningful to you, and why? Are there any you find surprising, object to, or think unnecessary?

5. Explain in your own words Edwards's view of how God the Son is eternally begotten from God the Father. And what place does the Holy Spirit have in the Trinity? Why is the Spirit's role not a lesser role than those of the Father and the Son?

6. Read John 1:1–5, 14–18. In what ways does this passage support what you have read of Edwards's theology in this chapter? Do these passages contradict Edwards in any way?

7. If someone were to accuse Edwards of believing in three gods and not one (tritheism), how do you think he would respond?

8. Delineate what role each Person of the Trinity has in the eternal covenant of redemption. Do any of Edwards's thoughts change how you understand God?

9. Read footnote 52 and then examine the Bible references Edwards used to deduce his ideas about the eternally begotten Son. Do you agree with his interpretation and use of these passages? Why is it important that Christ is begotten and not created by the Father?

10. Similarly, read footnotes 95 and 97 and examine the Bible references Edwards mentions to explain the Holy Spirit's ministry. How do Edwards and these passages change what you thought before about the Spirit?

11. Explain what "consent to being," "holiness," and "excellency" mean for Edwards, remembering that "excellency" has two dimensions to its meaning. Why are these ideas important to his understanding of the Trinity?

12. What new reflections about God has this chapter brought to your mind? What questions do you hope to have answered in upcoming chapters?

For Further Reading

As in subsequent chapters, the resources listed below are intended to supplement those that are mentioned in the bibliography. If you cannot find a source through the Internet or your local public library, consult the library of the nearest college, university, or seminary.

Bebbington, David W. "Remembered Around the World: The International Scope of Edwards's Legacy." In *Jonathan Edwards at Home and Abroad*, edited by David W. Kling and Douglas A. Sweeney. Columbia: University of South Carolina Press, 2003.

Dodds, Elisabeth D. *Marriage to a Difficult Man: The Uncommon Union of Jonathan and Sarah Edwards*. Philadelphia: Westminster, 1971; reprint: Audubon, 2005.

Edwards, Jonathan. *The Works of Jonathan Edwards, Vol. 26: Catalogues of Books*. Edited by Peter J. Thuesen. New Haven: Yale University Press, 2008. Among other things, this work presents lists of books that Edwards read and those he loaned to others.

Gura, Philip F. *Jonathan Edwards: America's Evangelical*. New York: Hill and Wang, 2005.

Hatch, Nathan O., and Harry S. Stout, editors. *Jonathan Edwards and the American Experience*. New York: Oxford University Press, 1988.

Lee, Sang Hyun, editor. *The Princeton Companion to Jonathan Edwards*. Princeton: Princeton University Press, 2005.

Lee, Sang Hyun, and Allen C. Guelzo, editors. *Edwards in Our Time: Jonathan Edwards and the Shaping of American Religion*. Grand Rapids: Eerdmans, 1999.

Lesser, M.X. *Jonathan Edwards*. Boston: Twayne, 1988.

———. *Reading Jonathan Edwards: An Annotated Bibliography in Three Parts, 1729-2005*. Grand Rapids: Eerdmans, 2008.

Marsden, George M. *Jonathan Edwards: A Life*. New Haven: Yale University Press, 2004.

———. *A Short Life of Jonathan Edwards*. Grand Rapids: Eerdmans, 2008.

McDermott, Gerald, editor. *Understanding Jonathan Edwards: An Introduction to America's Theologian*. New York: Oxford University Press, 2008.

Minkema, Kenneth P. "Jonathan Edwards in the Twentieth Century." *Journal of the Evangelical Theological Society* 47 (2004) 659-87.

Piper, John, and Justin Taylor. *A God Entranced Vision of All Things: The Legacy of Jonathan Edwards*. Wheaton, IL: Crossway, 2004.

Stein, Stephen J., editor. *The Cambridge Companion to Jonathan Edwards*. Cambridge; New York: Cambridge University Press, 2007.

Winslow, Ola. *Jonathan Edwards, 1703-1758: A Biography*. New York: Octagon, 1973.

2

The Trinity Revealed through Creation

EDWARDS'S EXPLANATIONS OF THE Trinity, and especially of the perfect mutual love the Persons of the Trinity enjoy within the Godhead, provide us with the basis for apprehending what comes to be the world as we know it. God creates physical reality out of nothing to serve as a means for his self-revelation and corresponding self-glorification.[1] Humanity has a special role in this creative design, a role that is not thwarted even by its sinful rebellion against God in refusing to obey his will. While sin and the detailed workings of the eternal covenant of redemption will be examined more closely in the next chapter, here our interest lies in exploring the divine purpose of creation, how creation exists within the being of God, and how the Holy Spirit serves as the agent of Christ to form and sustain all life in the universe. We will learn that there is an indivisible, interpenetrating bond between spiritual and physical realities: while God always remains distinct from creation, his intentions for himself and for his creatures ultimately blend into one. Creation is more than a divine exercise of curiosity, some experiment or tinker toy to keep God occupied in his eternal state. Rather, its existence, sustenance, and progress toward a divinely ordained goal add to the already overflowing glory and happiness of God.

Edwards's assertion of the specifically *Trinitarian* origin of creation can be found in various statements that must be dealt with due to their initial appearance of contradiction. For example, the pastor asserts that God the Father created the universe "to provide a kingdom for his Son in it."[2] The Father created heaven as part of the universe to be a "habita-

---

1. Based on Isa 41:18–20, "To 'create,' as the word is used in Scripture, is either to make out [of] nothing, or which is equivalent, to make out of that which has in itself no natural fitness . . . for such an effect" (*WJE 15*, 521).

2. *WJE 9*, 349.

tion for the redeemed and the Redeemer," complete with angels serving as ministering spirits while the plan of redemption is carried out.[3] In short, the cosmos "is made for the Son of God" in order that God the Father might glorify and reveal himself to other intelligent beings (that is, humans, angels, and demons), especially through Jesus Christ.[4]

But elsewhere, Edwards contends that Christ, and not the Father, was the Creator, leading us to believe that Christ made reality for himself while honoring the Father's wishes. In the creation of the world, Christ purposed to care for his Church: "all things were created by him and for him, viz. that he might obtain a spouse that he might give himself to and give himself for, on whom he might pour forth his love, and in whom his soul might be eternally delighted."[5] We find that just as the Father communicates himself to the Son and the Son reciprocates, the Son also desires to communicate his happiness in and through creation, particularly to humanity created in his own image.[6] Based on Gen 2:2, Edwards contends that Christ *did* perform the work of creation, "he being the Father's great officer and artificer, through whom he performs all his work, and executes his eternal counsels and purposes."[7] So while the Father did plan from all eternity to create, his means of doing so are through the Son, the Father's vicegerent, to whom dominion over the earth is given as part and parcel of the Trinitarian plan of redemption.

As we noted in the previous chapter, however, the Holy Spirit is the Godhead in action, and so behaves that way in creation. The Son of God, "by his immediate influence, gives being every moment, and by his Spirit actuates the world, because he inclines to communicate himself and his excellencies."[8] All life, whether physical or spiritual, is created

---

3. *WJE* 9, 118.

4. "Attempt," 337. Edwards explains, "God made the world that he might communicate, and the creature receive, his glory, but that it might [be] received both by the mind and heart.... Both these ways of God's glorifying himself come from the same cause, viz. the overflowing of God's internal glory, or an inclination in God to cause his internal glory to flow out *ad extra* [outward]. What God has in view ... neither in his manifesting his glory to the understanding nor communication to the heart, is not that he may receive, but that he [may] go forth" (*WJE* 13, 495).

5. *WJE* 15, 187.

6. *WJE* 13, 272. The image of God in humans will be discussed below.

7. *WJE* 15, 532. In "Discourse," Edwards states, "The world was made for the Son of God especially.... [T]he world is made to gratify divine love as exercised by Christ, or to gratify the love that is in Christ's heart, or to provide a spouse for Christ" (142).

8. *WJE* 13, 279.

and sustained at every moment by the ministry of the Holy Spirit, as we will consider again below.⁹ Just as the Spirit hovered above the void described in Gen 1:2, so he gladly and lovingly gives form and life to all things as the practicing agent of the Godhead's decrees, shaping and guiding them ultimately toward perfection.¹⁰ Consequently, all three of the Persons are intimately involved in the creation of the universe and of course humanity.¹¹

The Purpose of Creation

Edwards frequently points out that God creates not for the benefit of any creature but primarily for himself, to manifest and enjoy his own happiness. We noted in the first chapter the overflowing joy among the Persons of the Godhead and God's urge to express that joy to other beings. "God's joy is dependent on nothing besides his own act, which he exerts with an absolute and independent power."¹² God is not dependent upon creatures for anything, because anything he may receive from a creature is what he has given to it in the first place. God is always his own ultimate aim, and does not act selfishly or unjustly in valuing himself above all other things. Indeed, his holiness inherently requires that his own perfect being be that which is most esteemed in all reality.¹³ Edwards asserts that "the whole universe, including all creatures animate and inanimate, in all its actings, proceedings, revolutions, and entire series of events, should proceed from a regard and with a view to *God*, as the supreme and last end of all."¹⁴

But let us suppose for a moment that God chose not to make the universe as we know it. Suppose he chose to reside in his own complete sufficiency, eternally glorifying himself only within the Godhead. For Edwards, in theory, God would not in the least be diminished if the universe had never been created because his attributes would remain

---

9. *WJE* 15, 532.
10. *WJE* 15, 530.
11. "Threefold," 378.
12. "End," 447.
13. "End," 451. "God seeks the display of his own glory as a thing in itself excellent. . . . The excellency of God's nature appears in that . . . He loves and seeks whatever is in itself excellent" (*WJE 18*, 282).
14. "End," 424.

perfectly excellent, though not exercised "outwardly." On the other hand, the very nature of God's excellency calls out for conveyance of that excellency, so that his attributes are expanded and made even more excellent by their exhibition to other beings. God esteems his holy and perfect attributes because they are "valuable, and [he] delights in them, so 'tis natural to suppose that he delights in their proper exercise and expression."[15] So even though Edwards can maintain that God did not *need* to create the universe, and also was never required by his own nature to formulate the plan of redemption, there is a definite sense in which God is more fulfilled, happy, and glorified by doing so. To illustrate: although utterly perfect in himself before creating his spouse, the Church, "in whom his soul might be eternally delighted," Christ "was pleased not to look on himself as complete, but as wanting something, as Adam was not complete till he had obtained his Eve (Gen 2:20)."[16] God's consummate best becomes even better.

Edwards never doubts that God made the universe, and actually maintains that to be a self-evident fact. But his questions about the purpose and origin of creation are not merely intellectual exercises, as they can be today. The answers to these questions, which to him can only be correctly discerned according to scriptural principles, provide the groundwork for better understanding God's nature and intentions in everything he does. Humans may not understand many or most of the specific workings of creation and its divinely guided history, but what they are enabled to understand by the ministry of the Holy Spirit grants them insight into the goodness of their Creator. God's desire to glorify himself in, through, and to creatures is the most profound goodness that will ever be known.

> Goodness is the only end why he has created the world, and the ultimate end of every dispensation of whatever nature, even the damnation of the wicked for the happiness of the blessed. God's power, wisdom and justice, are exerted wholly and ultimately upon the feet of goodness.[17]

But why was this goodness expressed in the creation of humans, as opposed to some other creature or thing, known or unknown to us? After

---

15. "End," 430. "God's delight is not properly from the creature's communication to God, but in his to the creature; it is a delight in his own act" (*WJE* 13, 496).

16. *WJE* 15, 187.

17. "Apocalypse," 137.

all, God created angels as intelligent beings, so the question remains of why another kind of creature was vital for the reception and understanding of God's goodness.[18] While the Puritan cannot tell us why God chose to create physical reality as we know it *per se,* he does assert that God intended to have his works "exhibit an image of himself their author" consisting chiefly of his moral excellence "in the disposition of his heart."[19] Whatever kind of creature may have been created, it must have possessed moral, spiritual, and intellectual faculties so that God himself might be enjoyed, understood, glorified, and imitated by the creature. Creation would in fact be useless without intelligent beings of this kind, because "God could neither receive good himself nor communicate good," nor could such beings "behold and admire the doings of God."[20] So God in his wisdom made angels as spiritual beings. But he made humans to be spiritual beings *with bodies* whose exquisiteness shows "emanations of Christ's divine perfections," even while "the most proper image of the beauty of Christ" is seen in the beauty of the human soul.[21]

The difference between a human and an animal lies in the person's God-given capacity to be a moral agent and the ability to exercise excellence, or holiness, in that moral agency.[22] Christ's own capacities as a moral agent are shown in humans through their being created in God's image, thereby reflecting as well the holiness of God the Father.[23] Being created in the image of God enables people "to meditate on God, or the first cause of all things, to see him who is invisible, and see future and eternal things."[24] As we should expect, God's creation of humanity in

---

18. While angels will be discussed in more detail in chapter 7, here we simply note that angels are subordinate to humans in the order of creation because angels were created to serve humans and "be the universal ministers of God" (*WJE 13,* 271).

19. "End," 422.

20. *WJE 13,* 185. In "End," Edwards writes, "In the creature's knowing, esteeming, loving, rejoicing in, and praising God, the glory of God is both exhibited and acknowledged; his fullness is received and returned" (531).

21. *WJE 13,* 280. The human body and soul will be addressed more in chapter 4.

22. *WJE 1,* 166.

23. The natural aspects of the image of God involve reason, understanding, abilities appropriate to a being's nature, and dominion over lesser creatures. The moral or spiritual aspects include holiness and moral excellency. God's moral and natural attributes comprise the basis for those of humans (*WJE 2,* 255–56).

24. "Nothing," 147. In this quote Edwards is not declaring that people are innately capable of fortunetelling or ESP, but are able to join God in understanding time's meaning and progression.

his own image is intended to enhance his glory, his delight in his own glory, and his enjoyment in sharing that glory with intelligent life. But the knowledge of God that the image endows has the secondary purpose of making human happiness possible, particularly when our minds and hearts interact with God.[25] Humans were designed for joyful fellowship with God and to imitate his holiness in their thoughts, motives, and actions.[26]

A human's unique faculty of reason binds her to God through the knowledge of himself that God is always imparting to her.[27] The image of God in people and the love for God which is its intended fruit depend entirely and directly upon their "union and communion with God, or divine communications and influences of God's [S]pirit."[28] Ultimately, the desires and aspirations of the human heart and mind ought to be united with the heart and mind of God—in loving, happy consent to the being of God, one in intention, just as the persons of the Trinity are one in intention and happily consent to each other.[29]

For Edwards the human mind itself is a gift, part of the image of God that makes the divine mind's most excellent aspect, love, the standard for human thought and volition.[30] Notice that the theologian does not separate emotion, thought, and will from each other. Human reason with all these dimensions should be used as its Creator intended, "that it might be exercised and improved in spiritual things. The service of God is what we are created for, and our reason is given us to be improved

---

25. "Nothing," 151.

26. In "Holiness," Edwards notes that human "holiness is the image of God, his likeness, in [the person who] is holy," involving conformity to God's will, doing what God wills, and "acting holily and justly and wisely and mercifully, like him" (472).

27. "End," 441; see Rom 1:19–20. The image of God is the basis for human love; we love others purely when we love them because they are God's creatures.

28. WJE 3, 382.

29. The effects of sin upon the image of God will be considered in chapter 3. Here, we mention that for Edwards, the human soul prior to the Fall into sin loved all fellow creatures and the Creator completely, "and dispersed itself abroad in that infinite ocean of good and was, as it were, swallowed up by it, and become one with it" ("Charity," 253). But after rebelling and refusing to consent to God, the mind of man "shrunk from its primitive greatness and extensiveness into an exceeding diminution and confinedness" while his soul shrunk to be "wholly governed by narrow, selfish principles" ("Threefold," 378).

30. "Mind," 363. Though the divine nature is "vastly different from that of created spirits," humans still have will, idea, and love as God does, different chiefly in "degree and manner" ("Discourse," 113).

for that end."³¹ Not using reason for that end is actually beastly, because "intelligent perception and action" through the image of God is what distinguishes humans from all other earthly creatures.³² "Understanding and will are the highest kind of created existence. . . . And certainly the most excellent actual knowledge and will that can be in the creature is the knowledge and love of God."³³

But now we return to the divine origins of creation. In the eternal plan of God, humanity's appearance is not an accident or divine afterthought, but is a chief reason, subordinate only to God's glory, for which the universe was made. "Mankind is the principal part of the visible creation. . . . [T]hey have understanding and are voluntary agents, and can produce works of their own will, design and contrivance, as God does."³⁴ Not only that, humans can have communion with God and can participate with him in his own glory and happiness. Their existence and happiness are utterly dependent on God and are intertwined with his existence and happiness. In fact, there is no disjunction between the manifestation of God's glory and goodness to creatures and their own fulfillment, because both are mutually implied. "God in seeking their glory and happiness, seeks himself: and in seeking himself, i.e. himself diffused and expressed (which he delights in, as he delights in his own beauty and fullness), he seeks their glory and happiness."³⁵

However, Edwards points out that God's revelation of himself is not principally focused on individuals, but on God's fellowship with humanity as a whole. All of the activities of God are "works of goodness or mercy to his people."³⁶ Together they compose "a glorious society of created beings" dedicated to knowing and delighting in God and his attributes.³⁷ Thus God's goodness is to be praised, because he created humanity

---

31. "Hearers," 263.

32. *WJE* 20, 97.

33. "End," 454. Edwards continues on the same page by stating that the truest knowledge of God is knowledge of "his glory and moral excellence, and the most excellent exercise of the will consists in esteem and love and a delight in his glory." The relationship between will and faith will be addressed in chapter 4.

34. *WJE* 20, 96.

35. "End," 459.

36. "End," 510.

37. "End," 431.

for this very end, to make him happy in the enjoyment of himself, the Almighty, who was happy from the days of eternity in himself, in the beholding of his own infinite beauty: the Father in the beholding and love of his Son, his perfect and most excellent image, the brightness of his own glory; and the Son in the love and enjoyment of the Father.[38]

Such goodness, whether in the Trinity or among people, should be evidenced in loving relationships. While the Church will be described in chapter 5, we note here that the love-filled Trinitarian plurality of the Godhead is the model for divine-human fellowship and human-human fellowship. The diversity and plurality of humanity living in harmony is what richly reflects the glory of God.

The Value of Nature

The fact that the universe was created for humans so they might know and praise God does not mean that creation itself is without inherent value. Nature provides humanity with a window through which to see God's nature because physical reality is a reflection of him in the same way that a great artist's individual style can be discerned from her paintings.[39] Remembering from the first chapter that God's beauty blossoms from the harmonious consent within the Godhead, so also the "beauty of the world consists wholly of sweet mutual consents, either within itself, or with the Supreme Being."[40] But the beauty of the world is not only a *reflection* of God's beauty; it is also a manifestation of his *actual* beauty. The beauties of the natural world are "so immediately derived from God that they are but emanations of his beauty."[41] Because God is "the head of the universal system of existence; the foundation and fountain of all being and all beauty; from whom all is perfectly derived, and on whom all is most absolutely and perfectly dependent," God's "being and beauty

---

38. "Nothing," 153.
39. "Virtue," 550.
40. "Beauty," 305.
41. *WJE* 13, 331. McClymond explains, "The Trinity and the creation are thus the two great divine 'communications,' flowing from two great exercises of consent by God, the one *ad intra* [inward] and the other *ad extra* [outward]. Every creaturely consent is a miniature echo of the Trinity" (*Encounters*, 32).

is as it were the sum and comprehension of all existence and excellence."[42] Edwards saw "a calm, sweet cast, or appearance of divine glory, in almost everything."[43]

To state this point another way: because nature's beauty is predicated upon God's beauty so closely that they are essentially the same, Edwards concludes that all physical beauty is grounded upon spiritual beauty. In fact, the universe is beautiful *because* of its undergirding spiritual reality.[44] Nature's *secondary* beauty exhibits its own kind of consent to *primary*, spiritual beauty, thereby demonstrating God's pleasure in "beauty, good order and regulation, proportion and harmony."[45] Further, secondary beauty in creation communicates in a physical way the harmony within the Godhead: complexity in simplicity, and integrated plurality in relations among the Persons. Because he is Mediator and Vicegerent between God the Father and creation, Christ's spiritual beauty *is* the beauty of the universe.[46] Because he is the divine Act, the Holy Spirit is Christ's agent in creating, sustaining, and conveying beauty; indeed, the "Holy Spirit is the harmony and excellency and beauty of the Deity."[47] So creation shows that the Father, Son, and Holy Spirit all have a hand not only in its existence, but its wonderful form and marvelous appeal.

Because creation is beautiful and indicative of the harmony and balance of the Trinity, it should be expected then that individual parts of creation also express orderliness and regularity, a kind of pure constancy based on God's nature, wisdom, and design.[48] In creation,

> God does purposely make and order one thing to be in an agreeableness and harmony with another.... We see that even in the material world God makes one part of it strangely to agree with another; and why is it not reasonable to suppose he makes the whole as a shadow of the spiritual world?[49]

---

42. "Virtue," *WJE* 8, 551.

43. "Personal," 793–94.

44. "Beauty," 305. All parts of the universe direct us "to true and real greatness and excellency, and manifest the power and wisdom of God" (*WJE* 13, 224).

45. *WJE* 20, 97.

46. *WJE* 13, 330.

47. *WJE* 13, 384.

48. *WJE* 13, 410.

49. "Images," 53.

As the "Supreme Orderer of all things," God has premeditated and devised every part of nature to *typify* spiritual reality.[50] That is, the universe does more than just *represent* God's truth; it embodies and even "incarnates" his communications to intelligent life, pointing beyond its own beauty to the Creator and Origin of that beauty.[51] And the universe does so not in random or chaotic fashion, but with a high degree of predictability—a patterned reliability that provides the best means to reveal divine glory in the beautifully orderly plan of redemption.[52] Order *always* serves the ultimate goal of redemption and encompasses even the most infinitesimal part of reality. God's intricate government of the universe efficiently and surely brings to pass his loving intentions, ruling "every thought, and every purpose, every motion and action, not only of angels and men, but of every creature, great and small, even to every little atom in the whole creation, and that forever and ever."[53]

Edwards provides us therefore with an excellent case for our care of the environment. Nature is unmistakably God's, created for his glory. But because it was created to house humans, they should be concerned for it as a divine endowment and value it as an integral factor in God's eternal plan. Further, nature ought to be cared for due to its spiritual and typological significance, given that even a sub-atomic particle is imbued with divine meaning, in and of itself. Disease, accidents, and natural disasters, which for Edwards occur as a result of humanity's Fall into sin, are also part of an ultimately harmonious material system that reflects the Trinity: diverse while unified in interdependence. All of nature exhibits the government and goodness of God in physical and spiritual senses, and should be cultivated as a sacred gift pointing toward the goal of human redemption.

The Eternal Plan of Redemption

Just as there are laws created and used by God to order and manage the realm of secondary beauty in nature, so there are laws according to

---

50. *WJE* 15, 540.
51. *WJE* 13, 284.
52. "Threefold," *WJE* 14, 414.
53. "Excellencies," 422. Human will and determinism will be a topic in chapter 4.

which God maintains the spiritual dimension and its morality.[54] Made in God's image with "intelligent perception and action," every human consequently has a nature that subjects him to the moral government of his Creator.[55] Because humanity was made with the specific purpose of "remanating" (re-emanating) God's glory by worshipping and praising him, our moral responsibility is to fulfill that end by having our minds and wills "entirely conformed to the nature and will of the Creator and to those rules he gives that are expressive of it."[56] God's moral government does not consist of arbitrary rules, but of obligations that reflect God's holiness and expect every human's consent to him.

> [F]or there can be no such thing maintained, as a communication between God and men, as between intelligent voluntary agents, without moral government. For in maintaining communication, or converse, one must yield to the other, must comply with the other; there must be union of wills; one must be clothed with authority, the other with submission.[57]

This submission is fundamentally not to the *laws* of moral government, but to their source and end, Christ, who "is the head of the moral world, . . . the chief of God's servants, appointed to be the head of his saints and angels," and the "perfect pattern and example of goodness."[58] Just as Christ rules the natural realm through the ministry of the Holy Spirit, so he rules the moral realm in the same way, at the same time. All spiritual matters regarding "reasonable creatures . . . are ordered by sovereign providence according to absolute decrees," which by divine intention serve to fulfill the plan of redemption.[59]

"We see that all revolutions in the world are to subserve to this grand design, so that the Work of Redemption is . . . the sum of God's

---

54. *WJE* 15, 373.

55. *WJE* 20, 97.

56. "Judgment," 512. "'Tis reasonable that God should prescribe how we shall serve him, for he brought us out of nothing for this end, that we might serve him, and he keeps us from dropping into nothing every moment. All the being we have, and all the good of that being, is from him" ("Reasonable," 183).

57. *WJE* 20, 104. God's moral agency does not oblige him to keep sinners from sinning and incurring his punishment; doing so would actually compromise his own justice and the moral integrity of the creature ("Consideration," 108). For a more detailed treatment of sin, see chapter 3.

58. "End," 474.

59. "Judgment," 511.

works of providence."[60] Actually, redemption by Christ through the Holy Spirit's agency "is to be the grand design of all God's designs, and the *summum* and *ultimum* of all the divine operations and degrees."[61] In the loving work of human salvation from sin, "[a]ll the perfections of the Deity have their brightest manifestation"; in it "shines the glory of his face (II Cor 3:18)" and "are opened the infinite treasures of God's heart (Eph 3:8–10)."[62] As we saw in chapter 1, from all eternity God planned to reveal himself to humankind, so that to Edwards the redemption of just one soul as part of the plan of redemption is more glorious than the creation of the entire universe.[63]

Implicit to our treatment of creation so far has been the sovereignty of God exercised in his providential dealings and designs, especially in "his use of the world he has made."[64] For Edwards, God's sovereignty is a fact obvious to all intelligent beings; attempts to deny this run contrary not just to reason, but to the most basic premises of God's general revelation of himself in the universe. It is self-evident to all that God's sovereignty, the "ability and authority to do whatever pleases him,"[65] includes absolute and unconstrained power, independent will, and an "infinite all sufficient wisdom" that attends his will.[66] Not only do all people innately know that God is sovereign, but they know as well that all things worked in the world from its beginning were ordered by God according to his plan of salvation.[67]

Certainly finite creatures are capable of comprehending only a small portion of the outworkings of God's sovereignty because the nature, design, and ends of God's "general government of providential disposal . . . are secret things that belong to God" in which "man's understanding and will are no way concerned."[68] Still, it is not God's manner to hide his work totally since he desires his own glory, especially in fellowship with his chosen, redeemed people. He directs all things "to make his

60. *WJE* 9, 513.
61. "Trustees," 728.
62. "Pepperrell," 417.
63. "Thoughts," 334.
64. "End," 471.
65. *WJE* 1, 378.
66. *WJE* 1, 380.
67. "Threefold," 414.
68. *WJE* 20, 345.

hand visible, and his power conspicuous, and men's dependence on him most evident" so people are not justified to boast in their own abilities.[69] Indeed, the "providence of God preaches aloud to us our duty, and warns us of sin and danger; God so orders all his dispensations towards us, that his voice may be heard in them."[70]

While we will address the effects of sin and the need for special, divine revelation for salvation in the next chapter, here we observe that for Edwards, the Scriptures allow much greater insight into the sovereignty of God than revelation through nature alone. Due to sin, humans are crippled in their attempts to understand God and the spiritual dimension that pervades the universe. But through faith in Jesus Christ and with the indwelling guidance of the Holy Spirit, the Bible "reveals God to us and gives us a view of the grand design and glorious scheme of his providence, from the beginning to the end of the world."[71] God's written Word is the only sure guide and rule for properly appreciating the providence of events; nothing else can inform us of "what God is about or what he aims at in these works that he is doing in the world."[72]

What God *is* doing is regulating *everything*, and because God values people above the rest of creation, he regulates as well what pertains to their intelligence and voluntary acts.[73] God continuously exercises sovereignty over every person's health and use of reason,[74] afflictions and calamities,[75] duration of life,[76] volition,[77] temporal spiritual state,

---

69. WJE 2, 139; see Eph 2:8–10.

70. "Duty," 440. As part of creation, history (created time) is as revelatory as nature. Biblical history, because it is divinely inspired, serves as a model by which the rest of history can be interpreted. Edwards's premier analysis of the spiritual aspects of extra-biblical history can be found in *A History of the Work of Redemption*, WJE 9, especially sermons 21–24 (388–442), which discuss the history of the Church after AD 70. For an analysis of the ministry of providence in an individual's life, see WJE 7, especially 534–39, where Edwards describes the work of God as missionary David Brainerd (1718–47) approached death.

71. WJE 9, 290.

72. WJE 9, 520.

73. WJE 20, 98.

74. WJE 13, 352.

75. WJE 3, 207.

76. "Future," 369.

77. WJE 1, 433.

and eternal destiny.[78] Indeed, every breath is in God's hand and is "a mercy of God that we do not deserve."[79] As the most excellent, dignified, and perfect Being, the Creator of all, God is unreservedly worthy of such sovereignty. All things are his, "all creatures are wholly and entirely the fruits of God's power, and therefore it is fit that they should be subject to, and for, his pleasure."[80] For Edwards, God's sovereignty is a great part of his glory that demonstrates his holiness and loveliness: "The doctrines of God's absolute sovereignty, and free grace, in showing mercy to whom he would show mercy; and man's absolute dependence on the operations of God's Holy Spirit, have very often appeared to me as sweet and glorious doctrines."[81]

Not only is humanity totally reliant upon God and his care, but "all creatures . . . are wholly derived from and are wholly dependent on him every moment for being and all good, so that they are properly his possession."[82] And not only creatures, but every atom,[83] every planet,[84] every single thing affected by gravity is dependent upon God,[85] along with every other thing "in the universal system of existence."[86] So in nature there is harmony in plurality, interdependence with proportioned individuality (just as in the Godhead), and sheer reliance upon the Trinity who created it all.

Because nothing in the universe is contingent upon anything or anyone but God, and all things are eternally present to God, everything in the created realm is also thoroughly *foreknown* by him.[87] While foreknowledge's relation to human will is a matter for chapter 4, here we note that without foreknowledge, God would be inconsistent in his manner of sovereign, universal government and subject to various possibilities

---

78. *WJE* 13, 523.
79. "Self-Exam," 485.
80. "Consideration," 108.
81. "Personal," *WJE* 16, 799.
82. "Judgment," 512.
83. "Things," 265. Edwards also explains that "every atom in the universe is managed by Christ so as to be most to the advantage of the Christian" (*WJE* 13, 184).
84. "Sufficiency," 475.
85. "Things," 234–35.
86. *WJE* 3, 126.
87. *WJE* 1, 254.

related to the choices of other beings, particularly people.[88] In other words, God would be limited and ineffectual in carrying out the designs of providence—God would not really be God. But for Edwards, analyzing God's foreknowledge is simply another way of approaching God's implementation of the plan of redemption. Note this carefully: if an event is foreknown by God, it has the same certainty of occurrence as an event that has already happened, because God knows and sees all things in the realm of time from his state of ever-presence.[89] The entire concept of foreknowledge is really a human tool used to grasp at understanding God's eternal designs from our finite, time-bound vantage point. If we question the existence or scope of God's sovereignty even just in the dimension of time, which is itself created by him, we are not simply debating an interesting theological abstraction. Rather, we are questioning the power, sufficiency, and omniscience of God and acting contrarily to his drive toward fulfilling the eternal work of redemption.

There is no doubt then that for the theologian, God's sovereign communication of himself and his moral expectations obligates humans to a holy, obedient response. "The whole creation of God preaches to us; its creatures declare to us his majesty, his wisdom and power, and mercy."[90] Moral law, or the evidence of God's ways present in nature, guarantees that people know God and are without excuse to serve him.[91] It is "an eternal, unalterable rule, always the same," built into reality as one of the threads uniting the spiritual, corporeal, and temporal facets of the universe.[92] Moral law is a means of "common grace," or the assistance given to everyone by the Holy Spirit for religious and moral pursuits.[93] Moral law is and always has been "written in men's hearts, . . . [and is

---

88. *WJE* 1, 253.

89. *WJE* 1, 262. For two critiques of this point, compare Mavrodes with Plantinga. One of Plantinga's main concerns is that Edwards's God cannot foreknow anything without being time-bound and therefore finite. It is true that Edwards does not address specifically how a timeless God, for whom all things are eternally present, interacts with temporal matters. But Edwards does believe that God is involved with time as a separate, created thing, without God being limited by it. For Edwards, foreknowledge is basically a human construct for understanding the *logical* progression of divine acts within time, and is not directly related to the actual functions within God's *eternally present* mind.

90. "Duty," 440, based on Job 12:7–8; Ps 19:1–2; and Rom 1:19–20.

91. "Calamity," 489.

92. "Threefold," 399.

93. "Grace," 153.

that] by which men were exposed to death for personal sin."⁹⁴ In sum, natural law began with creation, was first understood and violated by Adam, and "is the original and universal rule of righteousness and judgment for all mankind."⁹⁵

Human knowledge of the moral law resides in the conscience. "And indeed natural conscience is implanted in all mankind, there to be as it were in God's stead, and to be an internal judge or rule to all, whereby to distinguish right and wrong."⁹⁶ Through conscience, all people know the reality of God, the demands of his holiness, and the temporal and eternal consequences for both righteousness and rebelliousness.⁹⁷ Since humanity's Fall into sinfulness, God has used the conscience to restrain people from utter wickedness.⁹⁸ The Holy Spirit also ministers to us through it to remind us of God's constant presence, enduring providence, supreme moral worth, and desire to fellowship with humanity. "God hath not left himself without witness in natural reason, in that he does us good, and gives us rain from heaven and fruitful seasons, filling our hearts with food and gladness."⁹⁹ It is, in the end, a great gift: "conscience is our best friend in this world when its rebukes are severest."¹⁰⁰

But what do we make of those in society, the despots and cold-blooded killers, who seem to have no conscience? For Edwards, their cruelty does not disprove the existence of conscience nor the Holy Spirit's power to communicate the reality of divine law through nature. Rather, persistent cruelty demonstrates humanity's ability to develop and savor a habit of sin to such an extent that the capacity to behave

---

94. "Torments," 314.

95. *WJE* 3, 339.

96. "Virtue," 613. In contrast to conscience, human *instinct* involves "various dispositions and inclinations . . . established chiefly for the preservation of mankind, though not only for this, but also for their comfortably subsisting in the world." Such instincts include "natural appetites and aversions," hunger, sexuality, sociability, and general benevolence (600). The difference between conscience and virtue will be discussed in chapter 4.

97. "Future," 357. In *WJE 13*, 373, Edwards notes that there is a "secret intimation and . . . inward testimony that men have upon occasion of the being of God . . . however they may endeavor to root it out."

98. "Virtue," 616.

99. *WJE 13*, 280.

100. "Self-Exam," 485.

morally is virtually obliterated.[101] Such evil is the persistent rejection of human and divine community, and a refusal to consent to God and others. It is deliberate rebellion against the Spirit's intention to reform the sin-fractured image of God in humans. But God still allows cruelty. As we will see in the discussion of original sin in chapter 3, God is under no obligation to restrain sin in his creatures. He does so only according to his sovereign mercy and wisdom, and may allow blatant evil for the higher purposes of his good and perfect plan. In the end, conscience is a treasure, but its rightful use is not forced upon those who crave its destruction.

Further Evidence of Divine Sovereignty

In his books and sermons, Jonathan Edwards strongly opposes deism, the belief that God created the universe but since has had little or no involvement with it. Instead, the Puritan contends that not only is the universe totally dependent on God, but the Spirit of Christ is continually creating all things out of nothing. Every single fraction of time is actually a new creation, "a present, remaining, continual act."[102] What to us seems to be the constant flow and perpetuation of time and reality is actually its constant, seamless re-creation. All things would cease to be "without a new exertion of the divine power to cause them to exist in the following moment."[103] So for you, the moments in time during which you turn to the next page will be created by God out of nothing for you to "live into," just as he planned before the world began.

As a result, the only difference between the initial creation of the universe, and every instance and effect of divine creation thereafter, is

---

[101] "Yet wickedness may by long habitual exercise greatly diminish a sense of conscience" ("Virtue," 615). The relations between will, habit, and morality will be discussed in chapter 4.

[102] *WJE 13*, 418, based on Job 9:9; Ps 65:6, 104:4; Isa 40:22, 44:24; and Amos 5:8, among others.

[103] *WJE 3*, 402. "God [doesn't] fully obtain his design in any one particular state that the world has been in at one time, but in the various successive states that the world is in, in different ages, connected in a scheme. But God is continually causing revolutions [i.e., changes]; providence makes a continual progress, and continually is bringing forth things new in the state of the world, and very different from what ever were before; he removes one that he may establish another. And perfection will not be obtained till the last revolution, when God's design will be fully reached" (*WJE 18*, 94).

circumstantial—initial creation just happened to be the first instance. God "so unites these successive new effects, that he *treats them as one*, by communicating to them like properties, relations, and circumstances; and so, leads us to regard and treat them as one."[104] Edwards deduces that all time and nature is a "constitution . . . which depends on nothing but the divine will; which *divine will* depends on nothing but the *divine wisdom*."[105]

Since all things continually depend on God and his wisdom, we remind ourselves not to segregate the physical, spiritual, and temporal realities of the universe. Rather, these facets are meticulously interpenetrating, and all simultaneously and directly reveal the Trinity. The existence of any material thing, any spirit, and both matter and spirit in the case of humans is a result of the Holy Spirit directly exercising divine power on behalf of the Father and Son.[106] The same power that maintains an ice crystal on Saturn's rings also continuously creates the angels, all while keeping a father's heart beating as he laughs and plays with his child. The body and soul of a human, and the awareness of self and the Divine that is provided and nurtured through the human image of God, rely in every way upon "the sovereign will and agency of God."[107]

The relationship between God and reality must be clarified further to preserve the distinction between the exercise of divine power and its effects in the universe. Edwards is very cautious to avoid pantheism, which holds that God, the universe, and all that is in it are really one, indistinguishably. Instead, as explained in chapter 1, God dwells in some kind of spiritual space that is not material, because God is not present anywhere in the way that our bodies or flowers are present.[108] Still, God is present in the universe, permeating it without being identical with that which he is continually creating. His creatures demonstrate that they are his workmanship, but his very essence is not imparted to

---

104. *WJE* 3, 403.

105. *WJE* 3, 404, original italics. In "Atoms," Edwards contends that divine continuous creation disallows all mechanistic views of reality in which "bodies act upon each other, purely and properly by themselves" (216).

106. "Things," 241. The implications of continuous creation for original sin will be addressed in chapter 3.

107. *WJE* 3, 399.

108. *WJE* 13, 335.

them.[109] True, the power of God is "exerted in an infinite number of places at once, even in every part of every atom of the universe. And since ... where his power is exercised, there his essence must be, his essence can be by nothing excluded."[110] But reality exists in God in such a way that it receives communications of God's glory and reveals that glory to all intelligent beings while remaining separate from God's identity.

To illustrate very simply, God creates a dog, is always present with the dog, and continuously sustains it until its appointed life cycle ends. The dog is beautiful, because its Creator is. Just as an artist shows a certain, unique style in her paintings, God's dog shows his style. But the dog never becomes God in any way, God never becomes a dog in any way, and when the dog dies, God still lives on perfectly and eternally.

If these notions of Edwards's aren't difficult enough to grasp, God's relation to the universe is made a bit more complicated when we consider Edwards's unique brand of idealism, or theology of God's own ideas.[111] This idealism requires a good bit of concentration to understand, so please read carefully. After this section Edwards's theology becomes much easier to grasp.

According to Edwards's idealism, because God's mind is unfluctuating, enduring, and all-knowing, we finite, sinful creatures should presume that there are things that exist only in the mind of God and that exist in our universe apart from human perception.[112] But what we *do* understand about God's mind is apprehended due to his revelation of those ideas to us. Our perception of them constitutes what we describe as time and history.[113] Edwards writes that "'Pastness,' if I may make such a word, is nothing but a mode of ideas," a way that we may comprehend God's thoughts in the finite context of time.[114] As our lives progress from day to day, what we knew and understood previously is ordinarily

---

109. "Unknown," 201.

110. "Atoms," 214.

111. For various treatments of John Locke's (1632–1704) influence on Edwards regarding idealism, see Anderson, "Editor's Introduction," *WJE* 6, 101–22; Jenson, 29–32; and Carse, 35–44.

112. "Mind," *WJE* 6, 356. Sang Lee explains that unperceived objects are real, much like the tree that falls in the forest with no one around ("Edwards on Nature," 47). Lee's article provides a helpful summary of why Edwards's idealism is not Neoplatonic: chiefly because it sees meaning and value in material reality.

113. Chapter 3 addresses more fully Edwards's theology of history.

114. "Mind," 371.

remembered, but also begins to fade, and becomes history. Our thoughts about what happened even an hour ago are not as vivid and clear as the thoughts we are having (or trying to have) at the present moment. But fading "pastness" not only reflects time's passage—it is moreover evidence that something in "the universe is conscious of its own being, and of what is done in it [by] the Creator and Governor."[115]

> For God to glorify himself is to discover himself in his works, or to communicate himself in his works, which is all one; for we are to remember that the world exists only [because of God's creative thought], so that the very [existence] of the world implies its being perceived or discovered [by people].[116]

Recall: the Son is the Idea of the Father, and the Holy Spirit is the love between them in action. Similarly, you and I are able to think (conceive ideas), then think about ourselves, then think and know that we thought about something in the prior moment. We thereby act in some way that refers back to prior thoughts. As all this happens, we imitate the Trinitarian God, albeit in a flawed, finite manner. So thought and memory, even fading memory, are good theological evidence that the image of God in humans is alive and kicking: God is gloriously communicating himself in and through that image, and the interconnected thoughts in our minds bear resemblance to the *intra*penetrating, pure relations among the Persons of the Trinity.[117]

When contemplating how we perceive time and reality, Edwards is not painting a subjective picture of reality, nor one that is fundamentally human-centered. A person's mind is neither the locus nor the ground of truth—the world really *doesn't* revolve around us, even though we often wish it did! And to the theologian, it is ridiculous to believe solipsistically "that the material world exists nowhere but in the soul of man, confined within his skull."[118] Rather, as has been stated, we are utterly dependent upon the Holy Spirit for the true perceptions of creation conveyed to our minds. While creation is incomplete without human perception to receive it as divine communication, the human mind is basically lost without material reality to provide its bearings. Without this physical

---

115. *WJE* 13, 197.
116. *WJE* 13, 360.
117. "Self-Exam," 485.
118. "Mind," 368.

context, we cannot begin to comprehend the spiritual reality of God's self-revelation because the human mind cannot receive, manufacture, or discern truth in a vacuum.[119] Further, only those with faith in Christ are granted by the Holy Spirit the ability to understand accurately the *spiritual* dimension of the universe; those lacking faith have only a skewed, shallow understanding.

To summarize: the harmonious agreement and inextricable bond between the universe's material and spiritual dimensions are revelatory products of God's creative mind. For Edwards the universe is dependent upon God's thought for its very existence, while creation's purpose as divine communication is validated by the human mind's Spirit-enabled perception of it. Stated another way, God operates through his image in people and through the corporeal world to join human consciousness, spirit, and thought with his own.[120] In this manner, we can know truth, which Edwards defines as "the consistency and agreement of our ideas with the ideas of God"—basically when our ideas *consent* with God's.[121] All reality therefore is a grand idea in the mind of God, expressed to finite minds that are enabled by the Holy Spirit to apprehend and experience the grand idea and its subsidiary ideas. This grand idea is precisely God's eternal plan of redemption for humanity, and the subsidiary ideas are the events we share in time and space. Above all else, the grand idea is a flawless representation of God's Trinitarian nature.

Crucial Spiritual Meaning in Nature

Because God is sovereign over every part of reality toward the goal of his own glorification through the plan of redemption, Edwards infers that all of those created parts serve as *types*. These are concrete representations of spiritual meanings and are illustrative of God's nature and intentions.[122] We have already observed that the secondary beauty of creation is based upon and expresses the primary, spiritual beauty of God. Edwards believed "that the whole visible creation, which is but the shadow of being, is so made and ordered by God as to typify and

---

119. "Mind," 384.
120. "Mind," 355.
121. "Mind," 341.
122. "Images," 129–30.

represent spiritual things."[123] Nature is a book that records the words of the still, small voice of God as he communicates himself, instilling corporeal reality with divine meaning.[124] God embeds types in nature to serve as the grammar of the divine language and as a "fit method of instruction" regarding the goal of created history: the glory of God in Christ.[125] Indeed, to "signify divine things by the constitution of the world is no mere trifling."[126]

The reason types involve "no mere trifling" is that for Edwards every single aspect of reality involves at least one type, and every type ultimately points toward the grand antitype, Christ himself. "The type is only the representation or shadow of the thing, but the antitype is the very substance, and is the true thing."[127] Unfortunately, due to sin types in creation can no longer be discerned by humans without God's help. Our primary tool to interpret creation's types is the Bible. Through it, the Holy Spirit is guiding us, "declaring to us those spiritual mysteries that are indeed signified or typified in the constitution of the natural world," and "actually making application of the signs and types in the book of nature."[128] The great value of types is actually demonstrated and authorized by the Spirit-inspired Scriptures. It only remains for us to learn how to use them so we may comprehend biblical revelation more deeply. In all, types in nature are "part of divine truth sufficiently and fully ascertained by the revelation God has made in the holy Scriptures."[129]

---

123. "Discourse," 138–39. In "Types," Edwards writes, "I am not ashamed to own that I believe that the whole universe, heaven and earth, air and seas, and the divine constitution and history of the holy Scriptures, be full of images of divine things, as full as a language is of words; and that the multitude of those things that I have mentioned are but a very small part of what is really intended to be signified and typified by these things: but that there is room for persons to be learning more and more of this language and seeing more of that which is declared in it to the end of the world without discovering all" (152).

124. "Types," 150.

125. "Messiah," 191. For Edwards, "typology represented an exegetical science that revealed God's progressive dispensation through history and human time while providing continuities between the Old and New Testaments and contemporary events" (Anderson et al., "Editor's Introduction to 'Types of the Messiah,'" WJE 11, 160).

126. "Images," 98.

127. "Images," 62.

128. "Images," 106. Typology in the Bible will be detailed in chapter 3.

129. "Discourse," 139.

Edwards held that the greatest of all natural types is the sun because it most fully reveals the personal attributes of God in Christ.[130] His statements about the sun vary widely, evidencing not only the biblically-bounded creativity Edwards expressed through typology, but also the numerous levels of spiritual meaning he believed could be legitimately discovered in nature. For example, he asserts that "as all the world is enlightened and brought out of darkness by the rising of the sun, so by Christ's rising we are begotten again to a living hope."[131] Just as the sunbeams cannot be scattered or interrupted by the wind, so is "heavenly light, communicated from Christ, the Sun of Righteousness, to the soul."[132] The sun's being eclipsed by the moon typifies the veiling of Christ's glory in his incarnation, death, and glorious shouldering of the Church's sins.[133]

Even the Trinity is typed by the sun, for the "Father is as the substance of the sun; the Son is as the brightness and glory of the disk of the sun; the holy Ghost is as the heat and continually emitted influence, the emanation by which the world is enlightened, warmed, enlivened and comforted."[134] Even if their meanings can only be partially discerned with the aid of the Bible, types such as the sun are God-designed, God-given keys to understanding the divine Being and his universe. The intertwined aspects of nature, spirit, and time compose a typological love poem from God to humanity that is constantly being re-created, yet is always calling humankind to holy conduct and holy fellowship with God and one another.

If we understand that the Trinitarian God's attributes and ministry provide the basis for creation, we can then apprehend that creation and its harmoniously interpenetrating physical and spiritual facets establish the foundation upon which the remainder of Edwards's theology is built. In a sense, creation as a topic in his theological system is itself typological, foreshadowing all the ways he expected to discover his continuously creating God through a scripturally informed interpretation

---

130. *WJE* 15, 340. "Unveiled by the gospel, these types and other figurative representations are as a glass [mirror] in which we see the image of Christ's face" (325).

131. "Images," 66.

132. "Images," 88. For an extended treatment of Christ as the Sun of Righteousness, see "Light," 540–43.

133. *WJE* 15, 290–91.

134. *WJE* 13, 434.

of history. Edwards's profound appreciation of God's condescension in communicating his glory and even himself to creatures who are made in his image is abundantly evident. The Puritan sought to capture the Godhead's dynamism of overflowing love in each fraction of time, each moment of human consciousness. The history of the work of redemption, with all of its intricate, providentially ordered divine acts, is the plan by which the Spirit expresses the Triune God's dynamism and permeates the universe with purpose: the goal of human salvation from sin. That plan, especially as described in Scripture, is the matter to which we turn next.

For Further Thought

1. In your own words, explain the part each person of the Trinity has in Edwards's theology of creation. Do his views impact how you see and interact with the natural environment?
2. Edwards uses Bible passages such as Gen 1:1—2:3; Isa 41:18–20; and John 1:1–14 to support his theology of creation. Read these passages and compare them with your own understanding of the origins of the universe.
3. Why does God create? List the reasons Edwards gives. How does the human creative process resemble and differ from God's?
4. What are the differences between angels, humans, and beasts? Do you agree with Edwards?
5. What is the image of God in humans? How does that image relate to conscience, reason, and evil, as Edwards defines them?
6. Do you agree that humans are created in God's image? Why? What are some alternative explanations for the existence of human personality, morality, and intelligence?
7. According to this chapter, what does God's sovereignty encompass? Do you see God as being sovereign in the same way that Edwards does? What objections might be raised against Edwards on this point?
8. How is God's sovereignty tied to moral law and humanity? What do nature, the Bible, and the Holy Spirit have to do with our ability to understand moral law?

9. Carefully read Rom 1:16–32. Make note of each point that either agrees with or contradicts Edwards's view of moral law.

10. Edwards believed that God is intimately involved in even the minor, mundane aspects of our lives. Does this idea bother you or comfort you? If he is correct, how might your understanding of God change?

11. What are your impressions about Edwards's concept of time and its continuous creation? If he is correct, how does this concept impact how you view and live your life?

12. What are types and antitypes? Do you see anything in nature (other than the sun) that could serve as a type for God? Do Edwards's types change your understanding of God? How?

For Further Reading

Bass, Diana Butler. "God's Visible Glory: The Beauty of Nature in the Thought of John Calvin and Jonathan Edwards." *Westminster Theological Journal* 52 (1990) 13–26.

Cherry, C. Conrad. *Nature and Religious Imagination: From Edwards to Bushnell.* Philadelphia: Fortress, 1980.

Colacurcio, Michael J. "The Example of Edwards: Idealist Imagination and the Metaphysics of Sovereignty." In *Puritan Influences in American Literature*, edited by Emory Elliott. Urbana: University of Illinois Press, 1979.

Cooey, Paula M. *Jonathan Edwards on Nature and Destiny: A Systematic Analysis.* Lewiston, NY: Edwin Mellen, 1985.

Daniel, Stephen H. *The Philosophy of Jonathan Edwards: A Study in Divine Semiotics.* Bloomington: Indiana University Press, 1994.

Lee, Sang Hyun. "The Concept of Habit in the Thought of Jonathan Edwards." PhD diss., Harvard University, 1972.

———. "Jonathan Edwards on Nature." In *Faithful Imagining: Essays in Honor of Richard R. Niebuhr,* edited by Lee et al. Atlanta: Scholars, 1995.

———. "Mental Activity and the Perception of Beauty in Jonathan Edwards." *Harvard Theological Review* 69, nos. 3–4 (1976) 369–96.

Schweitzer, William. "Rage against the Machine: Jonathan Edwards Versus the God of Deism." *Scottish Bulletin of Evangelical Theology* 25 (2007) 61–79.

Wainwright, William. "Jonathan Edwards and the Language of God." *Journal of the American Academy of Religion* 48 (1980) 519–30.

3

God's Solution to the Problem of Sin

WHEN JONATHAN EDWARDS WRITES that "the great work of providence, that is as it were the sum of all providences, is that work of mercy, the work of redemption," he is making a statement loaded with theological assumptions.[1] We have already observed that the meaning of providence for Edwards spans from the workings of a single atom to the most distant parts of the universe. We have seen that "the great work of providence" is manifest in the intricacies of intertwined spiritual and physical realities, merged in time to reveal the Creator and his nature. We've also seen that providence is grounded in the very being of God. Every part of reality begins as a divine idea and bears witness to God's identity when he creates that idea in time.

Edwards's God is a supremely good Being, incomprehensibly loving within the Trinity as well as in his care for every creature and thing. And this God is a God of purpose and orderly design who planned from all eternity to reveal himself to creatures and redeem part of humanity from its sinfulness. All of God's decrees belong to "that eternal covenant of redemption that was between the Father and the Son before the foundation of the world."[2]

Like everything else, the plan of salvation has the ultimate purpose of exalting God, who "is glorified in the work of redemption in this, that there appears in it so absolute and universal a dependence of the redeemed on him."[3] This dependence should not surprise us, because Edwards has already established that all things depend upon God for their existence. But the work of redemption is a special, superior case— the dependent redeemed are being redeemed *from* something (and *to*

---

1. *WJE* 15, 379.
2. *WJE* 9, 513.
3. "Dependence," 202.

something), and are redeemed despite their depraved indifference to God.[4] God glorifies himself by mercifully and lovingly forgiving them of their sinfulness and enabling them to love selflessly. In a word, the work of redemption is the *gospel*, which, all in all, is the good news of a grand act of divine love.

> Love is the principal thing which the gospel reveals in God and Christ. The gospel brings to light the love between the Father and the Son, and declares how that love has been manifested in mercy; how that Christ is God's beloved Son in whom he is well pleased.[5]

Given that God is omniscient and has eternally decreed a work of redemption, it logically follows that he knows from eternity those who will be forgiven of their sins. "The gospel teaches us the doctrine of the eternal electing love of God, and reveals how God loved those that are redeemed by Christ before the foundation of the world; and how he then gave them to the Son, and the Son loved them as his own."[6] God elects, or chooses, persons in sovereign love according to his own good pleasure and will, and not based upon his foreknowledge of anything they may do in their lives.[7] While Edwards notes that "God did choose men to eternal life upon a foresight of their faith," God also decreed that they would have faith, and that he would enable them to do so.[8] Election is itself a means of God's glorification, because it manifests his "sovereignty and supreme right to all his creatures."[9] In theory God could have elected

---

4. *WJE* 3, 353. On 354, Edwards notes that "the Scripture represents the redemption by Christ as a redemption from *deserved* destruction; and that [redemption] ... as the fruit of God's love to mankind." For further reflection, read Holbrook's "Editor's Introduction" in the same volume.

5. "Charity," 143; see Matt 3:17.

6. "Charity," 144.

7. *WJE* 13, 234. In "Charity," Edwards contends that "good practice is not the ground of election, as the Arminians suppose who imagine that God elects men upon a foresight of their good works. But Christian practice is the scope and end of salvation" (294). The role of the will and good works in faith will be addressed in chapter 4.

8. *WJE* 13, 478.

9. "Reasonable," 175. God has a sovereign right "to set bounds to the lives of his own creatures, be they sinful or not" (*WJE* 3, 206). He is just in doing so: "certainly the righteous Judge of all the earth won't bring death on thousands of millions, not only that are not worthy of death, but are worthy of no punishment at all" (209).

everyone to receive salvation, but did not in order to uphold his impeccable justice through the punishment of sin.[10]

God's choice of some people to receive salvation from their sin has numerous implications for Edwards, who saw election as part of God's design "to gather together in one all things in Christ in heaven and on earth."[11] Truly, election is the foundation for the establishment and fruition of the church. It enables each member of the church eventually to be glorified and exalted to sinless, mature personhood as part of the Body of Christ. Because one's election is grounded in the eternal plan of God and therefore rooted in his faithfulness, it is unchangeable and cannot be lost or have its benefits modified. And within the framework of God's great design, election ensures that human conformity to Christ's holy image, which is election's greatest gift, will result. "There is a certain measure of holiness and happiness, that each one of the elect is eternally appointed to; and all things that relate to him, work together to bring to pass this appointed measure of good."[12] Thus the elect are not only chosen to receive eternal life, which for Edwards is a phenomenal gift of fellowship with God, but are also granted the privilege of completing with joy and love the good works eternally ordained for them.[13]

Redemption in History: Jesus Christ Saves Sinners

Because humanity was first created to live out good deeds, it is not surprising that the everlasting covenant made by God with Adam in Gen 2:16–7 was a covenant of works. This covenant, or binding agreement, involves obedience to the natural, moral law that we examined in the last chapter. For Edwards, this is the only covenant God ever made with humankind.[14] Adam rejected his obligation to the covenant of works, so

---

10. Reprobation's purpose is for God to "glorify his vindictive justice," while election communicates God's goodness and glorifies his grace (*WJE 18*, 283).

11. *WJE* 9, 124.

12. "Gillespie," 230. Rev. Thomas Gillespie (1708–74) was a Scottish pastor who broke away from the established Presbyterian church to form a new communion opposing ecclesiastical tyranny. Initially called "The Presbytery of Relief," it became the United Presbyterian Church of Scotland in 1847.

13. "Thus God in the decree of election ordained that man should walk in good works" ("Charity," 295, based on Eph 1:4, 2:10). For elaboration of Edwards's childhood objections to the doctrine of election, see "Personal," 791–92.

14. While God does make covenants with Abraham and Israel in the Old Testament

its moral code remains the rule by which God judges people. Because sinful, wrecked people are never capable of meeting the covenant's requirements, it is not an adequate means for their redemption according to God's just and perfect standards.

On the other hand, the covenant of redemption is made between the Father and the Son to fulfill on behalf of humanity the sin-broken covenant of works.[15] God did not conjure up the covenant of redemption when Adam sinned; it was made from all eternity with the foreknowledge that Adam would fail in his works and need divine salvation. "Christ came into the world to fulfill and answer the covenant of works, that is the covenant that is to stand forever as a rule of judgment, . . . that is the covenant that we had broken, and that was the covenant that must be fulfilled."[16] So through the moral law that is part of the covenant of works, sinners are aware of their moral depravity and need for salvation, even if they choose to deny this awareness.[17] But through faith in Jesus Christ, who bears the penalty of God's judgment that they deserve, sinners can receive the free gift of salvation through the redemptive covenant of grace.[18] Edwards states that believers in Christ would perish if "God is not gracious to us, and don't make application of Christ's benefits to our souls. We are dependent on free grace, even for ability to lay hold in Christ already offered, so entirely is the gospel dispensation of mere grace."[19] Then it is the Holy Spirit who cares for the Father's elect, and applies the merits earned by Jesus Christ to their souls.

Edwards's basic thoughts about redemption, election, and covenants are not radically different from others in his Protestant, Reformed heritage. However, Edwards invests the incarnation of Jesus Christ and all that he accomplished during his ministry on earth with ramifications that are cosmic in scope and reach to the core of God's being. Edwards contends that Adam's Fall into sin resulted in a fracture or distortion of the created bond between physical and spiritual realities, so that the uni-

---

(Genesis 15, Exodus 19–20), these covenants are subsumed under Christ's covenant of redemption, and God assumes responsibility for fulfilling the human *and* divine obligations in those covenants.

15. *WJE 13*, 217.
16. *WJE 9*, 309.
17. *WJE 9*, 168.
18. "Inquiry," 205.
19. "Glorious Grace," *WJE 10*, 395.

verse is just as broken as humanity is. But Jesus Christ attains a healing of those realities simply through his fully *human*, fully *divine* constitution. He is the supreme antitype not only because he is God, and not only because his redemptive mission is the ultimate focus of creation and the Scriptures. He is the antitype who through his incarnate self personally commingles every natural type with its perfect spiritual complement.[20] In sum, as the chief Idea of God the Father and the Word made flesh, Jesus Christ unites all things within himself and paves the way for the healing of universal and human brokenness. His unification of the elect in the church is an integral part of the cosmic, restorative power in the incarnation.[21]

By default Christ also unites the reprobate, or those who are not granted salvation, in their damned state. In hell, which like heaven is created by God, all things exist because God thinks them into being. So even though the damned are totally separated from everything good, especially personal fellowship with God, they still exist and depend on God for that existence. Now, God could just let the reprobate cease to exist when their earthly lives end, a theory called annihilationism. Can it really be said that God's *good* will is to grant them miserable existence in hell? Edwards answers that the existence of the reprobate in hell is ultimately a good, though not of course for the sinners. Their continuing existence in hell manifests God's glory through his just and righteous hatred of sin.[22]

The elect will be delivered into heavenly fellowship at the consummation of time, when the full fruits of Jesus Christ's incarnation will be completely revealed. All of fallen creation, which has been groaning and

---

20. Cherry summarizes: "The Incarnation has made explicit in history what one could only infer from the natural order: that there is a harmonious resemblance between material and spiritual reality" ("Symbols of Spiritual Truth," 270).

21. In *WJE* 15, 325, Edwards contends that Christ's flesh typified the sin of the elect Church. "And the elect [C]hurch is Christ mystical, so that Christ, in taking flesh upon him, took their sin upon him; he was sin for us." But his assumption of flesh also represented the Old Testament Church and her manner of knowing God. "When Christ died, then there was an end to those Old Testament types, because they were then all fulfilled. [U]nveiled by the gospel, these types and other figurative representations are as a glass [or mirror] in which we see the image of Christ's face."

22. "The honor of God's justice won't suffer sin to go unpunished. 'Tis a dispute whether God's absolute justice obliges him to punish sin; but his *rectoral* justice . . . as judge and governor of the world, requires it, and as it belongs to him to see to the order of it" ("None Saved," 336). Hell will be addressed further in chapter 7.

in travail (Rom 8:20–22), will be restored and elevated to a greater state in which there will no longer be any brokenness or dichotomy between the material and the spiritual. Through the presence of the eternally incarnate Christ and the sustenance of all things by the Holy Spirit, reality will be a flawless blend of the material and the spiritual growing perpetually in holiness: this *is* heaven.[23] In that real place, the saints will have the ability to see Jesus Christ and each other "with their bodily eyes as well as by an intellectual view," such that they "will have two sorts of sight, intellectual and corporeal."[24]

So the incarnation of Christ has merits in restoring creation, making atonement for human sin, and reinstating divine-human fellowship. But the incarnation is also the paragonic antitype of holy behavior, the model the elect are empowered by the Spirit to imitate. Through "doctrine and precept" and "instance and example," Christ taught "true religion, in a greater degree than ever had been before."[25] Indeed, given Adam's Fall the "example of Jesus Christ is the only example that ever was set in the human nature, that was altogether perfect," thus exhibiting through his personhood the flawless fulfillment of the covenant of works.[26] Actually, "all his sufferings from the beginning were propitiatory, as every act of obedience was meritorious."[27]

Due to his peerless embodiment of the moral law that bespeaks the holy orderliness of the Godhead, his satisfaction of that law through his life, death, resurrection, and ascension, and his extension of forgiveness to the elect, Jesus Christ is the supreme revelation of the Trinitarian

---

23. Edwards contends that in heaven, saints and creation will continually become more perfect and complete because *finite* creation has *infinite* opportunity to reflect the glory of an *infinite* God. Saints will always grow more holy and creation will always grow in its revelation of God's glory, which itself will eternally increase. This will be explained more in chapter 7.

24. *WJE* 13, 501. Given Edwards's views of space, it could be that Jesus Christ's presence in heaven represents a higher "concentration" of manifest divinity. Edwards contends that God is everywhere, but "is said on some accounts more especially to be in some places rather than others. . . . [B]ut heaven is his dwelling place above all other places in the universe" ("Heaven," 369).

25. *WJE* 7, 89.

26. *WJE* 7, 91.

27. *WJE* 13, 539. Edwards explains, "though Christ's sufferings were but temporal, yet they were equivalent to our eternal sufferings by reason of the infinite dignity of his person. Though it was not infinite suffering, yet it was equivalent to infinite suffering, for it was infinite expense" ("The Sacrifice of Christ Acceptable," *WJE* 14, 452).

Godhead. The incarnation itself and Christ's earthly ministry clearly manifest "to men and angels the distinction of the persons of the Trinity." Christ's accomplishments display the infinite love between Father and Son—the Father forgiving an infinite debt and exalting Christ to "that high and mediatorial glory," and the Son "abasing himself for the vindicating of [the Father's] authority and the honor of his majesty." The Holy Spirit, in turn, is present as grace, a gift that is "a certain and infallible sign that a [person] shall have eternal life."[28] Thus, through the divine-human unification secured by the incarnation and the law's satisfaction, redeemed humanity can see the glory of the Trinity and imitate divine holiness by following the example of the God-Man, Jesus Christ.[29]

It follows then that the incarnation cements Christ's role as mediator between God and humanity. Christ was designated to be this mediator before the world was even created. But when humanity fell into sin through Adam's disobedience to God's moral law,

> Christ the eternal Son of God clothed himself with his mediatorial character and therein presented himself before the Father. He immediately stepped in between an holy, infinite, offended majesty and offending mankind, and was accepted in his interposition; and so wrath was prevented from going forth in the full execution of that ensuing curse that man had brought on himself.[30]

As mediator, Christ is the priestly intercessor and Word who communicates divine revelation to us through the active ministry of the Holy Spirit. And Jesus delights in communicating the elect's prayers, needs, and "communications of happiness" back to him.[31] Indeed Christ's mediatorial role is fundamentally one of mercy and compassion, for without it God could have justly destroyed all sinners. "There is no mercy exercised towards man but what is obtained through Christ's intercession."[32] Thus, even those who reject Christ still benefit from his mediation as he sustains creation through the Holy Spirit; human lives and every good in them are gifts from God.

An underlying assumption of Edwards's concept of election is "atonement," which involves three main factors: the voluntary bond

28. *WJE* 13, 406.
29. *WJE* 13, 526.
30. *WJE* 9, 130.
31. *WJE* 13, 264; "Christ's Sacrifice," *WJE* 10, 598.
32. *WJE* 9, 130.

Christ made with the elect by becoming a human, the Father's acceptance of Christ's representation of them as the Second Adam, and the imputation of Christ's victories over sin and death to the elect. The atonement restores those chosen to be redeemed and adopted as God's children by removing the guilt of their sins and setting them "in the same state that Adam was in the first moment of creation."[33] In this "federal theology," Adam stands as the representative for all humanity before the moral law of God and Christ stands as the elect's representative before God—their Savior from the punishment for sin the law demands.

> [B]elievers are represented in Scripture as being so *in* Christ, as that they are legally one, or accepted as one, by the Supreme Judge: Christ has assumed our nature, and has so assumed all, in that nature, that belongs to him, into such an union with himself, that he is become their head, and has taken them to be his members.[34]

But did Christ die for the sins of *everyone*, or just the elect? Edwards states, "Christ did die for all in this sense, that all by his death have an opportunity of being [saved]."[35] But Christ did *not* die for all in "that he did not die intending and designing that such and such particular persons should be the better for it."[36] Therefore, Christ's death provided everyone with the *option* for salvation from sin, but God eternally knew that some would reject it.

Edwards admits that the concept of divine imputation is a mystery that cannot be fully comprehended.[37] Nevertheless, it basically means that the elect are granted proper standing and holiness before God as if they had earned it themselves. "That righteousness of Christ is accepted for us, and admitted instead of that perfect inherent righteousness that ought to be in ourselves" but is not due to sin.[38]

Some think only of Christ's crucifixion when they hear the term "atonement." But Edwards maintains that we cannot neglect the corresponding power of Christ's historical resurrection from the dead and ascension (Matt 27–28). The resurrection was imperative to complete

33. "Justification," 187.
34. "Justification," 191, original italics.
35. *WJE* 13, 478.
36. *WJE* 13, 174.
37. "Threefold," 401.
38. "Justification," 185–86.

"that work that God required," the triumphant "conquest of death."[39] His resurrection validates and seals the elect's eternal future while his ascension establishes heaven as the church's eternal domain.[40] In effect, his resurrection was also meritorious in that it purchased "eternal life and glory" for the elect, who in a very real way rose from the dead with Christ.[41] Because Jesus Christ was raised from death by the Father, and ascended to heaven through the Spirit's power, we have proof of the sufficiency of Jesus' righteousness to satisfy and fulfill the Trinity's eternal plan of redemption.[42] This proof affirms that the designs of that plan are nearly complete, waiting only for the outworkings of God's agenda until the end of time as we know it.[43] For this reason, the theologian contends that the resurrection and ascension of Christ are "in general by far the greatest manifestation and the brightest effulgence of the moral perfection and glory of the divine Being that ever was."[44]

The Holy Spirit in the Life of the Savior

To Jonathan Edwards, the Holy Spirit had an integral role in the life of Jesus Christ from the very beginning. Christ was "formed in [Mary] by the Holy Ghost coming upon [her], and the power of the Highest overshadowing her, which is a lively representation of the manner in which the new creature is formed in the saints."[45] Jesus was conceived "of the

---

39. *WJE 13*, 211. Consult 1 Cor 15:42–49.
40. "Future," 361.
41. *WJE 9*, 358.
42. "Threefold," 393, based on Rom 8:34 and 1 Tim 3:16.
43. Edwards's beliefs about the end times ("eschatology") and Christ's defeat of Satan will be examined in chapter 7.
44. *WJE 15*, 591.
45. *WJE 15*, 288. While Christ is ordinarily the agent of creation through the Holy Spirit, the incarnation was a special case. "All the works of God . . . are wrought by Christ excepting those that are immediately wrought upon or about Christ, . . . and these are more immediately from God the Father. . . . [T]he human nature of Christ and what belongs to it is by the Spirit as the Spirit of the Father. But all the rest are by the Spirit as the Spirit of the Son" (*WJE 20*, 234). The human nature of Jesus Christ includes his conception in Mary's womb; the instruction, care, strength, and wisdom given to him through the course of his life; his resurrection; and his ascension.

substance of her body" and born sinless because of the Spirit's powerful influence.[46]

But the Holy Spirit did not simply form Christ in Mary and then have nothing to do with him. We know that the Spirit has the Trinitarian role of continuously sustaining the entire universe, so the birth and daily life of Jesus would certainly be included in that. But even more, the unique divine-human nature of Christ was very much a union accomplished through "the Spirit . . . dwelling in him after a peculiar [or unique] manner and without measure. . . . There is no other way of God's dwelling in a creature but by his Spirit."[47] It was the Spirit who made the incarnation possible, sealing the divine-human bond and subsequently enabling the elect to be united with the *Logos* and filled with the same indwelling Holy Spirit.[48] It was the Spirit who helped Jesus to resist temptation and maintain his holiness in accordance with the pure nature of the Godhead.[49] "It was by this Spirit that his sacrifice of himself was sanctified, being an offering to God in the pure and fervent flame of divine love, which burnt in his heart as well as in the flame of God's vindictive justice and wrath into which he was cast." In short, it "was by the eternal Spirit that Christ offered up himself without spot to God."[50]

For Edwards the Spirit's work in Jesus' life was most publicly evident at his baptism (Matt 3), which was "his solemn inauguration, and by which he entered on his ministry; and was attended with his anointing with the Holy [Spirit], in a solemn and visible manner."[51] When the Spirit descended like a dove, Christ "was filled with the fullness of God, but also Christ mystical, and every individual member of his mystical body effectively was filled."[52] So when the Spirit indwells believers, he conveys to them the same "meekness, harmlessness, peace and love"

---

46. *WJE* 9, 297.

47. *WJE* 13, 528.

48. *WJE* 15, 575. "All divine communion, or communion of the creatures with God or with one another in God, seems to be by the Holy Ghost. 'Tis by this that believers have communion with Christ. . . . The Spirit of God is the bond of perfectness by which God, Jesus Christ, and the [C]hurch are united together" (*WJE* 13, 529–30).

49. *WJE* 1, 281–82.

50. *WJE* 15, 575.

51. *WJE* 9, 315.

52. *WJE* 15, 530.

that he communicated to Christ at his baptism, along with all the other blessed benefits of fellowship with God.[53]

"The inheritance that Christ has purchased for the elect, is the Spirit of God; not in any extraordinary gifts, but in his vital indwelling in the heart, exerting and communicating himself there, in his own proper, holy or divine nature."[54] This inheritance blesses the elect with continual communion with God as well as sanctification, the process by which each believer in Christ gradually comes to resemble the flawless image of God in Christ. Although "the blood of Christ washes us from our guilt, yet 'tis the Spirit of Christ that washes from the pollution and stain of sin. . . . [T]he blood of Christ washes also from the filth of sin, so it purchases sanctification; it makes way for it . . . and purchases it by merit."[55] As Christ's messenger, the Spirit convinces believers about the reality of sin, righteousness, and judgment, all while gifting them with the privilege of knowing and loving of God.[56] Edwards concludes, "Christ Jesus, as applied by the Spirit of God in our enlightening, effectual calling and sanctification, is the only nourishment of the soul."[57]

To recap: we have noted the concrete expressions of the eternal plan of redemption, which is rooted in God's desire to communicate himself to creatures in the universe, which is itself rooted in his loving, holy nature. God does not redeem all people; some choose to remain in their sin and its just punishment for all time. The elect, though, have been granted forgiveness for their sins based upon the meritorious work of Christ, who not only fulfills the Godhead's redemptive purposes but also serves as the Second Adam to fulfill humanity's covenantal obligations to God. And based upon Christ's efforts, the Holy Spirit is bestowed to Christians as a sanctifying gift who begins to restore the image of God in them. When they pass from this world and partake of eternal, heavenly fellowship with the Trinity, they also experience the perfection of God's image in themselves, otherwise known as "glorification." Still, it remains for us to explore why the plan of redemption exists in the first place: the intrusion of sin into history through Adam.

---

53. *WJE* 2, 348.
54. *WJE* 2, 236.
55. *WJE* 13, 496. Sanctification will be further considered in chapter 4.
56. "Attempt," 330.
57. "Feast," 284.

Adam, History, and the Bible

Unlike many scholars today, Edwards never questions whether any part of the biblical account of Christ's atoning ministry is historically true, so he also never questions whether there was a historical person named Adam. Since history and revelation are integral to Edwards's conception of God and creation, it naturally follows that he has a high view of the authority of Scripture—authority divinely endowed through inspiration by the Holy Spirit. In fact, Edwards's view of Scripture serves as the single most fundamental assumption of his entire theology. Upon this one presupposition, that the Scriptures are the perfect, inspired revelation of God, is built his understanding of the Trinity, the plan of redemption, and every topic we will investigate from this point on.

Edwards did not adhere to this view of the Scriptures merely out of convention, blindly following the teachings of his prominent family, Puritan friends, or Reformed predecessors. The Scriptures for him are not just words on a page, but are completely the inscribed, paginated rendering of the incarnate Christ, and every truth in the Bible is a truth ordained to reveal God and his gospel.[58] Christ is the *Word made flesh*, but the Scriptures are Christ the *Word recorded* for the Church through all time.[59] Indeed, the Scriptures and the teachings they contain "are the holiness of God in writing, and, when the soul is conformed to them, [saints] have holiness of God upon their hearts."[60]

The Puritan did not expect everyone to agree with his opinion of the Scriptures, and herein lies his second most important theological presupposition. Even though Edwards maintains that their authority as divine revelation is self-evident, a person who rejects Jesus Christ as Savior will also reject the Bible's authority and thus lack insight into its veracity. "The being of God is evident by the Scriptures, and the Scriptures themselves are an evidence of their own divine authority" in much the same way that human existence and thought are evidenced by a body.[61] But proof of the Bible's authority is worthless to one who does not have the indwelling guidance of the Holy Spirit to celebrate God's

---

58. *WJE* 9, 520–22.
59. "Life," 526.
60. "Holiness," 473.
61. *WJE* 13, 410.

glory and endorse all of the truths the Bible explains.[62] So while God the Father is the fountain of all truth, and the Son is the Word incarnate, the Spirit is the author of the Scriptures who grants humans the spiritual insight to accept and understand them.[63]

Edwards was especially critical of those who elevated their own reason above the wisdom of the Scriptures, particularly the deists if his era.[64] To him, learned men such as the deists are fools before God because they "scorn to submit their reason to divine revelation, to believe anything that is above their comprehension."[65] Philosophers' doubts about original sin, the divinity of Christ, the historicity of the Bible, or the expectation of a cataclysmic, literal Judgment Day did not surprise him. For Edwards, their notions demonstrate a basic, stubborn unwillingness to submit to God's supremacy and revelation of himself. Biblical truths are valid for all times and places; if they seem foreign or unbelievable, it is not the fault of the divine Author or his biblical text, but the proud, faithless human reader. Instead, humility and devotion to God must drive human reason: "The eye which God has given to man is the eye of reason; and the eye of a Christian is reason sanctified, regulated, and enlightened by a principle of Christian love."[66] The Holy Spirit through the Scriptures reveals truth to this eye of reason. Every person's privilege and responsibility is to cherish it as holy, divine revelation and behave according to its precepts.[67]

Edwards did not presume that all Christians would agree with each other about the Bible's contents. Though Christians have the Holy Spirit indwelling them and thus have been spiritually recreated, they are still hindered by sin and still growing in faith until they reach heavenly perfection. The theologian also recognized that the Scriptures can at times

---

62. *WJE* 15, 94.

63. "Excellencies," 415. For passages dealing specifically with the Holy Spirit's involvement in prophecy and in the writing of the Old Testament, see *WJE* 9, 268–69.

64. *WJE* 23, 353.

65. *WJE* 9, 441. For McClymond, Edwards's "God was simply not confined by the contemporary standards of reasonableness. Like his Puritan predecessors, Edwards worshipped the mighty Jehovah, who thundered with his voice and performed mighty deeds that we cannot comprehend. Much in God remained mysterious, and even scandalous to natural reason" (*Encounters*, 64). For a more detailed examination of Edwards's opposition to deists, see McClymond, *Encounters*, 80–106.

66. "Inquiry," 185.

67. *WJE* 13, 479.

be difficult to grasp. It could take a hundred pages to explain partially just one divine concept, while in other cases using only a few words can represent an idea to our minds in "lively pictures."[68] Though the major tenets of Christian belief are clear to the elect, also called "saints," there are lesser biblical and theological points that are not so clear—when holy love is lacking these can give rise to disagreement and lead to division in the church. In any case, the problem of incomprehensibility lies not with the Scriptures, but with the capacity of a person to accept the truth of God and apply this truth to daily life through the power of the Spirit. To use Edwards's terminology, one reading the Bible must have an idea that corresponds with the ideas presented on the pages he reads, and must desire to understand those scriptural ideas, consenting harmoniously to divine revelation. Through this kind of consent, "we learn, in what sense the Word of God is said to be written in the hearts of believers."[69]

Adam and the Fall

According to Edwards's view of Scripture, Adam must be a historical person, because he is treated as such in the Bible and because he cannot serve as merely a mythical or theoretical figure in Edwards's federal theology. Sin and salvation are *temporal* realities that must be dealt with *in time* by a savior. Plus, if Adam was not a specific, historical person, then sin is just an *abstract* idea requiring only an *abstract* redeemer. Instead, Adam and sin must be acknowledged to be real, historical, and concrete since the work of redemption has really been concretely manifest in time. In fact, sin is *very* concrete—a deadly, genetically transmitted disease that has ravaged *real* people created in God's image and has spread mortality throughout creation. Therefore, the biblical description of the Fall is a "history of Adam's sin," and

> that history which gives us an account of the origin of all things. And doubtless it was expected, by the great Author of the Bible, that the account in the three first chapters of Genesis should be taken as a plain account of the introduction of both natural and moral evil, into the world.[70]

68. *WJE* 13, 181.
69. *WJE* 13, 290.
70. *WJE* 3, 272.

Adam, the head of mankind, was created to be the federal representative of his posterity.[71] To Edwards, if Adam had glorified God by fulfilling the covenant of works he was given in Eden, theoretically he and his descendants would have been granted eternal life.[72] Adam was created innocent and morally upright, enjoyed every finite benefit of God's favor, and for a time did everything out of his love for God.[73] The Holy Spirit dwelt in his heart fully.[74] He was created holy, because "it would have been a disparagement to the holiness of God's nature, if he had made an intelligent creature unholy."[75] Consequently, there was in him no propensity whatsoever to sin.[76]

So what happened? Why *did* Adam sin? Edwards's explanation attempts a challenging balancing act, with Adam's liberty of will as an innocent being on the one hand and God's allowance of evil into a pure context on the other. Edwards insists that Adam "had no sinful inclinations to hurry him on to sin; he did it of his own free and mere choice."[77] God gave Adam and Eve sufficient grace to be agents with free wills so they could act with liberty according to their desires.[78] Though they knew only good, they still chose to reject God, to disobey the covenant of works, and to refuse to consent to holy Being.[79]

But Edwards still has not addressed the problem: why did Adam do it? Edwards concedes that to desire to overthrow a good inclination is itself sin, so the desire must be rooted in a prior sinful inclination, or "inferior appetite."[80] Since Adam was created holy, having such a negative

---

71. *WJE* 3, 251.

72. *WJE* 3, 238. Referring to Rom 5:12–21, Edwards asserts that it was for Adam's transgression "and not Eve's, that the sentence of death was pronounced on mankind after the fall (Gen 3:9). It appears unreasonable to suppose the Apostle means to include Eve, when he speaks of Adam: for he lays great stress on it, that it was *by one* [that humanity fell], repeating it no less than seven times" (*WJE* 3, 310).

73. *WJE* 3, 231.

74. "Threefold," 378.

75. "Dependence," 204.

76. *WJE* 3, 203.

77. "Reasonable," 168.

78. *WJE* 13, 485.

79. "Glorious Grace," *WJE* 10, 392.

80. *WJE* 13, 486. Edwards states that Adam as an innocent and free moral agent was "obligated even then to be *inclined* to act right," and that "Adam's sin, with relation to the forbidden fruit, was the *first* sin he committed" (*WJE* 3, 228). Unfortunately, Edwards

inclination is out of the question. If we consider the outside influence of Satan, whose rebellion against God will be discussed in chapter 7, even that approach is insufficient. Adam still has to bear responsibility for his actions as a free agent and no reason exists for Adam to choose evil over good. Actually, while living in the blissful presence of God in Eden, Adam had every reason to prefer good!

In the spirit of Sherlock Holmes, whom I believe Edwards would have appreciated, we persist: why did Adam do it? Not because his will was flawed—he was created perfect. Not because Satan in serpent form was more engaging than God himself. And not because Eden left anything to be desired—after all, it was paradise. We know the butler didn't have anything to do with it, so the explanation must be found with the sovereign God. The devil tempted Adam, but didn't *make* him do it. God did—sort of.

While this answer may shock some, for Edwards there is no question that Adam's Fall was in a sense *planned by God*. Actually, this is a fundamental assumption of the eternal plan of redemption. "So man's fall was intended that God might glorify himself this way, by manifesting his mercy and his just wrath, for that is properly the end of God's determining the fall; and all that is after the fall is later in intention to that end."[81] For the sake of God's glory, it was "necessary that God's awful majesty, his authority and dreadful greatness, and justice and holiness [should be manifest]; and this could not be [unless] sin and punishment were decreed."[82] When Adam chose evil over good and disobeyed God's moral law, "it was absolutely certain from all eternity that the man should make such a choice."[83]

---

later contradicts himself on 390 when he asserts that Adam's first sin occurred at the rise of an evil inclination in his heart; his evil disposition thereafter was a punishment for this first transgression.

81. *WJE* 13, 384. "Man's fall was God's opportunity, to show how far his device and contrivance was beyond that of all creatures" (461).

82. *WJE* 13, 419–20. "There is no evil decreed for any other end but the glory of God's justice" (*WJE* 18, 321).

83. "Reasonable," 168. The balance between divine sovereignty and human will is a topic for chapter 4. In Edwards's view, it does not matter that the particular man Adam was involved, because any person in his shoes or after him would have responded comparably. "Adam was *as likely*, on account of his capacity and natural talents, to *persevere* in obedience, as his posterity . . . if they had all been put on the trial singly for themselves" (*WJE* 3, 396).

Edwards proposes that God did not predetermine the Fall by influencing Adam's will, in effect *forcing* him to choose evil. Rather, God *permitted* Adam's choice despite how offensive sin is to the divine sensibilities. As mentioned already, Adam in his flawless created state had no inclination to sin. But "God did not prevent him [from sinning] by his confirming grace."[84] In other words, God was not required to offer the grace that would have restrained Adam, so he withheld it "for the sake of the great good that . . . shall be the consequence" of the plan of redemption.[85] Edwards explains that God

> did not take away that grace from him while he was perfectly innocent, which grace was his original righteousness; but he only withheld his confirming grace, that grace which is given now in heaven, such grace as shall fit the soul to surmount every temptation. . . . This grace God was not obliged to grant him.[86]

So God was not the agent of sin but he did determine by default that it would be committed.[87] Even though God withheld some of the Holy Spirit's ministry, he charged the responsibility and guilt for sin to Adam and his offspring.[88] Edwards then admits that God *is* the author of sin in the sense that he permitted its existence and infiltration, and is "a disposer of the state of events, in such a manner, for wise, holy and most excellent ends and purposes, that sin, if it be permitted or not hindered, will most certainly and infallibly follow."[89] But God is still not the *first cause* of sin; Adam is.[90] "God decrees that it shall be sinful for the sake of the good that he causes to arise from the sinfulness thereof, whereas man decrees it for the sake of the evil that is in it."[91] Is this unfair of God? Edwards answers:

> Notwithstanding the plausibleness of such an objection, the very principal reason of such thoughts arising in the mind is a want

---

84. "Reasonable," 168.
85. *WJE 1*, 408.
86. *WJE 13*, 382.
87. "Reasonable," 167.
88. "Threefold," 385.
89. *WJE 1*, 399.
90. *WJE 1*, 413.
91. *WJE 13*, 250.

of the sense of the horrible evil of sin. . . . This makes us pity the sufferer and this raises objections against God.[92]

Let's pause for a moment. By now, you may have thought it ridiculous that Edwards goes into so much detail about something so apparently incomprehensible or unknowable. Why spend so much time thinking about stuff like this? Or you may have wondered why he bothers with such arguments when there is no explicit scriptural support for any of this reasoning, especially given how important it was to him to support his theology with Scripture. What really is the point of all this abstract, theological gymnastics? It's this kind of cerebral debate that gives many people a headache and turns them off to the value of theology or the integrity of theologians—they're too smart for their own good, should stop wasting time on trivialities, and come down from their ivory towers!

First of all, these arguments made by Edwards *do* have relevance as we survey the rest of his theology. Beyond that, the Puritan never pretended to be able to capture God completely or to state with certainty things that Scripture did not directly teach or clearly imply. Edwards knew that with this kind of a topic and others we will examine, he was merely speculating. What is key to remember is that he saw no problem with speculating about God as long as the speculations were guided and guarded by biblical principles. Today, some Christians fear creativity, especially theological creativity. They are suspicious of those who think and act "outside the box," in part because it is not clear to them whether the Bible supports such activity. To Edwards creativity is a gift from God; he saw no issue with theological experimentation or any other kind of creative expression, so long as its methods and results were both faithful to God and intended to glorify him. Above all he had an insatiable curiosity, and if his curiosity enabled him to know and love God one little bit better, he was exhilarated and further driven to know and love his Lord.

So let's return to the problem of Adam, sin, and God. Sherlock Holmes probably would not be satisfied with Edwards's reasoning, but then again, no theologian in history has produced an airtight explanation for the origin of sin under God's sovereign rule. The mystery may never be solved unless the answer is revealed to the elect in heaven.

---

92. *WJE* 20, 107. We must value and love God's holiness, justice, and sovereignty more than the fate of humanity.

Though the Puritan admits reluctantly that God is the author of sin in a restricted sense, we must impel him to go further, following his own line of thought. Like everything else, sin can only exist if it is first an idea in the mind of God. And sin can only exist in Adam's mind if it is first presented to him by God, either directly or through natural means (as in the demonic serpent).[93] But then God would directly or indirectly be the tempter, contradicting Jas 1:13, which states that God does not tempt anyone.

Another problem is that it would be unholy of God to "leave men's volitions, and all moral events, to the determination and disposition of blind and unmeaning causes"; instead, human will is "determined by circumstances which are ordered and disposed by divine wisdom."[94] In Adam's case those circumstances involved God placing him in a situation that influenced him to sin, or that enticed him with the idea of sin, or involved God deliberately withholding the grace that would have prevented him from sinning—or all of the above.

Again, Edwards logically concludes that God placed innocent Adam in a situation in which his finite will was not strong enough to resist temptation because the Spirit withheld adequate grace to help. We might think that God is unfair, negligent, or even malicious in this—Adam could exclaim, "What choice did I really have?! It was all a set-up!" Edwards wanted to avoid having God be labeled sin's author, since most would perceive that to be contrary to his holiness.

But that *is* the logical conclusion of Edwards's rationale. According to his idealism it is not a problem for a holy, sovereign God to be the author or creator of sin: God is never identical with his creations, and uses even the lowliest and ugliest of them for his good purposes. Further, Edwards cannot explain why Adam would prefer evil over good without

---

93. God was not obliged to grant confirming grace "and so the sin certainly followed the temptation [by] the devil. So that, as to the sin of mankind, it came from the devil. Then the question is, how came the devil by it, seeing he had no tempter? I answer, 'tis probable, some extraordinary manifestation of God's sovereignty was his temptation, the occasion of his sin and rebellion" (*WJE* 13, 382–83). This quote only adds to Edwards's problems regarding inclination in the will, for he still must explain why a good angel went bad, assuming that angelic will is like human will. The fall of some angels into sin will be a topic for chapter 7.

94. *WJE* 1, 405. In the same way, those who crucified Christ were responsible for doing so even though "God ordered the fact which they committed, who were concerned in Christ's death; and that therein they did but fulfill God's designs"—every aspect of the crucifixion, like the rest of history, "was ordered in God's providence" (402).

prior knowledge of evil, or why Adam should bear full responsibility for his choice of sin.[95] However, no theologian has answered these questions adequately, so we are left to evaluate for ourselves the truth and quality of Edwards's reasoning, keeping in mind the presuppositions we use to make our own judgments.

The Domino Effect: Sin's Impact

As humanity's representative, Adam incurred on himself and his posterity the just punishment of God for his sin—his sin was imputed to his descendants for all time in such a way that they share in his violation.[96] All people derive their "guilt and pollution" from him.[97] But for Edwards humanity shares only in the guilt of his first sin and not in any sins he committed after he and Eve were expelled from Eden (Gen 3). The guilt of Adam's descendants excludes his "peculiar [unique] personal aggravations," and

> concerns his posterity only as it was a direct breach of God's covenant, and an act of rebellion against God's express law. And only those aggravations are imputed to us, that arise from circumstances that would have been common to all mankind, if they had been then living in an unfallen state and under the same law.[98]

---

95. Logan points out that some of Edwards's successors, such as clergymen Samuel Hopkins (1721–1803) and Joseph Bellamy (1719–90) and his theologian son, Jonathan Edwards Jr. (1745–1801), developed theologies in which God actively and blatantly created sin for a greater good. See Logan, "The Doctrine of Justification," 26–52.

96. WJE 3, 348. A common objection to imputation is that people who did not even exist when Adam sinned are charged with the guilt of a man they never knew. But the elect and the reprobate in the mass of humanity have existed in God's mind as long as the plan of redemption has. In God's wisdom they are seen corporately, either in terms of the imputation of sin due to the First Adam, or the imputation of righteousness due to the Second Adam, Jesus Christ.

97. WJE 3, 346. The sin of Adam's posterity "is not theirs, merely because God *imputes* it to them; but it is *truly* and *properly* theirs, and on that ground, God imputes it to them" (408). In Edwards's view of Adam's headship within the covenant of works, everyone essentially is Adam and so is just as guilty. Based on covenant identity, "that corruption of nature with which Adam's posterity are born is not the consequence of imputation. It is an essential element of the imputation itself" (Storms, *Tragedy in Eden*, 232).

98. WJE 13, 447.

When Adam fell, the most crucial immediate effect, and the chief effect that Christ corrects in his redemptive ministry, was the separation of humanity from God. Loving, idyllic divine-human fellowship ceased.[99] God's holiness could not tolerate the presence of sin so the Spirit ceased to dwell in Adam and Eve: "The Holy Spirit, that divine inhabitant, forsook the house."[100] Adam and his descendants were condemned to know God only through skewed natural means unless God in his mercy might extend redemptive revelation to them.

Another grievous consequence of the Fall, which is concomitant with separation from God, is physical and spiritual death, or "being given over to everlasting wickedness and misery, in separation from God and in enduring his wrath."[101] Referring to Gen 2:17, Edwards asserts that God's phrase "shalt die" refers to the certainty and extremity of death "in the superlative and to the utmost degree; and so it properly extends to the second death, the death of the soul, for damnation is nothing but extreme death."[102] This deadness of soul is denoted by the term "original sin," the *"innate sinful depravity of the heart."*[103] The day Adam sinned, he

> died spiritually; he lost his innocence and original righteousness, and the favor of God; a dismal alteration was made in his soul, by the loss of that holy divine principle, which was in the highest sense the life of the soul. . . . And the alteration then made in his body and external state, was the beginning of temporal death. . . . Not only was Adam's soul ruined that day, but his body was ruined; it lost its beauty and vigor, and became a poor, dull, decaying, dying thing.[104]

Original sin and guilt due to a corrupt nature are essentially the same and all people are born with them, continuing Adam's "first apostasy."[105] As a result of the Fall, every person "became wholly governed by narrow, selfish principles. Self-love became absolute master of his soul, the

---

99. *WJE* 9, 131.
100. *WJE* 3, 382.
101. *WJE* 3, 238.
102. *WJE* 15, 72.
103. *WJE* 3, 107, original italics.
104. *WJE* 3, 258–59. Edwards believed, though, that based on the revelation of the gospel of Christ in Gen 3:16, Adam and Eve were redeemed through faith before they had any children.
105. *WJE* 13, 452.

more noble and spiritual principles having taken warning and fled."[106] So original sin and the habit of sin which festers from its wound in the soul yield a complete depravity "whereby his heart is wholly under the power of sin, and he is utterly unable, without the interposition of sovereign grace, savingly to love God, believe in Christ, or do anything that is truly good and acceptable in God's sight."[107]

Christ's life, death, resurrection, and ascension not only restore the spiritual and physical natures that were originally perfectly intertwined in creation, but also enliven them toward the goal of peaceful fellowship between God and his elect. Christ's work serves to refurbish the ruined image of God, the corrupted human soul that is dead in sin, and enables that soul to stand before God recreated and guilt-free.[108] By the Holy Spirit's grace the believer is enabled to love God above self, to consent to his Being, and to love herself and others as she ought.[109] Original sin transmitted from Adam is a doctrine of great importance, because if

> all mankind are by nature in a state of total ruin, both with respect to the moral evil they are subjects of, and the afflictive evil they are exposed to, the one as the consequence and punishment of the other, then doubtless the great salvation by Christ stands in direct relation to this ruin, as the remedy to the disease; and the whole gospel or doctrine of salvation, must suppose it; and all real belief, or true notion of that gospel, must be built upon it.[110]

The remedy for the disease of sin that Christ the Great Physician (Mark 2:17) delivers is described by the doctrine of justification, which is the application of the atonement, or the imputation of Christ's righteousness, to the elect. The justified person is absolved of all guilt (original and earned), is free from the entirety of the punishment sin deserves, is seen in the eyes of God as having the righteousness and obedience of Christ, and is therefore deemed worthy of eternal life in God's mag-

---

106. "Charity," 253. In this manner, God uses sin itself as a punishment for sin (*WJE* 3, 206).

107. *WJE* 1, 432; see Rom 3:10–20.

108. *WJE* 9, 124.

109. Sin "weakens and breaks the bonds of union instead of making a people subservient to one another's good, which is [the] end [or goal] of society" ("Calamity," 492). The proper nature of community will be considered in chapter 5.

110. *WJE* 3, 103.

nificent presence.[111] Justification, which Jesus Christ earned through his life and death and which was sealed by his resurrection and ascension, is "a privilege belonging only to some, and that which is peculiar [or unique] to distinguished favorites . . . who had been sinners; implying . . . reconciliation and forgiveness of sin, and special privilege in nearness to God, above the rest of the world."[112] Based upon election in the eternal plan of redemption, which in turn is based in the very being of God, justification is "decisive and final."[113] Those whom God the Father chooses to receive the gift of faith in Christ can *never* lose their salvation and will *always* be reconciled with God.

Justification's Instrument: Special Revelation

For Edwards, how we may be justified, or made right with God, is "the main thing for which fallen men stood in need of divine revelation for, to teach us how we that have sinned, may come to be again accepted of God."[114] In the period between Adam and Moses, God conveyed the message of the gospel through nature and tradition. But through Moses, God committed his revelation to writing as a "steady rule throughout the ages."[115] Subsequently, the "written word of God is this main instrument Christ has made use of to carry on his Work of Redemption in all ages since it was given."[116] Though God may choose to redeem a soul in any manner he sees fit, nature and tradition are generally no longer sufficient to impart the gospel message by which people may be saved through faith in Christ.[117] Only the Scriptures provide the perfect, divinely inspired, "special revelation" of what constitutes upright conduct according to the image of God in Christ. The Bible is "a revelation of the

---

111. "Justification," 177.

112. *WJE* 3, 321.

113. "Justification," 203. For a discussion of justification based on Rom 1:16-8, see *WJE* 15, 294-96.

114. "Justification," 239. On the same page, the theologian asks, "What is the gospel, but only the glad tidings of a new way of acceptance with God unto life, a way wherein sinners may come to be free from the guilt of sin, and obtain a title to eternal life?"

115. *WJE* 9, 182. See Exodus 19–31 as well as the book of Leviticus.

116. *WJE* 9, 182. To understand how Edwards read the Bible for himself and made notes for preaching and teaching on specific passages, consult *WJE* 24.

117. *WJE* 9, 520.

will of God as directing our actions and behavior, and a revelation of the reason and foundation of it."[118]

Given the view of history Edwards held, it was not a leap of faith for him to see historical accounts in the Scriptures as accurate, divinely documented revelations of God's nature and purposes in the gospel. Prior to Christ's incarnation, God revealed himself chiefly through nature, history, prophecy, and "events he brought to pass by his special providence to that end, or by things that he appointed and commanded be done for that end."[119] The Scriptures do not contain a "proper history of the whole," that is, a complete history of the world and God's workings in it.[120] But the Bible *does* reveal the essential points of the eternal plan of redemption and the nature of the Creator, "considering all parts of the grand scheme in their historical order," so people may know how to receive the gift of salvation from sin.[121]

> Without divine history, we can't properly see the grounds and foundation of divine administrations in God's moral kingdom, the first formation or erection of God's moral kingdom, the nature and manner of the main revolutions that it has been the subject of, which are the ground of future designs, and to which future events and intended revolutions [they] have a relation. . . . And prophecy is needful to reveal the future designs and aims of government, and what good things are to be expected. . . . Without 'em, divine government, or [government] of an infinitely wise and good head, is not sensible [understandable].[122]

In fact, Old Testament narratives are "inspired history."[123] The entire account of Israel recorded in the Old Testament is comprised of particular types, especially the "constitution of the nation and their state and circumstances," and rituals related to the Law of Moses.[124] For Edwards,

---

118. "Hearers," 250. "The Christian revelation gives us a most rational account of the design of God in his providential disposition of things—a design most worthy of an infinitely wise, holy, and perfect Being" (*WJE 14*, 95).

119. "Messiah," 194. See Anderson's introduction to "Images" and Lowance's introduction to "Messiah" for their analyses of Edwards's biblical typology.

120. *WJE 9*, 242.

121. "Trustees," 728.

122. *WJE 23*, 352.

123. *WJE 9*, 288.

124. "Types," 146. Not only does the Law of Moses depend on history to be understood, "but the manner of writing the law shows plainly that law and history were

"the historical events of the Old Testament in the whole series of them . . . were typical things, and . . . under the whole history was hid, in a mystery or parable, a glorious system of divine truth concerning greater things than those."[125] That glorious system was fully revealed in Jesus Christ and documented in the pages of the New Testament. The New Testament's revelation "is essentially the same revelation with that which was given in the Old Testament, but only the subjects of divine revelation are now more clearly revealed in the New Testament than they were in the Old."[126]

We already observed in the last chapter that history and nature are filled with types, all of which ultimately point to Christ as their antitype. Edwards states, "I am not ashamed to own that I believe that the whole universe, heaven and earth, air and seas, and the divine constitution and history of the holy Scriptures, be full of images of divine things, as full as a language is of words."[127] But types in the Bible are a special, superior case, not only because they are described *in* the inspired Word of God, but because they *are* the Word of God. "Now types are a sort of word; they are a language, or signs of things, God would reveal, point forth, and teach as well as vocal or written words, and they are called 'the word of the Lord,' in Zech 4:6, and 11:11."[128] Since biblical types are in and of themselves the very communications of God himself, the Scriptures interpret the rest of reality "by declaring to us those spiritual mysteries that are indeed signified or typified in the constitution of the natural world; and secondly, in actually making application of the signs and types in the book of nature as representations of those spiritual mysteries."[129]

---

written together. . . . The history is part of the law. . . . The laws, as they stand, are parts of the continued history; and the history of the facts is only as an introduction and preamble, or reason and enforcement, of the laws, all flowing in a continued series, as the several parts of one uninterrupted stream" (*WJE 15*, 440).

125. "Messiah," 217, referring to Ps 78:2.

126. *WJE 9*, 443. To Minkema, Edwards held "that the Old and New Testaments cannot be understood apart from each other; the former prophetically and typologically anticipates the latter and the latter interprets the former" ("The Other Unfinished 'Great Work,'" 59).

127. "Types," 152.

128. *WJE 15*, 580.

129. "Images," 106. Edwards advises that people be careful in interpreting types, not giving in to "wild fancy; not to fix an interpretation unless warranted by some hint in the New Testament of its being the true interpretation, or . . . by an analogy to other types that we interpret on sure grounds" ("Types," 148).

Without the Scriptures, humanity is "like a parcel of beasts with respect to their knowledge in all important truths."[130] Edwards observes that some people are "full of endless disputes about the very being of a God, whether the world was from eternity or not, and whether the form and order of the world don't result from the mere nature of matter."[131] (These "endless disputes" have continued and changed little over the past three hundred years!) Those who engage in these disputes ignore or reject the Scriptures and deprive themselves of the redeeming and enlightening power of Christ. "Jesus Christ himself is the essential Word of God, of whom the word written and preached is but an emanation: Christ is the sun, and the word written and preached are the rays."[132]

While most people in our time have the opportunity to read the Bible in their own languages, reading itself does not guarantee a proper comprehension of even basic biblical concepts. Only those who have been spiritually recreated by the Holy Spirit, or "born again," may truly enjoy and apprehend this special revelation.[133] The Scriptures are a distinctive gift for the elect, the Church. Understanding the Bible requires prayer to God the Father, in which we "beg of him to teach. He is the fountain of both Word and Spirit, and he has reserved to himself this work of enlightening the mind with spiritual knowledge, and there is no other can do it; there is none teaches like God."[134] Certainly God may use a person's reading of the Scriptures and exposure to its gospel message as the means by which salvation initially comes to him. Only then will he be enabled to grasp the truth that "knowledge and understanding of these great things of the Word of God are only given by the illumination of the Spirit of God. Men by study can make no approaches to such an understanding without God's teaching accompanying."[135] Through the influence of the indwelling Holy Spirit, who is the blessed inheritance merited by Christ for the elect, God's glory can be understood

---

130. *WJE 13*, 424.

131. *WJE 13*, 421.

132. "Light," 542.

133. Some today assume the phrase "born again" is a term coined by fundamentalists or evangelicals, but it actually is taken directly from Jesus' words to Nicodemus in John 3:1–21.

134. "Hearers," 266.

135. "Hearers," 254.

and celebrated by sinful, but redeemed and forgiven, people.[136] In the next chapter, we will consider the practical influence of the Holy Spirit in daily life.

For Further Thought

1. In your own words but based on Edwards's understanding of them, define these terms: providence, sin, election, original sin, justification, and special revelation. Do you agree with him regarding the meaning of each term? Why?
2. Why was it important to Edwards that Adam was a historical person? Do you agree? How do your beliefs on this subject impact your views about sin and redemption?
3. What is sin? Does sin impact you as greatly as Edwards contends it does?
4. Compare how Edwards explains the origin of sin in the world with your own thoughts. Do you believe that God is responsible for sin and humanity's Fall? Provide support for your argument. How do you think Edwards would respond to your opinion on the topic?
5. According to Edwards's definitions, are you "elect" or "reprobate"? Do you believe that God chooses only some people to receive salvation? Why?
6. What were Edwards's main assumptions about the Bible? Do you share those assumptions, and why? What place, if any, does the Bible have in your life and how you view the world?
7. Why did Edwards not expect all Christians to agree about the Bible's meaning? What, if any, are the limits of what we can learn from the Bible?
8. Regarding redemption, why was it crucial that Jesus Christ be both human and divine? What role did the Holy Spirit play in Christ's incarnation?
9. Go back through the pages of this chapter. For each section, note what place each Person of the Trinity has in the topic being addressed.

---

136. *WJE* 15, 221.

10. Throughout this chapter, there were numerous references to the Bible in support of Edwards's perspectives. If you have not already done so, review the chapter (including the footnotes) and look up those Bible references. Make a note of how you think each passage validates or contradicts Edwards's thoughts.

For Further Reading

Beck, Peter. "The Fall of Man and the Failure of Jonathan Edwards." *Evangelical Quarterly* 79 (2007) 209–25.

Bogue, Carl. *Jonathan Edwards and the Covenant of Grace.* Cherry Hill, NJ: Mack, 1975, especially chapters 7–9.

Brown, Robert E. *Jonathan Edwards and the Bible.* Bloomington: Indiana University Press, 2002.

Clark, Stephen M. "Jonathan Edwards: The History of the Work of Redemption." *Westminster Theological Journal* 56 (1994) 45–58.

Crisp, Oliver D. *Jonathan Edwards and the Metaphysics of Sin.* Aldershot, UK: Ashgate, 2005.

Edwards, Jonathan. "Christ's Example." In *The Works of Jonathan Edwards, Vol. 21: Writings on the Trinity, Grace, and Faith,* edited by Sang Hyun Lee. New Haven: Yale University Press, 2003.

Fiering, Norman. "The Rationalist Foundations of Jonathan Edwards's Metaphysics." In *Jonathan Edwards and the American Experience,* edited by Nathan O. Hatch and Harry S. Stout. New York: Oxford University Press, 1988.

German, James D. "The Political Economy of Depravity: The Irrelevance (and Relevance) of Jonathan Edwards." In *Jonathan Edwards at Home and Abroad,* edited by David W. Kling and Douglas A. Sweeney. Columbia: University of South Carolina Press, 2003.

Gerstner, John H. "Jonathan Edwards and the Bible." In *Inerrancy and the Church,* edited by John D. Hannah. Chicago: Moody, 1984.

Howe, Daniel Walker. "Franklin, Edwards, and the Problem of Human Nature." In *Benjamin Franklin, Jonathan Edwards, and the Representation of American Culture,* edited by Barbara B. Oberg and Harry S. Stout. New York: Oxford University Press, 1993.

Logan, Samuel T. "The Hermeneutics of Jonathan Edwards." *Westminster Theological Journal* 43 (1980) 79–96.

Otto, Randall E. "Justification and Justice: An Edwardsean Proposal." *Evangelical Quarterly* 65 (1993) 131–45.

———. "The Solidarity of Mankind in Jonathan Edwards' Doctrine of Original Sin." *Evangelical Quarterly* 62 (1990) 205–21.

Schafer, Thomas A. "Jonathan Edwards and Justification by Faith." *Church History* 20 (1951) 55–67.

Stein, Stephen J. "The Spirit and the Word: Jonathan Edwards and Scriptural Exegesis." In *Jonathan Edwards and the American Experience,* edited by Nathan O. Hatch and Harry S. Stout. New York: Oxford University Press, 1988.

Wainwright, William. "Original Sin." In *Philosophy and the Christian Faith,* edited by Thomas V. Morris. Notre Dame: University of Notre Dame Press, 1988.

Zakai, Avihu. *Jonathan Edwards's Philosophy of History: The Reenchantment of the World in the Age of the Enlightenment.* Princeton: Princeton University Press, 2003.

4

Personal Experience of God

So far, we have noted that although damaged by sin's effects on the universe, the material and spiritual realms are so intertwined that they practically serve as one means used by God toward his self-glorification. For Jonathan Edwards, the union of body and soul in sinners then is not only a microcosm of that union which pervades the entire universe, but also an imitation, an image, of the perfect union inherent to the divine-human nature of Jesus Christ.

Reflecting on human spirituality, Edwards immediately admits that we "find a great deal of difficulty in conceiving exactly of the nature of our own souls."[1] Of course, this difficulty does not restrain him from trying to hypothesize about that nature anyway, though it does explain his interchangeable use of terms to describe the soul. For Edwards, the term "soul" is generally congruent with the terms "person," "mind," "spirit," and "consciousness."[2] He uses each term to define the others: for example, "consciousness is the mind's perceiving what is in itself—its ideas, actions, passions, and everything that is there perceivable."[3] The soul and the mind are congruent, and both are made by God in his image. Human spirits are created by "the great original Spirit."[4] The soul has two faculties, understanding and inclination, which are both interchangeably called will, mind, love, and heart.[5] But whatever the terminology Edwards settles on, chiefly for contextual purposes rather than fine theological distinctions, there is no doubt that in God's eyes, the "soul is in effect the man, and the body without it is no more than a stick

1. *WJE* 1, 376.
2. "Mind," 342.
3. "Things," 245.
4. "Mind," 363.
5. *WJE* 2, 96.

or a stone. 'Tis the soul that thinks, that perceives pleasure, that enjoys good, and the body without the soul enjoys nothing."[6]

To Edwards, the soul is immaterial and can think independently of the body.[7] Created by God with eternal duration of life, the soul is of inestimable worth, as reflected in the great pains God has taken to redeem lost souls and restore them to a right relationship with him.[8] The soul provides the capacity for the highest human pleasures through its divinely designed receptivity toward communications from God.[9] Regarding morality, the soul's decisions direct and govern motions of the body according to whether the inclination of the soul is holy or evil, resulting of course in either holy or evil practice.[10] In this way the soul can enslave the body in sin, because the body in and of itself does not have moral traits.[11] In short, it is the foundation of personal consciousness and action, dependent of course "on the sovereign pleasure of God" for its existence and sustenance.[12]

Though Edwards does esteem the soul more than the body due to its ability to perceive both the natural *and* spiritual dimensions, he still concludes that bodies are a fine creation of God and "a world of wonders."[13] Like the rest of creation, the beauty of a human body shows "emanations of Christ's divine perfections. . . . But we see [by] far the most proper image of the beauty of Christ, when we see beauty in the human soul."[14] Part of the soul's beauty lies in its inherent inclination to adhere to the body. In Christians, the body is bound to the soul "so that with the soul it becomes partaker of the union with Christ."[15] The recreated Christian soul may use the body to glorify God as a living sacrifice that is accepted by God due to Christ's reconciling ministry

6. "Value," 326.
7. "Future," 359.
8. "Value," 320.
9. "Pleasantness," 107.
10. *WJE* 2, 450.
11. *WJE* 3, 278.
12. *WJE* 3, 399. Body and soul have a "union and mutual communication" that "has existence, and is entirely regulated and limited, according to the sovereign pleasure of God, and the constitution he has been pleased to establish" (398).
13. "Sufficiency," 480.
14. *WJE* 13, 280.
15. *WJE* 13, 178.

of mediation between the Father and the elect.[16] The Christian soul pervades the entire body, just as the spiritual dimension pervades the material universe. The Holy Spirit dwelled in Jesus Christ in this kind of pervasive way, and so dwells in believers.[17]

In those who do not believe in Christ, though, the soul's relationship with the body is mortally damaged, and they are incapable of consenting to God in love.[18] Not surprisingly such people harbor an active animosity toward God and divine matters, have self-centered dispositions, cannot accurately discern spiritual matters, and are spiritually dead.[19] They may practice religion but their comprehension of it is restricted to "the speculative faculty, or the understanding strictly so-called, or as spoken of in distinction from the will or disposition of the soul."[20] They are, in fact, "under the dominion of Satan," and "have their reason and all their other faculties lorded over by impure lusts and vile affections."[21] They possess hardened hearts, involving "blindness of mind, and the depravation of the faculties of the mind in general, and the perversion of their exercises."[22] Sin causes a fracture that corrupts the natural inclination of the soul toward the body; that fracture will only be exacerbated in their experience of hell's torments.[23]

These comments about non-Christians may seem quite harsh, especially since all of us know fine people who do decent things without professing allegiance to Christ. From our previous chapters, we know that the Holy Spirit works to influence non-Christians, or "natural" people, and that they still may resist God.[24] The Spirit sustains their very lives and stirs their consciences to restrain wanton immorality. They may be pleasant, kind, and try to do good, but the Holy Spirit is not their indwelling principle, the foundation of their dispositions. They are not spiritually united with him, do not derive moral character from him,

---

16. "Dedication," 551; see Rom 12:1–2.
17. "Images," 57.
18. "Denied," 76.
19. "Denied," 83–85.
20. "Divine," 414.
21. "Glorying," 466.
22. *WJE 15*, 55. For an explanation of Pharoah's hardness of heart in Exodus 7, see 379.
23. *WJE 13*, 79.
24. "Threefold," 384, based on Acts 7:51 and Heb 6:4.

and do not desire to place God first in their lives.[25] These "unregenerate" have not been spiritually born again, and thus are not able to see the Christian faith's "moral and holy excellency" and appreciate its truth.[26] In sum, the Holy Spirit does not impart salvific, or redemptive, grace to them but does conserve the natural principles in them that are commonly part of a sinner's broken image of God.[27]

Those who disdain even this divine assistance, who are hypocrites or commit the unpardonable sin of openly scorning the Holy Spirit, are undoubtedly the worst of sinners. They willfully, maliciously, and insolently spite the Spirit of grace.[28] They are "most out of the reach of means of conviction and repentance."[29] They are indeed apostates who may use the gospel for their own gain and "don't sincerely receive Christianity; their faith is built upon a rotten foundation; the Word has no rooting, and so will not bear fruit."[30] They are openly rebellious to the precepts of divine law. If they show any obedience to God, it is feigned, desperately lacking in sincerity and consistency.[31] In sum, the souls of hypocrites and apostates yield "false, superficial, external, unsound, unripe and fading, withering fruits."[32]

The Holy Spirit and Conversion to Faith in Jesus Christ

We've already drawn some distinctions between Christians and those who reject God outright, or those who pretend to be Christians but are hypocrites and apostates. But what is the difference between the activity of the Holy Spirit in the life of one who *is* elect but has yet to be spiritually converted to Christ, and one who is *not* elect and will never be

---

25. WJE 2, 201.
26. WJE 2, 309.
27. WJE 2, 262–76.
28. WJE 15, 177. "Whereas the Father acts only in his own name, the Son in his own name and the name of the Father, but the Holy Ghost in the name of both. Hence a reproaching him only is the unpardonable sin, is looked upon as reproaching the whole Trinity" ("Equality," 147).
29. WJE 2, 197.
30. "Nobleness," 231.
31. "Hearers," 259–60.
32. "Hearers," 261. For comparisons of hypocrites and blasphemers with saints, see WJE 2, 365–74 and 379–82.

saved? Or, on the flip side of the issue, what distinguishes the *response* of one who *will believe* from one who *will always refuse* to do so? Through the Holy Spirit's ministry, the sinner who will be converted undergoes a process of spiritual conviction and "evangelical humiliation," or growing humility in light of God's gospel message. This process is unique to every individual but nevertheless usually follows a pattern.[33] The would-be convert initially possesses some kind of notional knowledge of religious matters and things of the gospel, though that knowledge may be minimal.[34] He or she then has a discomfiting experience that is itself a work of God's grace, so that the abased, mortified awareness and "sense of the mind should be in the same order as the state of the soul."[35]

This discomfiting or even terrifying experience occurs to prepare the heart to humble itself sincerely before God and to make undeniable its dangerous condition before God's law and justice.[36] The experience involves at the same time an increasing sense and acknowledgment of God's love, majesty, and glory, a sense that only grace can impart.[37] Indeed, though conceptual knowledge and external factors from daily

---

33. "As to preparatory work before conversion, there is undoubtedly always, except very extraordinary cases, such a thing. For we have shown . . . that conversion is wrought in a moment. Now who can believe that the Spirit of God takes a man in his career in sin, without any forethought, or foreconcern or any such thing, or any preparatory circumstances to introduce it?" (*WJE 13*, 173). For an extended description of evangelical humiliation and conversion, see *WJE 4*, 159–91.

34. "Hearers," 265.

35. *WJE 13*, 428. "A being terrified with fears of wrath and seeing the dismal consequences of sin has in itself no tendency to wean the heart from sin. For true weanedness from sin don't consist in being afraid of the mischief that will follow from sin, but in hating sin itself, and don't arise from a sight of the dreadful consequences of sin, but from a sight of the odiousness of sin in its own nature. But yet one may be a good preparation for the other and is commonly so made use of by God" (*WJE 18*, 352).

36. "Erskine C," 469. John Erskine (1721–1803) was a Scottish Presbyterian pastor and theologian who was a leader during the revivals of the Great Awakening.

37. *WJE 13*, 508. "The design of the spirit of God in these legal terrors seems most evidently to be, to make way for, and to bring persons to a conviction of their absolute dependence upon his sovereign power and grace, and universal necessity of a Mediator, by leading them into a sense of their exceeding wickedness and guiltiness in his sight, the pollution and insufficiency of their own righteousness, that they can in no wise help themselves, and that God would be just and righteous in casting them off forever" ("Benjamin Colman's Abridgment, November 1736," *WJE 4*, 123). Colman (1673–1747) was a fellow and overseer of Harvard College, missionary to New England Native Americans, pastor of Boston's Brattle Street Church, and an ardent supporter of revivals.

life are used by the Spirit to awaken sinners from their spiritually dead slumbers, genuine conviction arises only from "an apprehension of the spiritual beauty and glory of divine things."[38] Even as he shudders and despairs at his own sinfulness in the face of God's glory, the abased one knows "a rest of soul in submission and resignation to God, in a complacential acknowledgment of his sovereignty and mercy."[39] People usually hate being humiliated, but in this case, it is a supremely and eternally good thing!

Edwards went to great lengths to stress that though the Holy Spirit often utilizes "evangelical humiliation" in the process of regeneration, or spiritual recreation, God is not bound to any pattern and may bring about conversion through any means he sees fit.[40] "These operations are most arbitrary and bound to no knowable law, any more than any actions of the Deity whatever."[41] There may be varying degrees of spiritual discoveries prior to the moment of conversion, and the length of time the Holy Spirit employs to prepare a person for conversion may be moments or years long.[42] On the other hand, while a person may be converted without distinct steps and methods, a person may experience those steps and *never* be converted. She may resist the gospel's offer of salvation or be deceived by herself, others, or Satan to imitate what the process of conversion seems to involve. Satan "can't *exactly* imitate divine operations in their nature, though his counterfeits may be very much like them in external appearance; but he can exactly imitate their order."[43] Consequently, "no order or method of operations and experiences, is any certain sign of their divinity" or their falsehood.[44] The only

---

38. *WJE* 2, 307.

39. *WJE* 13, 456.

40. For a discussion about Puritan thoughts on conversion and the historical background of Edwards's observations during the Great Awakening, see Goen's introduction to *WJE* 4.

41. *WJE* 13, 235. "The Spirit of God is sovereign in his operations; and we know that he uses a great variety; and we can't tell how great a variety he may use, within the compass of the rules he himself had fixed. We ought not to limit God where he has not limited himself" ("Marks," 229).

42. "Colman," 55.

43. *WJE* 2, 159. Satan's activity, especially in conversion and revival, will be discussed more in chapters six and seven.

44. *WJE* 2, 159.

certain signs of genuine conversion and faith in Jesus Christ are the "exercise and fruits of grace in a holy life."[45]

So "experience plainly shows, that God's Spirit is unsearchable and untraceable, in some of the best of Christians, in the method of his operations, in their conversion."[46] The genuine convert will bear the fruit of a holy life while at the same time publicly professing his experience of salvation for the benefit and edification of the church, to the glory of God. He need not and often cannot describe in intricate detail the workings of the Spirit in his heart in order to confess true faith. But the convert must be able to discern the change God has made in him, and express "understandingly and honestly . . . what he is conscious of in his own heart."[47] "We are often in Scripture expressly directed to try ourselves by the *nature* of the fruits of the Spirit; but nowhere by the Spirit's *method* of producing them."[48] And after this sincere confession, he must endeavor to live not merely a *moral* life, but a *holy* life resembling Christ's. "His conversation [will] be such, that he [will] carry with him a sweet odor of Christian graces and heavenly dispositions, wherever he goes."[49]

Thus, the greatest concern of an unconverted person whose interest in Christ has been stirred should not be adherence to a certain spiritual regimen or schedule, but striving toward heartfelt obedience, for this is the primary way God leads persons to salvation.[50] Prior to conversion, the sinner will not be able to forsake sin utterly. But if he is earnest and diligent in seeking to humble himself and understand God's ways, and if he strives to be obedient "to all his commandments to the utmost of his ability," God *may* have mercy on his soul.[51] When sinners seeking salvation "have done all, God is perfectly at liberty, whether to show them

---

45. *WJE* 13, 475.
46. *WJE* 2, 162.
47. *WJE* 2, 416.
48. *WJE* 2, 162.
49. *WJE* 2, 419.
50. *WJE* 13, 533. For an example of Edwards's pastoral advice to seekers of salvation through Jesus Christ, see "Denied," 91–95.
51. "None Saved," 353. "Hence we learn that nothing appears in the reason and nature of things . . . that can justly lead us to determine that God will certainly reveal Christ, and give the necessary means of grace, or some way or other bestow true holiness and saving grace, and so eternal salvation, to those heathens that are sincere . . . in their endeavors to find out the will of the Deity" (*WJE* 23, 56).

mercy, or not; ... they are wholly in the hands of God's sovereignty."[52] The reception of salvation is never predictable or earned, but is *always* a gift from God.

As mentioned, the elect are beneficiaries of the eternal covenant of redemption and the fulfillment of that covenant's requirements by Jesus Christ. The only way that they experience conversion is through the ministry of the Holy Spirit.[53] For Edwards, the actual moment of conversion involves numerous facets. It is instantaneous, a sudden infusion of salvific grace, the very presence of the Holy Spirit arriving in a passive soul.[54] The presence of the Holy Spirit establishes a new "disposition," or a fresh foundation for previously unknown holy thoughts and habits that are consistent with the image of God in Christ—the very kind of disposition that first directed Adam's heart.[55] "Regeneration is that work of God's Spirit whereby the soul is brought back from that state of sin into which we fell by the first apostasy of mankind and restoring it to its former state of holiness, restoring the image of God to it that was lost by the fall."[56] It is a one-time event of spiritual rebirth, "a dying unto sin and an emptying of self that Christ may be all in all, what in the Scripture is called 'hating our own life.'"[57] Through repentance for sinfulness, conversion expresses a compliance with the covenant of grace in "giving our souls to Christ as his spouse."[58] Above all, regeneration is a new capacity for knowing and loving God and consenting to his being; it is "a plant transplanted into the soul out of heaven; it is something divine, something from the holy and blessed Spirit of God, and so has its foundation in God, and not in self."[59] God grants to the new convert

---

52. "To the First Church of Christ, Northampton, [June 1752]," *WJE* 16, 482.

53. *WJE* 13, 458. For Edwards's observations about some specific historical examples of conversion, see "Faithful," 191–205, for Abigail Hutchinson and Phebe Bartlet; and *WJE* 7, 506–10, 522–24, and 543–44, for David Brainerd.

54. "Grace," 154–65. In "every man that becomes good, there is a last moment of his being bad and a first moment of his being good," a defined boundary between the state of salvation and of damnation (*WJE* 13, 168). Christ's miracles were nearly all examples of "the instantaneous work of conversion" ("Grace," 162).

55. "Divine," 411.

56. *WJE* 20, 71.

57. *WJE* 13, 214; see Luke 14:25–27. "What is done in a particular soul to make way for the setting up Christ's kingdom is to destroy Babel in him" (*WJE* 9, 154).

58. "Inquiry," 205.

59. "Charity," 264.

a discovery of [God's] own excellency, and shows the glory of the Mediator, and convinces of the truth of those great and wonderful things that are declared in his Word, and that [discovery] changes the nature, gives a new heart and a right spirit, and inclines the soul to obedience, to walk in God's ways and do his commandments.[60]

The Bible describes regeneration as a resurrection from the dead, as the creation of a new being, and as the giving of new eyes to the blind; for Edwards these are more than mere literary devices.[61] Justification before God includes a literal, fundamental change in one's soul involving spiritual baptism, "a cleansing from moral filthiness.... So the washing of regeneration or the new birth, is a change from a state of wickedness (Titus 3:3–5)."[62] Edwards even calls conversion an event of "re-existence," because a soul that was as good as dead in its state of judgment for depravity is given new, eternal life.[63] So the soul is recreated by the Spirit such that loving Jesus Christ and hating sin are the paramount concerns of the believer. Christ is *really* and mystically born in her heart, so she is endowed with fresh conformity and consent to him.[64] As a result, converts are "renewed not only within, but without" and "walk in newness of life, that . . . their bodies are new, that whereas they before were the servants of sin, . . . now they yield [their bodies to be] servants of righteousness unto holiness."[65] But further, a new world is opened for the eyes of the soul, showing "the glory of all the perfections of God, and of everything appertaining to the divine being: for . . . the beauty of

---

60. "Hearers," 263.

61. *WJE* 3, 302. See Isa 29:18; Matt 11:2–6; Luke 7:22; John 9; Rom 7:4, 8:11; 1 Cor 15; 2 Cor 5:14–9; and Col 2:9–15. "Regeneration is in Scripture represented as the raising the soul from the dead, but the whole sanctifying work of God's Spirit is a raising the soul from the dead. In every step of this work the same exceeding greatness of power is exerted that wrought in Christ Jesus when he was raised from the dead.... 'Tis as it were a raising the soul from its grave. All that death which came upon the soul when it died in the fall is removed in that spiritual resurrection that it has in Christ, and therefore that resurrection is not finished till the soul is thoroughly sanctified" (*WJE* 20, 71).

62. *WJE* 3, 370.

63. *WJE* 13, 324.

64. "Attempt," 351. For a typological treatment of the activity of Christ the Sun of Righteousness in conversion, see "Light," 540–43.

65. "Gillespie," 228.

all arises from God's moral perfection. This shows the glory of all God's works, both of creation and providence."[66]

The Spirit's Transformative Ministry of Holiness

At this point our study expands beyond the alteration made in the soul at the moment of conversion. That alteration is caused by the Holy Spirit but the Spirit does not simply recreate a soul and then withdraw. He does not instill a new disposition and then distance himself as the convert seeks to make the best of her new heart. Rather, the Spirit remains permanently, establishing a relationship with and within the believer, literally uniting her with the Trinity and enjoining her in God's plans and purposes.[67] The convert is not only the *subject* of the plan of redemption and a *recipient* of eternal love, but now a *participant* in that plan and an eternally living *lover and glorifier* of God. The Spirit's indwelling in a soul is a matter of cosmic import, planned before history and extending beyond its consummation. This indwelling is the ultimate divine communication and expression, concretely impacting individuals and their communities and rippling throughout all creation in the intricacies of providence.

In order to prevent exercises of the imagination from being mistaken for the Spirit's presence in a soul, Edwards explains what it means that the Spirit "indwells" believers. Being guided by the indwelling Holy Spirit involves no new precepts that supersede scriptural teachings and no inward suggestions or revelations that override or replace human personality: in sum, no guidance for which human thought, judgment, and wisdom are not required.[68] The Spirit works *in tandem* with the Scriptures and personal experience to mature human knowledge and discernment.[69] By stating a certain definition of "indwelling" Edwards

---

66. *WJE* 2, 273.

67. The Spirit makes "the soul a partaker of God's beauty and Christ's joy, so that the saint has truly fellowship with the Father, and with his Son Jesus Christ, in thus having the communion or participation of the Holy Ghost" (*WJE* 2, 201). Because of this union, the believer literally possesses all things "because Christ, who certainly doth possess all things, is entirely his" (*WJE* 13, 184).

68. *WJE* 2, 285.

69. The Scriptures are "the great and standing rule which God has given to his church, to guide them in all things relating to the great concerns of their souls; and 'tis an infallible and sufficient rule" ("Marks," 227).

does not intend to place limits upon God or his methods. Instead, the theologian recognizes that the Spirit never bifurcates the human faculties of mind and heart, which are already broken apart by sin, but instead unites them to recreate an intelligent, spiritual creature in the image of God. Therefore, any phenomenon that sets aside intellect for impression or implies that a person is somehow sharing in God's essence must be a product of either imagination or demonic influence.[70]

More specifically, the indwelling of the Holy Spirit is the means through which Christ himself resides and reigns in a saint.[71] As we have observed, the Spirit's ministry is one of the benefits Christ earned for the elect through his redemptive work.[72] It is Christ alone, then, who "can send into our hearts the Holy Spirit to dwell in us, to teach us heavenly things."[73]

> Christ himself lives in the soul of a true Christian, and influences and actuates him by his Holy Spirit.... [H]e enlivens and actuates the Christian by his Holy Spirit as by refreshing, warming beams of light diffused around in the soul, which scatter the darkness and is like a vital heat which destroys the coldness and deadness of the heart.[74]

Through the agency of the Spirit, Christ in a merciful act of reconciliation bonds the convert to himself and thus to the entire Godhead, serving thereafter as the "principle of life in the soul."[75] "The soul is united

---

70. *WJE* 2, 286.

71. "Consider the excellent and gracious manner of Christ's governing his people by communicating vital influences to them and governing their hearts. His powerful, inward influence is exceeding pleasant. The soul is never so happy as when it is under the strongest influences of Christ, and [the Christian's] heart is most irresistibly governed by him. Christ don't drive, but he draws the heart; he draws by light and love" ("Threefold," 432).

72. *WJE* 2, 236.

73. "Life," 525. We remind ourselves that God continually creates all souls. But regenerate souls are essentially continually recreated, their new principle continually reinstated. Edwards likens this to breathing, for "the spiritual life is constantly maintained by the Spirit of God entering into the soul" ("Images," 70).

74. "Living," 570. Edwards does not of course mean here light in the sense of that emitted by the sun, but nevertheless does intend a spiritual kind of light, a literal power of illumination emanated by God to grant spiritual insight. "Jesus Christ, when he enlightens the mind, sends for the Holy Spirit to dwell in the soul, to be as a continual internal light to manifest and make known spiritual things to the believer" ("Light," 543).

75. "Living," 571. God "gives his Spirit to be united to the faculties of the soul, and to dwell there after the manner of a principle of nature; so that the soul, in being indued

to Christ, and therefore partakes of his life: he lives in Christ and Christ lives in him, yea, not only lives in him but *is his life*. He is invigorated with him, with his Holy Spirit which is diffused as new life all over his soul."[76]

The indwelling Spirit of Christ establishes an everlasting principle of love of God, self, and others. "The nature of the Holy Spirit is love; it is by communicating himself, or his own nature, that the hearts of the saints are filled with love or charity. Hence the saints are said to be 'partakers of the divine nature' [2 Pet 1:4]."[77] But the Spirit's union with the human soul is not a form of absolute identity: Creator and creature always remain distinct, just as spouses do in their common life. Saints *partake* of God's holiness, fullness, and "spiritual beauty and happiness," but God does not impart any of his core essence to them.[78] The presence and blessing of the Spirit, also called grace, is a redemptive indwelling that serves as a new foundation of love for the soul, yet without a person becoming a "mini God" or blending indistinguishably with God.[79]

This principle of love is in turn generally synonymous with what Edwards calls the "sense of the heart."[80] This sense enables the saint to enjoy God through a "Divine taste" by which spiritual, supernatural matters can be accurately discerned.[81] Without the sense, knowledge of God is uncertain and abstract. But with the sense of the heart, "the mind don't only speculate and behold, but relishes and feels."[82] Through illumination by the Holy Spirit, the sense literally unifies one's relationship with the Godhead, the truths of biblical revelation, and the human mind, body, and soul, so that for the Christian divine glory and beauty

---

with grace, is indued with a new nature. . . . In the soul where Christ savingly is, there he lives" (*WJE* 2, 342).

76. "Living," 570, my italics.

77. "Charity," 132.

78. *WJE* 2, 203; see also *WJE* 13, 513. Edwards walks a fine line: the Spirit imparts his *love* to the godly, but not his *very being*, though his being *is* present as he indwells and continuously creates a new spiritual principle.

79. *WJE* 2, 206.

80. For a comparison of the sense of the heart with the beating of a heart in an unborn child, see "Images," 122. For Edwards's description of how the disciples might have experienced the sense of the heart at Christ's transfiguration (Matt 17:1–13) see *WJE* 15, 214.

81. "Grace," 175.

82. *WJE* 2, 272.

are self-evident everywhere.[83] Saints know intellectually, spiritually, and experientially the power of God in salvation and the presence of the Spirit in their souls.[84] They thereby possess an immediate, intuitive comprehension of divine matters, and consequently are able to understand the will, nature, and being of God in a manner far better than they could before conversion.[85] In other words, the sense of the heart or divine light is spiritual knowledge of holiness unique to the regenerate, and a gift of God in Christ of which the Holy Spirit is the "immediate efficient cause."[86] Then gradually the believer's thoughts, emotions, and indeed his entire being conform to God's image, holiness, and moral excellency.[87] "Holiness is a thing that has its seat in the heart and is from the secret influence of the Spirit of God there."[88]

From Edwards's perspective, human holiness especially conforms to the perfections of Christ through faith, hope, and love.[89] These three gifts of charity, the greatest of which is love, "when joined together and united in one, constituteth saving faith, or the soul's savingly embracing Christ and Christianity."[90] Exercising charity as a "fruit" or result of the Spirit's influence in turn yields even greater virtue and holiness, as a convert's disposition to loving God establishes stronger and stronger habits of love.[91] And stronger habits of love constitute holy wisdom, a spiritual acumen which can only be given through the instruction of the Holy Spirit and is "the highest and most excellent gift that ever God bestows on any creature: in this the highest excellency and perfection of a rational creature exists."[92]

83. *WJE* 2, 298. "The spiritualized regenerate soul sees a beauty and an amiableness, and tastes an incomparable sweetness, that is altogether hidden from the wicked" ("Denied," 79).

84. *WJE* 2, 141.

85. "Denied," 74. The believer "understands those divine and spiritual doctrines which once were foolishness to him" (*WJE* 2, 268). Consult *WJE* 18, 249.

86. "Denied," 88.

87. "End," 441–42.

88. "Hearers," 251.

89. "Holiness," 472.

90. *WJE* 15, 276. For representative essays on these topics, see "Charity," 123–397, and "Poverty of Spirit," *WJE* 10, 493–505.

91. *WJE* 13, 287. For comments on the meaning of virtue as "true grace and real holiness" ("Virtue," 560), see *WJE* 1, 315–40, *passim*; "Virtue," 539–627; and *WJE* 9, 320–25.

92. "Divine," 422.

It follows that for Edwards, only believers in Jesus Christ can be spiritually wise, because only they are being conformed to him through the influence of the Holy Spirit. Jesus is called in Scripture the Wisdom of God not just in a figurative sense; "he is the real proper wisdom of God."[93] "Every one of the true members of Christ's invisible [C]hurch [is] possessed of this fruit of the Spirit in their hearts. Divine or Christian love is implanted there, and dwells there, and reigns there, and [wisdom] is an everlasting fruit of the Spirit."[94] Any wisdom that unregenerate persons may display is based only on their learning about God through general revelation. And a person may memorize the entire Bible, but without the empowering influence of the Spirit has only another form of speculative knowledge and is not capable of valuing God's excellency or sincerely loving him.

Because holiness, the sense of the heart, the divine light, and the indwelling of the Spirit so overlap, we can see why Edwards states that "the graces of God's Spirit and the spiritual fruits of holiness and happiness are interwoven with one another, and are connected together, and depend one on another as it were by a concatenation," or continuous integration.[95] Spiritual growth is infused by the Holy Spirit, who as the giver of life is "the spiritual heavenly food with which God feeds the saints."[96] Through the Spirit's sanctifying ministry, the Christian will continue to grow in faith, holiness, and beauty of soul through all eternity.[97] Having now the mind of Christ, she will experience spiritual discoveries and insights which "not only make an alteration of the present

---

93. "Equality," 148.
94. "Charity," 358.
95. *WJE 15*, 230.

96. *WJE 15*, 208. "Rightly to understand the nature of the habit of grace, it must be observed that the Spirit of God in the heart of a saint acts both as a natural vital principle and also as a voluntary agent manifesting care of that heart that it is in, lest [the heart] should be overcome by temptations and lest it should fall away.... But yet the indwelling Spirit takes care of the heart and wonderfully and with great care and wisdom conducts it, preserves it, and restores it.... That indwelling vital Spirit acts so as to punish miscarriages and reward diligence and to answer prayer" (*WJE 18*, 528–29).

97. *WJE 15*, 544. "'Tis a wonder that a creature should ever be so highly honored, as to be made conformed to the image of God, as much a wonder as that they should be allowed the enjoyment of him. Sanctification is as great, yea, a greater favor done to the creature, than glorification: the creature is more honored by being made like unto God in holiness, than in happiness; the image and likeness of God upon the creature exalts it and honors it more" ("Excellencies," 430).

exercise, sensation and frame of the soul; but such power and efficacy have they, that they make an alteration in the very nature of the soul."[98] The Christian soul is *always* being transformed and renewed, even when unaware of it.

Conversion does not immediately eliminate all sin from the believer; sanctification is inherently a purification process that may have its setbacks even as she makes significant steps toward holiness at other times.[99] "Yea, a Christian's life may be attended with many and exceedingly great imperfections, and yet be a holy life, a truly Christian life."[100] The crucial factor is that there exists a new, holy disposition based upon which choices for goodness and righteousness are made, for the glory of God.[101] "The best and most just man upon earth is not free from actual sins, but what a vast difference is there between a man before and after repentance and regeneration. The life of a man before . . . is one continued act of sin."[102] But the gift of salvation through faith in Jesus Christ "mortifies . . . our natural depravity and enmity against God."[103] Thanks to the presence and power of redemptive grace, a "universal change" occurs in the soul, and as a result corruption no longer has dominion over an individual—God does.[104] Yet the saint remains a participant in the process, as we have already noted, "so that all that men do in real religion is entirely their own act, and yet every tittle is wrought by the Spirit of God."[105]

It is not possible to overemphasize that for Edwards holiness and consistent, godly practice are crucial to religious experience following conversion.[106] The believer earnestly desires to behave in a Christlike manner and part with sinful ways because they are so deeply offensive to

---

98. *WJE* 2, 340.

99. "The gradual progress we make from childhood to manhood is a type of the gradual progress of the saints in grace, and the gradual progress the [C]hurch makes towards perfection of knowledge, holiness and blessedness," based on 1 Cor 13:11 ("Images," 61).

100. "Charity," 309. If a person "has once believed in Christ, he is sure of heaven; and it is impossible he should miss of it, how many sins soever he has been guilty of before, and though he falls into great sins afterwards" ("Threefold," 428).

101. "True Love," 637.

102. "True Repentance Required," *WJE 10*, 513.

103. "True Love," 636.

104. *WJE* 2, 341.

105. *WJE* 13, 240.

106. *WJE* 3, 191.

God.[107] But remembering that the spiritual and material are for Edwards intertwined, a new spiritual principle must impact the material realm in order to show its validity. Genuine faith will inevitably bear fruit in good works. The power of the Holy Spirit in a heart will not lie dormant and unexpressed, for it is God's very nature to express himself, as we have seen. So in sanctification the Spirit shapes the convert's will to match God's, so that "all true grace tends to practice."[108]

Though external behavior is not an infallible guide to the state of a soul, when charity is consistently evident it can be concluded that the human will has been forever changed by grace to obey and serve God.[109] But we must remind ourselves that Edwards views Christian faith and practice from an eternal perspective: the entire purpose of spiritual rebirth is to fulfill God's plan of redemption. Holiness is the goal and "practice is the aim of that eternal election which is the first ground of the bestowment of all true grace."[110] So when holiness is evident, election is as well.[111] The Holy Spirit is putting into effect the work of redemption by calling and regenerating the elect, a ministry that simply will not fail, and behavior sanctified by the Spirit exists only with true conversion as its starting point.[112] Eternal election, however, is the key to it all.

Because of the power and vitality of the Spirit's indwelling presence, for Edwards there is no doubt that any individual can discern through self-examination whether he or she is in fact regenerate or "born again." An unregenerate person can manufacture phony assurance of salvation based on arrogance or self-deception, being "prompted by false joys and comforts, excited by some pleasing imaginations impressed by Satan, transforming himself into an angel of light."[113] Saints, on the other hand, may have doubts about their eternal destiny through spiritual immaturity or neglect, "owing to their own sloth, and giving way to their sinful dispositions."[114] But when true faith is indeed present, "the lively exercises of faith do naturally produce satisfaction of a good estate *as*

---

107. "Charity," 301–10, *passim*.
108. "Charity," 297.
109. WJE 2, 420–22, 452–55.
110. "Charity," 294.
111. WJE 13, 223.
112. "Inquiry," 189.
113. WJE 2, 172.
114. "Inquiry," 298.

their immediate effect."¹¹⁵ A spiritually healthy person's eyes of faith can perceive the unmistakable testimony of the Holy Spirit's indwelling presence; can know of Christ's faithfulness and the sufficiency of salvation through him; can see the changes grace makes in his own heart; and can demonstrate the Spirit's gracious influence through holy living.¹¹⁶ Edwards summarizes:

> when a person feels the Spirit of God in those divine dispositions and exercises, it assures him that God does not hold him as an enemy, but that he is in a state of favor with God. . . . Thus the Spirit of God bears witness together with our spirits, that we are the children of God, Rom. 8:16.¹¹⁷

Human Will and True Faith

In addition to Edwards's insatiable curiosity and sheer brilliance, his pastoral responsibilities also drove him to explore the vagaries of spiritual life. Up to this point we have largely examined personal religious experience from the divine viewpoint, without much consideration of the human perspective. A person may examine herself to confirm whether or not she is a child of God, yet ultimately her salvation hinges upon whether God in his mercy has elected her, and will consequently regenerate and sanctify her. Election, from God's perspective, is a cut-and-dried matter: you are either chosen or not. But regarding sinful humans who are subject to pride and confusion, the practical workings of salvation can be a blurry matter that leaves the answers to some theological questions only to be guessed.

For the Puritan, human will has been crippled by sin and is inclined only to wickedness.¹¹⁸ A person has two components of the will, the

---

115. *WJE* 2, 510. Missionary David Brainerd's assurance of salvation "was by feeling within himself the lively actings of a holy temper and heavenly disposition, the vigorous exercises of that divine love which casts out fear" (*WJE* 7, 504).

116. *WJE* 2, 452. "All the fruit of the Spirit, upon which we are to lay weight as evidential of grace, is summed up in charity or Christian love, because this is the sum of all grace. And the way, therefore, that we and all others are to argue [for our salvation] is by discerning the exercises of grace in our hearts, some exercise of this divine charity, and comparing this with the rule of God's Word, and so to conclude our good estate" ("Charity," 169).

117. *WJE* 13, 447.

118. *WJE* 13, 486.

rational will and the appetite. Due to sin, the rational will is subject to the appetite, so he acts contrary to righteous, proper reason and thus sins.[119] Spiritual rebirth establishes a new principle, inclination, or disposition that enables the saint to exercise his rational will toward holy ends and master the appetites through self-control.[120] The Holy Spirit then ministers through the will to strengthen a habit of good choices until heavenly glory, when the saint will never fail to choose what is pleasing to God.

Especially in *A Careful and Strict Enquiry Into the Modern Prevailing Notions of That Freedom of Will*, Edwards insists that the will should not be conceived of as an independent *psychological* faculty, but as being synonymous with the *soul's* active preference. The will is a subordinate expression of the mind choosing according to its strongest motive.[121] An unconverted sinner possesses the liberty to choose anything good, including faith in God, and therefore can be held accountable for her moral actions.[122] But she *does not will* to choose good because she does not have the desire, and does not have the desire because she does not have the inclination, or disposition.[123] "The inclination is unable to change itself; and that for this plain reason, that it is unable to incline to change itself."[124] Therefore, such a sinner suffers from a "*general and habitual* moral inability."[125]

Because of this chronic moral inability ("original sin"), Edwards maintains that it is preposterous for people to believe that they possess free wills and genuine self-determination. Such freedom and self-determination eliminate the need for redemptive grace by placing the event of conversion on the shoulders of human choice.[126] People really

---

119. *WJE 13*, 484.
120. "Grace," 172.
121. *WJE 1*, 137.
122. *WJE 1*, 312.
123. *WJE 1*, 162. It is impossible to "do what is necessary in order to salvation ... without the almighty operation of the Holy Spirit of God, yea, except everything be entirely wrought by the Spirit of God. True and saving faith in Christ is not a thing out of the power of man, but infinitely easy. 'Tis entirely in a man's power to submit to Jesus Christ as a Savior, if he will; but the thing is, it never will be that he should will it, except God works it in him" (*WJE 13*, 238).
124. *WJE 1*, 305.
125. *WJE 1*, 160.
126. "Erskine B," 723.

have no need for God's help if they can act freely on their own.[127] If human free will is not totally dependent on God, then God's omniscience, providence, and omnipotence are negated. If the will is absolutely free, a person can make a choice that overrides God's will and subjugates God's foreknowledge and redemptive plan. For Edwards all of these suggestions are unbiblical and unacceptable.

Either events are certainly established in the mind of God, or not. If they are, a foreknown event is basically a divine decree that *will happen*, without a doubt.[128] If they are not, God can foreknow only those events "he would bring to pass himself by the extraordinary interposition of his immediate power," and the traditional biblical conception of God is shattered.[129] If human will is totally free, then we rule, and God does not.

In some circles today, the preservation or even sanctity of human free will is so important that the very idea of declaring that we do not have free will seems ludicrous. Yet Edwards attempts to demonstrate that free will is both illogical and unbiblical, especially with reference both to God's nature and to human, sinful finitude. But neither does Edwards believe that humans are God's robots. He explains that

> man is entirely, perfectly and unspeakably different from a mere machine, in that he has reason and understanding, and has a faculty of will, and so is capable of volition and choice; and in that, his will is guided by the dictates or views of his understanding; and in that his external actions and behavior, and in many respects also his thoughts, and the exercises of his mind, are subject to his will; so that he has liberty to act according to his choice, and do what he pleases; and by means of these things, is capable of moral habits and moral acts.[130]

Edwards attempts to balance the interplay between God's foreordination and human will. This is the all-important point: human liberty entails a *circumscribed* freedom to act according to human nature, within the material world, according to God's design. Prior to the Fall, Adam and Eve did *not* have absolute free will, but this very same *circumscribed* freedom. Even today, finite, sinful people experience circumscribed freedom when they act according to their natures, just as God freely acts

---

127. "Erskine C," 470.
128. *WJE 1*, 262.
129. *WJE 1*, 250.
130. *WJE 1*, 370.

according to his perfectly holy nature. To illustrate, a bear is most free when it acts like a bear, not when it performs human-like tricks in a circus. A tiger is still a tiger in a zoo exhibit, but its lack of freedom is not only physical due to walls and cages; it is unable to fulfill its God-given creaturehood in the wild.

Similarly, human will is at its height when its liberty is "determined by circumstances which are ordered and disposed by divine wisdom."[131] Every person has the freedom to choose simply because he enjoys the freedom to act. In fact, the entire history of humanity has depended in "innumerable ways on the acts of men's wills" and their sheer multitude.[132] But God provides the spiritual-material structure in which the human will is active, exercising his providence over creation and human action without infringing on the "real liberty of mankind."[133] Nature's seasons, the flow of time, the chemical elements, and even basic cause-and-effect do not imprison humanity. They are instituted by God to comprise nature's regularity and allow us the real freedom that utter chaos and meaninglessness would not. As Strauss explains, humans "choose, and choose freely, but their choices are in the midst of a world which their choices did not make."[134] So God's universal moral and natural laws do not imprison us, but give us and all other creatures the opportunity to fulfill who we are and be the best we can be.

That leads us at last to the definition of true faith: the exercise of the will in the greatest possible moral act, "the soul's savingly embracing Christ and Christianity."[135] With the new disposition of will provided as a gift by the Holy Spirit, at the moment of conversion the elect soul (including the intellect, will, emotions, and senses) freely chooses to submit completely to Jesus Christ as its Master, Lord, Mediator, and King. The soul trusts in him and loves him with a readiness "to do and undergo all that he requires, in expectation of his redemption."[136] True faith expresses "evangelical humiliation" and acknowledges absolute dependence upon God; in consenting to God's being, "faith is a sensibleness of what is

---

131. *WJE* 1, 405.
132. *WJE* 1, 248.
133. *WJE* 1, 406.
134. Strauss, "A Puritan," 247.
135. *WJE* 15, 277.
136. *WJE* 13, 408.

real in the work of redemption."[137] In other words, faith according to Edwards "implies a disposition to give all the glory of our salvation to God and Christ."[138] It fulfills in the most practical manner the eternal plan of redemption's utmost goal: the glorification of God through creatures made in his image—lovable and loving creatures with minds, wills, spiritual capacities, and unique personal identities.

To elaborate a bit more: faith in Jesus Christ does not *precede* the moment of conversion. Faith is an expression of a soul *already* transformed by the Spirit of God, a soul *already* granted the spiritual illumination that yields the "sense of the heart."[139] Faith is the sincere, heartfelt loving of God above all else, a love that is the soul's "working, operative principle or nature."[140] Once the Holy Spirit has entered a soul to dwell there, faithful confession is the soul's response and that "by which men are *brought into* a good estate."[141] Faith therefore affirms the justification merited by the ministry of Jesus Christ.[142] The righteousness of faith is "not perfect holiness, but a justified state or freedom [from] guilt; and the imputation of [Christ's] righteousness."[143] Thus, justification by faith is "something peculiar [unique] to believers, who had been sinners; implying some reconciliation and forgiveness of sin, and special privilege in nearness to God, above the rest of the world."[144]

Religious Affections and the Christian Life

The Holy Spirit's ministry of sanctification, or spiritual purification from sin, begins immediately after regeneration and produces good works that imitate the holy disposition and behavior of Jesus Christ. These "good works" occur first in the soul as the Christian wrestles internally to be more like Jesus, and then are manifest in daily life in relation to others. The righteous are never made right with God by their deeds, only by the merit of Christ, but "their works shall be brought forth as the evidence

137. "Dependence," 213.
138. "Erskine B," 722.
139. "Reasonable," 181.
140. "Charity," 330.
141. WJE 2, 178, original italics.
142. WJE 13, 458.
143. WJE 13, 197.
144. WJE 3, 321.

of their having believed."[145] True faith is a faith that is manifest through works and gives consent for biblical principles to govern one's thoughts and behavior.[146]

Religious affections unite all of the components of religious experience we have discussed in this chapter and serve in Edwards's theology as the basis for how Christians are to live out their faith. He defines affections strictly as "the more vigorous and sensible [sensory] exercises of the inclination and will of the soul."[147] More broadly, they are manifestations of divine power in the marvelous transformation of a feeble sinner into a servant of God. Through the religious affections, the Holy Spirit stirs body and soul to prepare a heart for conversion. Conversion to faith in Christ is rooted in the affections, and after this the fruit of good thoughts and deeds grows as faith expresses itself through the affections. "The essential point is that the affections manifest the center and unity of the self; they express the whole man and give insight into the basic orientation of his life."[148]

Evoked and spurred on by Christian books, preaching, sacraments, prayer, praise songs, and the Word of God itself (the greatest producer of spiritual blossoming), the "religious affections" are personal, experiential expressions of romance to God. They are of divine origin, to enhance and purify a believer's life.[149] Then, these expressions flow back to God as the believer's loving, heartfelt declarations of a passionate desire to be holy, and of thanks for the holiness thus far granted to him by God. "And the more he experiences, the more he knows this excellent, unparalleled, exquisite, and satisfying sweetness, the more earnestly he will hunger and thirst for more, till he comes to perfection."[150]

Herein lies what distinguishes genuine religious experience from false, and holy affections from evil. "For evil affections radically consist in inordinate love to other things besides God."[151] But true affections, constituting true religion, are not humanly mustered or demonically encouraged, but imitate those manifest by Christ himself and exhibit

145. "Judgment," 527.
146. "Charity," 299.
147. WJE 2, 96.
148. "Editor's Introduction," WJE 2, 14.
149. WJE 2, 348.
150. WJE 2, 379. "Conversation between God and mankind in this world is maintained by God's word on his part, and prayer on ours" (WJE 23, 350).
151. WJE 3, 146. For more about natural affections, see "Virtue," 601–5.

devotion to him as saving, ruling Lord. Edwards makes special mention of the example of Jesus' high priestly prayer in John 17, stating that "of all the discourses ever penned, or uttered by the mouth of any man, this seems to be the most affectionate, and affecting."[152] As the perfectly virtuous God-man, Christ displayed impeccable affections through absolute devotion to his Father and incomparable compassion to humankind. Edwards observes,

> even the Lord Jesus Christ, was a person who was remarkably of a tender and affectionate heart; and his virtue was expressed very much in the exercise of holy affections. He was the greatest instance of ardency, vigor and strength of love, to both God and man, that ever was.[153]

You may have noticed by now that "religious affections" is a broad term with numerous aspects. A religious affection can be expressed through feelings and good works, but is chiefly composed of a love for God and others that displays a constant, enduring temperament of kindness, gentleness, sincerity, purity, and spirituality.[154] True Christians are childlike in that they have "hearts tender, and easily affected and moved in spiritual and divine things, as little children have in other things."[155] They clearly display a bond with their heavenly Father "because they are born of the Spirit, and because of the indwelling and holy influences of the Spirit of God in them."[156] Through the Spirit's transforming grace, believers are clothed with Christ's qualities of righteousness.[157] Living out religious affections, the Christian

> has more holy boldness, so he has less of self-confidence ... and more modesty.... He is less apt than others to be shaken in faith; but more apt than others to be moved with solemn warnings, and with God's frowns, and with the calamities of others. He has the firmest comfort, but the softest heart: richer than others, but poorest of all in spirit: the tallest and strongest saint, but the least and tenderest child among them.[158]

---

152. *WJE* 2, 112.
153. *WJE* 2, 111.
154. *WJE* 2, 146.
155. *WJE* 2, 117.
156. *WJE* 2, 198.
157. *WJE* 2, 347.
158. *WJE* 2, 364.

Unfortunately, *false* religious affections also exist. Love and humility, being the greatest components of genuine virtue, are the qualities most avidly counterfeited by Satan.[159] The presence of one affection, or even many affections, is thus not indisputable evidence for one's genuine conversion to faith in Jesus Christ.[160] Whether in the unregenerate person or in the Christian who strays from holy living, false affections may be intense and move him to perform seemingly good works, but they are always weak in power and duration. The Puritan explains, "Passing affections easily produce words; and words are cheap; and godliness is more easily feigned in words than in actions. . . . Hypocrites may much more easily be brought to talk like saints, than to act like saints."[161]

On the other hand, the true religious affections of a healthy believer endure by God's grace in an abiding calm, irrespective of the storms that surround her. Real religious affections are grounded on both a rational and a spiritual conviction, a grace-granted certainty of the gospel's truth. They are based upon the doctrines central to the Scriptures, including Jesus' Messiahship, his atonement for elect sinners, the unmistakable human needs for sincere repentance, devotion to God alone, and complete reliance upon him. The authentic believer does not simply have a strong intellectual conviction of the gospel's truth, but "he that truly sees the divine, transcendent, supreme glory of those things which are divine, does as it were know their divinity intuitively; he not only argues that they are divine, but he sees that they are divine."[162] And seeing that they are divine, he clings to them with a tenacity that can only exist and be sustained through the power of the Spirit of God in Christ.

The capacity for religious affections in all people is a remnant of humanity's pre-Fall fellowship with God in Eden. We have been created to have unadulterated affections in a pure relationship with the living God. But due to sin, our affections are shamefully bent toward the self and are morally inadequate for fellowship with God. Consequently, the "natural" or unconverted person may feel a sort of love toward God, may feel guilt and then repent, and may strive to behave religiously and piously. But without a soul that has been recreated by the Holy Spirit, he remains unable to understand God meaningfully, is ignorant of the

---

159. *WJE* 2, 113.
160. *WJE* 2, 132.
161. *WJE* 2, 411.
162. *WJE* 2, 298.

wonderful truth of divine things, and has "no sense of the beauty and amiableness of the moral and holy excellency . . . that is in the things of religion."[163] Though this probably sounds harsh, an unregenerate person is like the demons, who apprehend God's terrible majesty and power but cannot love him for his beauty and holiness.[164] Such a person may be religious in a Christian way, expressing this natural religiosity through Christian means. But behaving "in a Christian way" does not necessarily mean that a person has the Holy Spirit's indwelling presence and real faith in Jesus Christ.

This is why Jonathan Edwards strenuously emphasizes that the presence of "natural" affections is not evidence of salvation. In fact, spirituality and religiosity that lack genuine faith are ghastly offenses to God because they endorse the Satanic delusions that God may be placated by religiosity and that salvation may be obtained apart from Christ. The religious affections of hypocrites and apostates are built upon the shifting sand of the sinful self. Meanwhile, the saints' joyful affections are founded upon "evangelical humiliation" in a steady, reverent acknowledgement that their repugnant sin offends God's holiness and that they are undeserving of his mercy and grace.

We conclude then that holy, religious affections are the only valid basis for true religion, or "the exercise and expressions of regard to the Divine Being."[165] Love is the core of this regard, being the "very quintessence of all religion, the very thing wherein lies summarily the sincerity, spirituality, and divinity of religion."[166] Since only the elect are enabled to love God properly, only the elect know true religion; all other religious endeavors, labeled Christian or otherwise, are false, idolatrous contrivances of humans, Satan, or both.[167] Only the elect are capable of applying the "divine and supernatural light" to daily life.[168] And only the elect are drawn by the Spirit to follow Jesus Christ, who is the "perfect example of true religion and virtue, for the imitation of all."[169] "That principle of true

---

163. WJE 2, 309.
164. WJE 2, 263.
165. "Grace," 171.
166. "Grace," 169.
167. WJE 7, 578. Edwards's ideas about non-Christian religions will be examined more in chapters five and seven.
168. WJE 2, 99.
169. WJE 2, 111.

religion which is in them, is a communication of the religion of heaven; their grace is the dawn of glory; and God fits them for that world by conforming them to it."[170] As we will see in the next chapter, this divine fitting for the heavenly world is hardly an individualistic process of sanctification. Rather, corporate religion is the primary manifestation of the Kingdom of God on earth and is a crucial component in the fulfillment of the plan of redemption.

For Further Thought

1. How would you define the word "soul"? Compare your definition with Edwards's. Do you believe the soul and the body interact the way he describes?

2. What are the spiritual and intellectual distinctions that Edwards draws between Christians and non-Christians throughout this chapter? Do you agree with him? Why?

3. How does Edwards define conversion? What are the general steps that the Holy Spirit uses to bring about conversion? Why is God not confined always to follow these steps?

4. How does Edwards define "justification by faith"? What are the roles of humans and the Holy Spirit in it?

5. What effects does the indwelling of the Holy Spirit have on a Christian? What does the Spirit have to do with the "sense of the heart"?

6. What places do sin and good works have in the life of a genuine Christian? To Edwards, how can it be that good works may not be proof of true faith in Christ?

7. What is the only way a person can know if he or she is a Christian? Do you agree that this is the only way?

8. Do you believe that humans have free will? What points do you like and dislike about Edwards's view of human free will?

9. What are "religious affections," in your own words? What are the differences between true and false religious affections? Have you ever experienced such affections?

---

170. *WJE* 2, 114.

10. Consult footnote 61. Having examined each of the Bible passages, how well do you think Edwards's thoughts agree with these Scriptural references?

11. Read 2 Cor 1:20–22 and 5:1–5. Do these Bible passages support or contradict Edwards's ideas about the presence of the Holy Spirit in the lives of Christians?

12. Read 1 Cor 4:1–5. Does this Bible passage support or contradict Edwards's view of the human ability to judge our own spiritual state?

For Further Reading

Chamberlain, Ava. "Self-Deception as a Theological Problem in Jonathan Edwards's 'Treatise Concerning Religious Affections.'" *Church History* 63 (1994) 541–56.

Danaher, William J. "Beauty, Benevolence, and Virtue in Jonathan Edwards's *The Nature of True Virtue*." *Journal of Religion* 87 (2007) 386–410.

Edwards, Jonathan. "'Controversies': Efficacious Grace," "'Controversies': Justification," "Efficacious Grace," and "Faith." In *The Works of Jonathan Edwards, Vol. 21: Writings on the Trinity, Grace, and Faith*, edited by Sang Hyun Lee. New Haven: Yale University Press, 2003.

Fisk, P. J. "Jonathan Edwards's *Freedom of the Will* and His Defence of the Impeccability of Jesus Christ." *Scottish Journal of Theology* 60 (2007) 309–25.

Gerstner, John H., and Jonathan Neil Gerstner. "Edwardsean Preparation for Salvation." *Westminster Theological Journal* 42, (1979) 5–71.

Guelzo, Allen C. *Edwards on the Will: A Century of American Theological Debate.* Middletown, CT: Wesleyan University Press, 1989, especially 17–40, 54–72.

Hoopes, James. "Jonathan Edwards's Religious Psychology." *Journal of American History* 69 (1983) 849–65.

McClymond, Michael J. "Spiritual Perception in Jonathan Edwards." *Journal of Religion* 77 (1997) 195–216.

Nichols, Stephen J. *Heaven on Earth: Capturing Jonathan Edwards' Vision of Living in Between.* Wheaton, IL: Crossway, 2006.

Smith, John E. "Editor's Introduction." In *The Works of Jonathan Edwards, Vol. 2: Religious Affections.* New Haven: Yale University Press, 1959.

———. "Testing the Spirits: Jonathan Edwards and the Religious Affections." *Union Seminary Quarterly Review* 37 (1981–82) 27–37.

Spohn, William C. "Sovereign Beauty: Jonathan Edwards and the Nature of True Virtue." *Theological Studies* 42 (1981) 394–421.

Steele, Richard B. *"Gracious Affection" and "True Virtue" According to Jonathan Edwards and John Wesley.* Metuchen, NJ: Scarecrow, 1994.

Stein, Stephen J. "The Quest for the Spiritual Sense: The Biblical Hermeneutics of Jonathan Edwards." *Harvard Theological Review* 70 (1977) 99–113.

Storms, C. Samuel. "Jonathan Edwards on the Freedom of the Will." *Trinity Journal* 3 (1982) 131–69.

Veto, Miklos. "Spiritual Knowledge According to Jonathan Edwards." Translated by Michael J. McClymond. *Calvin Theological Journal* 31 (1996) 161–81.

5

The Religious Experience of Christ's Church

THOUGH MANY OF JONATHAN Edwards's writings detail personal religious psychology and relations with the Divine, underlying the experience of the individual lies the cosmic dimension of religion to which we have often referred. Like the intramutual, relational nature of the Godhead, the entire scope of reality is an enterprise in universal community in which individual religious experience, though important, is only a small part of the vast, eternal plan of redemption. Whether one accepts or rejects the offer of salvation through Jesus Christ, that offer is made in a historical context by messengers of the gospel—in other words, in community.

Edwards agrees with John Donne that no man is an island.[1] All people lives in the midst of a natural world that reveals the existence of God to them and in a dimension of time created for the express purpose of bringing them into fellowship with God. Even if someone lives where Christian influence is minimal, that person is nevertheless exposed to the gospel through general revelation. Meanwhile, the church of Jesus Christ is his witness through the fruits of the Holy Spirit, all of the good works that flow from true conversion. Not only are particular souls sanctified, or made holy, to be like Christ.[2] All Christians as one organism, the Body of Christ, are sanctified and inevitably impact society by exhibiting, expressing, and advocating humanity's love for God and God's love for us. In the universal system of existence, all beings are in some

---

1. "No man is an *Iland*, intire of it selfe, every man is a peece of the *Continent*, a part of the *maine*; if a *Clod* be washed away by the *Sea*, *Europe* is the lesse, as well as if a *Promontorie* were, as well as if a *Mannor* of thy *friends* or of *thine own* were; any mans *death* diminishes *mee*, because I am involved in *Mankinde*; and therefore never send to know for whom the *bell* tolls; It tolls for *thee*" (Donne [1572–1631]).

2. *WJE* 2, 454.

way dependent on other beings; the church's mission in that system is to exemplify loving, mutual dependence, to the glory of God.[3]

For Edwards, the church universal refers to God's people everywhere throughout the ages, while "by a particular true church must be meant a society of men [and women] that are visibly God's people . . . in the eye of Christian judgment, and that are indeed joined together in the Christian holy public worship."[4] The church is thoroughly theocentric because like creation and time, she was from all eternity intended to glorify God in Christ. [5] But that theocentrism is not chiefly a *human* activity that regards God. Instead this theocentrism is evidenced by the love *God* manifests in and through the saints as a whole, for "God in all his works, in laying the foundation of the world, and ever since the foundation of it, had been preparing this kingdom and glory for them."[6] God continually preserves, maintains, and provides for the church through the Holy Spirit's ministries of grace and revelation.[7] And just as an individual gradually progresses in sanctification, so Christ's universal Kingdom is established from place to place and grows in degrees. Such advancement magnifies God's wisdom to be "more visible to the creature's observation" and to triumph over Satan more gloriously.[8] This Kingdom "is by far the most happy Kingdom in the world. He that is their king is their father, their brother and husband, one that has a love stronger than death to his people, has infinite wisdom to guide him in governing [them and] infinite strength to defend them."[9]

Those who comprise the church of Christ on earth are not unified only by common religious experience based on election, regeneration, and sanctification. Their unity is grounded upon the reality that because of the merit of Christ, every true convert, or "saint," is indwelt by the Holy Spirit. The Spirit works in each toward the overall spiritual prosperity of God's Kingdom; the sanctification of one soul effectively benefits every other believer, even in generations to come.[10] In the church,

3. *WJE* 3, 126.
4. *WJE* 13, 414.
5. "Attempt," 337.
6. "End," 511.
7. *WJE* 9, 449.
8. *WJE* 9, 355.
9. "Glorying," 466.
10. *WJE* 13, 342, based on 2 Cor 13:14.

Christ is "mystically born into the world, in the advancement and flourishing of true religion, and great increase of the number of true converts, who are spoken of as having 'Christ formed in them.'"[11] Because it "was the design of Christ, to bring it to pass, that he, and his Father, and his people, might all be united in one," they are "one society, one family; that the church should be as it were admitted into the society of the blessed Trinity."[12] Consequently, every saint through the agency of the Holy Spirit enjoys this communion, a fellowship that is hinted at on earth and perfectly consummated in heaven "to the constant full satisfaction of the enlarged desires of the soul."[13] "There is the nearest union and a holy friendship between Christ and believers. They are Christ's dear ones, his jewels; and Christ is their jewel, their pearl of great price."[14]

When one thinks of Christian mysticism, Jonathan Edwards's name is not likely to spring to mind immediately. Nevertheless, the theologian describes a mystical dimension to the Body of Christ that complements the legal unity Jesus Christ accomplished as the covenant representative or federal head of the elect. Thus, "Christ and his church are one in law; that is, they are one in respect of the covenant."[15] Yet it is also true that this unbreakable union is one of supreme beauty, love, pleasure, and intimacy.[16] In the mystical Body of Christ there is great human and divine joy as the elect are somehow knit together by the Holy Spirit and are brought "to perfect excellency and beauty in his image and in holiness which is the proper beauty of spiritual beings."[17] Christ is glorified and exalted even as the saints are also glorified and exalted, body and soul, "giving them a participation of his elevation of nature. . . . Herein, in this whole work of restoration and exaltation of Christ mystical, is above all

---

11. "Attempt," 351.

12. "Christ," 594.

13. "Excellencies," 429. Heaven and the earthly-heavenly union of the church will be considered in chapter 7.

14. "Feast," 286. Edwards's reference to jewels and pearls is reminiscent of Matt 13:44–6, among other Bible passages.

15. WJE 13, 199.

16. "Fragment: Application on Love to Christ," WJE 10, 617.

17. WJE 9, 125. Schafer explains that the covenant of grace "is made with the saints not as separate individuals, but only as in Christ. The Church, which is elect mankind and the body of Christ, is seen to be a universal, not merely a collection of particulars; it is the new man which is in Christ and, in some sense, *is* Christ" ("Conception of the Church," 54).

things manifested the power of God in the new creation."[18] As a result, the covenant union between God and the church will eternally grow to resemble more and more the Spirit-bond between the Father and Jesus Christ, "who are so united, that their interest is perfectly one."[19] Indeed, the saints "are united with one mind to breathe forth their whole souls in love to their eternal Father, and to Jesus Christ, their common head."[20]

We recall from an earlier chapter that though God is perfectly self-sufficient, he nevertheless has a personality that longs to express his loving goodness to others; thus results the plan of creation and redemption for humanity.[21] For Jesus Christ in particular, the church answers that longing, satisfying his tender inclination to communicate himself.[22] Edwards proposes here a reciprocal partaking between Christ and his spouse, a perpetual, mutual infilling of goodness, joy, and glory through the faithfully constant ministry of the Holy Spirit.[23] The church is wholly possessed by God, and yet the church wholly possesses God and indeed the entire universe because she is united with the Ruler of all.[24] "The Son is the fullness of God, and the church is the fullness of the Son of God" even though she would be utterly destitute without him.[25]

How Christians Partake of God

Edwards elucidates the union between Christ and the saints through the concept of "partaking." As with the Holy Spirit's indwelling, partaking does not mean that a person shares in God's *essence* but in his "spiritual beauty and happiness."[26] As adopted children of God, believers share in the Son's enjoyment of God the Father and experience the joy Christ has in his own personal relationships with them.[27] This living, vibrant

---

18. *WJE 15*, 600–601.
19. "End," 533.
20. "Charity," 374.
21. "[R]ational beings' communion with God is the very highest end and only end of the whole universe" (*WJE 13*, 281).
22. *WJE 15*, 53.
23. *WJE 15*, 186.
24. *WJE 13*, 183–85.
25. *WJE 13*, 273. Consult "End," *WJE 8*, 439, based on 1 Cor 11:7 and Isa 46:13.
26. *WJE 2*, 203, based on Eph 3:17–19 and John 1:16.
27. "Christ," 593.

connection allows Christians to participate in God's own goodness in daily life, just as a guest might participate in conversation and dining as she takes part in a feast.[28]

One of the highest privileges of being elect, partaking of God is much more than a nice feeling or a metaphor for a spiritual idea.[29] It is a very real aspect of union with the Godhead in which Christ *is* the believer's life: the saint is "invigorated with him, with his Holy Spirit which is diffused as new life all over his soul" in a refreshing shower of grace.[30] As believers in Christ are being sanctified, God expresses his excellency to them by gently imposing his glorious image upon their souls. "The saint hath spiritual joy and pleasure by a kind of effusion of God on the soul. In these things the redeemed have communion with God; that is, they partake with him and of him."[31]

This common partaking of God and participation in his nature is actually what establishes the true Kingdom of God. Christ's first interest, according to Edwards, is to rule the hearts of his people by grace, so he sets up his Kingdom there and governs their wills and inclinations through the Scriptures and the influence of the Holy Spirit.[32] This Kingdom will spread throughout the globe "not by outward force, but inward overcoming influence, by his Word and Spirit making them 'his willing people in the day of his power' [Ps. 110: 3]."[33] They are a people willingly focused upon the things of God in gratefulness to Christ for the gift of salvation. Having claimed their hearts, the Holy Spirit then works through and in them to quell "contentions among men, and gives a spirit of peace and goodwill, excites to acts of outward kindness and earnest desires of the salvation of others' souls; and causes a delight in those that appear as the children of God and followers of Christ."[34] Saints truly submitted to God bear the fruit of righteous works that establish in society what is equally real in the human heart: God is growing a holy Kingdom, rooted first in Christian souls. Paul Ramsey explains that "the Kingdom

---

28. *WJE* 15, 186, based on 1 John 1:3.
29. "Grace," 156. Consult 1 Pet 4:13 and 2 Pet 1:4.
30. "Living," 570.
31. "Dependence," 208.
32. "Threefold," 422.
33. "Attempt," 309.
34. "Marks," 256.

of Christ building up in the souls of men should never be separated from the Kingdom of Christ building up in the world among men."[35]

The increase and prosperity of this Kingdom should be paramount to every Christian, who is to be soberly concerned with the "spiritual and eternal good" of the public, and "for the universal church and the world of mankind, has an universal benevolence."[36] Contrary to Alexis's opinion that Edwards was "other-worldly" and had a "lack of concern with the social order,"[37] Edwards believed that "to be of a Christian spirit is to be public-spirited."[38] Being a genuine Christian inherently implies wholeheartedly extending the love of God to all, being Christ's ambassadors of the gospel, and emulating the loving consent of the Trinitarian Godhead. Though Christians are called to love all people, the welfare of the *saints* is to be every believer's special joy because it is the glory of Christ's church everywhere to be "one holy society, one city, one family, one body," just as the Trinity is.[39] Union in the church

> is very much her beauty; and the mutual friendly correspondence of the various members, in distant parts of the world, is a thing well-becoming this union (at least when employed about things appertaining to the glory of their common head, and their common spiritual interest and happiness), and therefore is a thing decent and beautiful, and very profitable.[40]

The Jewish Church

When using the term "church," Jonathan Edwards is not simply referring to the entire body of believers since the ascension of Jesus Christ and the outpouring of the Holy Spirit at Pentecost (Acts 2). The church's ultimate origin is found in the eternal plan of redemption, but begins *in time* with Adam. In the Old Testament era, people were redeemed *only* by faith in

---

35. Ramsey, "Editor's Introduction," *WJE 8*, 71.

36. "Nobleness," 238. "Moral agents are social agents; affairs of morality are affairs of society" (*WJE 23*, 349).

37. Alexis, "Theocratic Ideal," 333.

38. "Nobleness," 238. In social benevolence, "there must be an assumption of [others'] happiness into the will and love of our own happiness, as Christ assumed our own nature into his" (Ramsey, "Editor's Introduction," *WJE 8*, 27).

39. "Attempt," 365.

40. "Scotland," 444.

the promised Messiah, Jesus Christ.[41] Just as the church has a special bond with God today, prior to Jesus' birth "the Jews had the true worship and communion of the one great and holy God, and that no other nation upon earth had."[42] Despite its many weaknesses and failures, what we know as the Old Testament church was preserved by the Holy Spirit to be a testimony of the one true God to her heathen neighbors.[43] The covenant of grace extended to us today is the very same covenant of grace that was extended to Adam, Noah, Abraham, David, and all of the other saints who preceded the incarnation of Christ. That covenant applies to elect humanity throughout the ages.[44]

The Old Testament church is especially important because it prepared the way for the New Testament church and serves as a "type of the invisible church, the true people of Jesus Christ in all ages."[45] But just as not all who profess to be Christians really are redeemed, not all in ancient Israel were faithful to the living God.[46] For Edwards, wickedness has prevailed in all peoples throughout history and is much more the norm than the righteousness that ought to be displayed by the church.[47] By Christ's time, the Jewish church had so strayed from God that it "was become exceeding corrupt, overrun with superstition and self-righteousness."[48] Yet even this decline prepared the way for Christ, allowing his saving gospel message to contrast the Law more strikingly and making "the glory of God's power in the great effects of Christ's redemption the more conspicuous."[49] How much more glorifying of God it was when wayward Jews were converted during the ministry of Jesus and his disciples! And how much more glorifying of God's justice it was

---

41. "Life," 523.

42. *WJE* 13, 448.

43. *WJE* 9, 129; also, *WJE* 3, 170–81. Edwards's *A History of the Work of Redemption* in *WJE* 9 analyzes the role of the church of Israel in God's providence and how Israel laid the foundation for what became the New Testament church. To review numerous types Edwards found for the church, please see the "Addendum" at the end of this chapter.

44. "Inquiry," 269.

45. "Glorying," 461.

46. "Inquiry," 184–85.

47. *WJE* 3, 163–66.

48. *WJE* 9, 230.

49. *WJE* 9, 231. For a summary of the differences between Old and New Testament times, see "Inquiry," 279–83.

when the apostate Jewish church shamefully ended in AD 70 with the destruction of Jerusalem.[50]

During the time of Christ, the Jewish church "was rejected and became barren" because so many Jews despised him; it was no longer blessed by the Holy Spirit, and the Gentile church flourished in its place.[51] Indeed the Jews as a people lost their special favor with God and "were broken off from the church, and ceased any longer to be visible saints, by their open and obstinate unbelief."[52] Since the time of Christ Jews may receive the gift of salvation in the same manner as everyone else, through faith, but without faith "surely they are not God's covenant people, in the sense that visible Christians are."[53] The Savior's ministry not only brought closure to the Jewish church, but also to the period of Old Testament biblical revelation: "then there was an end to those types and shadows, because they were then all fulfilled" in Jesus Christ.[54]

Edwards's comments about the Jewish church, especially that it was rejected by God for rejecting Christ, should not be construed as anti-Semitism. The Puritan believed that *all sinners* are rejected by God because by their sins *all* have crucified Christ.[55] Throughout his works Edwards marvels at God's mercy and grace in choosing the Jews as his own people, and believes that the Jews will receive unique blessings at the end of time because of the special place they had in the plan of redemption.[56] But due to their treatment of Christ during the time of his ministry on earth, Jews have the same status as adherents of any other religion. Edwards lumps them together with pagans, heathens, deists, Muslims, and professors of false Christian religion as being equally in need of salvation through the gospel. Christ serves in this respect as the Great Equalizer: he no longer extends preference in the offer of salvation

---

50. *WJE 15*, 115. The "whole church of God is still God's Jerusalem: they are his spiritual Jerusalem and are, as it were, only added to the church that was begun in the literal Jerusalem" (*WJE 9*, 377).

51. *WJE 15*, 301.

52. "Inquiry," 273.

53. "Inquiry," 271, based on Lev 26:42.

54. *WJE 15*, 325. For types of Christ in Old Testament history, see "Messiah," 217–22 and 294–305.

55. "Images," 52.

56. "Inquiry," 271.

to one nation, but fulfills the divine promise made to Abraham that he would be the father of many nations (Genesis 12, 15).

God's promise to Abraham was markedly fulfilled at Pentecost (Acts 1–2), when "God fed his people with spiritual dainties, and filled them with the Spirit, and gave 'em joy in the Holy Ghost."[57] Prior to Pentecost, the Holy Spirit merely "came upon" certain people temporarily to empower them for a specific calling or task. On the day of Pentecost, the indwelling of the Spirit became the *permanent* blessing of *all* who have faith in Jesus Christ. This event in Edwards's mind bore forth the "first fruits of Christ's redemption."[58] But even more, it established a firm spiritual foundation for the new church era, building up those converted directly by Jesus and freshly converting young and old, male and female, Jew and Gentile.[59] On Pentecost, "the Holy Ghost was not only given in ordinary, sanctifying, saving influences, but also in extraordinary gifts of inspiration for the revealing the mind and will of God, and establishing the standing rule of the faith, worship, and manners of the Christian church."[60]

The extraordinary gifts of which Edwards speaks include prophesying (as in preaching and foretelling), speaking in tongues (preaching in various languages), working miracles, and having an "understanding of the deep things of religion by immediate revelation, or inspiration."[61] The purpose of these gifts was to establish the fledgling church quickly and firmly, "to promote and establish true religion, and propagate the gospel."[62] By "means of these extraordinary gifts of the Holy Ghost, the apostles and others were enabled to write the New Testament to be an infallible rule of faith and works and manners to the church to the end of the world."[63]

In the context of the spiritual revivals Edwards encountered during the First Great Awakening, it was important for him to define the nature and value of extraordinary gifts in order to distinguish true religious activity from that which was a product of human imagination or demonic

---

57. "Thoughts," 367.
58. "Thoughts," 359.
59. "Charity," 149.
60. WJE 15, 392.
61. "Charity," 151, based on 1 Cor 12:8.
62. "Charity," 161–62.
63. WJE 9, 365.

influence.⁶⁴ Edwards contends that extraordinary gifts were generally restricted to the apostolic era and totally ceased when the books that comprise the New Testament (the "canon") were settled by the early church.⁶⁵ For him, any assertion that extraordinary gifts are evident or necessary in the post-apostolic era implies that the Bible is imperfect, and needs supplementary revelation and miraculous activity to complete and validate it. "Prophecy and miracles argue the imperfection of the state of the church rather than the perfection," and thus were intended only for an infant church.⁶⁶ In fact, these extraordinary gifts will never be evident again, because the glorified, heavenly church will relish God's perfect presence and have no need of them.

Moreover, arguing for the continuing presence of these extraordinary gifts also denigrates the powerful activity of the Holy Spirit since Pentecost. For Edwards, it is more than enough that the "Spirit of God be poured out only in his gracious influences in converting souls, and infusing divine love into them in such a measure as he may."⁶⁷ Extraordinary gifts have never been evidence of a greater degree of virtue or even of saving faith, and phenomena in the post-apostolic era resembling them should not be given any weight because they are nothing more than delusions.

Rather, it is much more important for believers to pursue holiness through the "ordinary," or conventional, workings of the Holy Spirit. They are actually *more* extraordinary than so-called "extraordinary" gifts, because the latter do nothing to sanctify a soul. While the extraordinary gifts seem flashy and appealing, the Spirit's ordinary influences in conversion and sanctification are more desirable because they impart

---

64. The First Great Awakening (1730s–40s) was a renewal of Christian religion in Europe and North America that emphasized guilt due to sin, everyone's need for salvation through Christ, and personal morality. The influence of demons was thought to be a factor in the opposition to the revivals, and will be examined in the next chapter.

65. The history of the New Testament canon is complex, but for our sake here it was "closed" by church leaders around AD 400.

66. "Charity," 362.

67. "Charity," 363. Edwards notes that while it was necessary and profitable for God to use extraordinary gifts in Israel and the apostolic church, it "is no way necessary, nor at all suitable to the gospel state of the church.... Is it not better that God should give the world a book that should be the summary of his will, to which all nations in all ages may resort, to know the mind of God?... God now communicates himself to his church in a much more excellent and glorious way than that by miracles, etc., by the communications of his Spirit of holiness to the hearts" of his people (*WJE 13*, 449).

"the spiritual image of God" and the holiness it entails.[68] The love of God and saving grace are far preferable to any unusual gifts, and are indeed the greatest privileges any human can be given. Even the prophets and the apostle Paul did not comfort themselves with their extraordinary gifts of the Spirit, but with the integrity, faith, and sincere commitment to God they were granted by his grace (Romans 12; 1 Corinthians 12–14).[69] That such unusual gifts have expired teaches the church to cherish divine love, which is "of an immortal nature, and which will be a sure evidence of our own blessed immortality, and the beginning of eternal life in our souls."[70]

Let's review for just a moment. Having discussed the foundation of human community in the Godhead, we have also examined how God expresses that intratrinitarian, harmonious set of relations through the establishment and growth of the Kingdom of God. Like everything else in the universe, the church is utterly dependent upon God for its existence and prosperity. But the church is a special case in that she is composed of people who have been granted salvation from sin through Jesus Christ in accordance with their election in the eternal plan of redemption. The Holy Spirit knits them together across all times and places, even across death's boundary into heaven. When God draws time to its close, the church will savor fellowship in God's eternal paradise. But for now, the divine bond that members of the Body of Christ share is manifest concretely in its worship, leadership, prayer, and impact upon the world.

God's People Worship

For Edwards worship is the gathering of God's people for singing, confession of sin, preaching, prayer, and praise, but it is also much more than this. Worship is the purpose for which humanity was really created, and the concrete act of worship shows "the high esteem and love of the heart, exalting thoughts of God, and complacence in his excellence and perfection."[71] Certainly, part of worship's beauty lies in its public nature, honoring God and praising him in the midst of broader society. "'Tis

---

68. "Charity," 159.
69. "Charity," 160.
70. "Charity," 365.
71. "End," 522.

fit that God's honor should not be concealed, but made known in the great congregation, . . . to the utmost ends of the earth."[72] But it is not enough that one's soul desires to praise God; the presentation of our whole selves, body and soul, is the greatest of all Christian duties, giving of ourselves entirely to him as a community of living sacrifices.[73] United worship, particularly on the Sabbath, shows people to be "one holy society, and great congregation of worshipers, and servants of God . . . for the greater glory of their common Lord, and the greater edification and comfort of the whole body."[74]

Worship is also the utmost human way to imitate the loving consent within the Trinity. As such, Edwards took the matter quite seriously, even making a personal resolution "never to speak anything that is ridiculous, or matter of laughter on the Lord's day."[75] He advocated orderly worship, thinking that even the greatest zeal for the Lord requires structure and a sense of propriety because these best promote "the designs of Christ's glory and the church's prosperity."[76] And though he was a great proponent of singing in Sunday services, seeing it as a natural fruit of the Spirit's influences, he also thought it should be done with "reverence and solemnity" as a holy act, respecting and honoring God as if he were "visibly present."[77]

The sacraments of baptism and the Lord's Supper are of equal gravity, chiefly because they are the ordinances through which Christ rules

72. "Thoughts," 492. Formal worship is an outward gesture and "profession of inward worship" (523).

73. "Dedication," 551; see 1 Pet 2:4–10. Until "we have given ourselves to God, and have offered ourselves as a sacrifice to him, we belong to the devil and he claims a right to us" (553).

74. "Attempt," 373; see Heb 10:25. For an explanation of the importance of worship on the Sabbath, see *WJE 13*, 310–19.

75. "Resolutions," *WJE 16*, 756. On 95 of that volume, Edwards advises one Deborah Hatheway, "Don't talk of things of religion and matters of experience with an air of lightness and laughter, which is too much the manner in many places" ("To Deborah Hatheway, June 3, 1741"). Hatheway was an eighteen-year-old new convert who asked Edwards for advice about how to pursue her Christian life.

76. "Thoughts," 455.

77. "Thoughts," 489. "There are many things in Scripture, that seem to intimate that praising God, both in speeches and songs, will be what the church of God will very much abound in, in the approaching glorious day" (406). Unlike some of his contemporaries, Edwards saw no reason to exclude hymns from worship. His congregations sang the works of Isaac Watts (1674–1748), the "Father of English Hymnody," during their afternoon Sabbath services.

his people and is especially present with them through the Holy Spirit.[78] The only reason the two sacraments exist and have any meaning is because they are appropriated by the Word of God and immediately bless the Christians who partake of them.[79] They are appointed by God "as means and expressions of true religion."[80] The sacraments are "covenant privileges" and "seals of the covenant" of grace.[81] In sum, "'tis only the Word of God in the Holy Scriptures, that gives a man a right to worship the Supreme Being in this sacramental manner, and to come to him in this way, or any other, as one in covenant with him."[82]

While Edwards did not write extensively on the theological nature of the Lord's Supper, we do know that he believed it to be a formal acceptance of the covenant of grace that should be part of worship every Sunday.[83] The Lord's Supper, also called Holy Communion, is an intensely spiritual rite that should not be taken lightly—a "solemn profession" of believers that Christ is "their only Savior and chief good."[84] Those who are not genuinely redeemed or Christians who are not fully reconciled with others should not take part in the sacrament until they are at peace (1 Cor 11:27–34). So participation in the Lord's Supper requires a living faith and sanctified heart that "capacitates men to discern the Lord's body in the sacrament with that spiritual sensation or spiritual gist, which is suitable to the nature and design of the ordinance."[85] Though a serious matter, Lord's Supper is also a wonderful type of the heavenly gospel feast that will be held after Judgment Day, and signifies Christ's provision of salvation for believers and the intimate communion he shares with them.[86] In total, the Lord's Supper is

> the Christian church's great feast of love; wherein Christ's people sit together as brethren in the family of God, at their father's table, to feast on the love of their Redeemer, commemorating his

---

78. "Threefold," 421.
79. *WJE* 9, 135.
80. *WJE* 2, 114.
81. "Corrected," 412–13.
82. "Inquiry," 294.
83. "Erskine A," 366.
84. "Inquiry," 256. Cf. 1 Cor 10:16.
85. "Inquiry," 262.
86. "Feast," 288. "The ordinances of the external worship of the Christian church are typical of things belonging to its heavenly state" ("Messiah," 192).

sufferings for them, and his dying love to them, and sealing their love to him and one another.[87]

Baptism, on the other hand, was a practice adopted by the early church for new converts as "an exhibition and token of their being visibly regenerated."[88] In the case of adults who are baptized, the sacrament entails a dedication of oneself to God and "a profession of being buried with Christ and rising with him."[89] But in the case of an infant who is baptized, parents stand before God on the child's behalf. They declare their dedication of the child to God and intent to raise the child with the hope that he or she will eventually profess faith in Jesus Christ and lay claim to the covenant of grace. Based upon the parents' faith,

> if that child dies in infancy, the parents have good grounds to hope for its salvation; and have also good grounds to hope, that if the child don't die in infancy, that the blessing of God will attend their thorough care and pains to bring up their child in the nurture and admonition of the Lord. So that by that means it may be brought to salvation.[90]

Thus, if "the adult person does sincerely and believingly give up himself to God, baptism seals salvation to him: so if the parent sincerely and believingly dedicates the infant to God, baptism seals salvation to it."[91]

From these few references, Edwards may seem to view baptism as a work of merit in which sincerity and earnestness of faith is crucial and performance of the ritual absolutely confirms the eternal salvation of the participant. Though baptism does not *guarantee* salvation, for Edwards its great efficacy lies in the power of the covenant of grace for redemption. If the adult convert has taken the acceptance of that covenant as seriously as it deserves, his profession of faith in baptism is as natural and meaningful as the holiness he strives to exhibit in daily life.

Meanwhile, the "baptism of infants is the seal of these promises made to the seed of the righteous."[92] Through parents, infants are given

---

87. "Inquiry," 255.
88. "Inquiry," 196, based on Romans 6.
89. *WJE* 20, 114.
90. *WJE* 18, 115–16; see also *WJE* 20, 79.
91. *WJE* 18, 129. In the spiritually prosperous season of the millennium, the thousand-year period before Judgment Day, "children will be sanctified in their infancy" (*WJE* 20, 163).
92. "Corrected," 484.

to God as first fruits, are visibly made part of that eternal covenant, and thereafter "stand fair for being really God's people and [part] of his church in God's ordinary way of dealing with mankind."[93] As children grow, they more and more come to be seen by God as responsible for themselves, according to their developing capacities. In adulthood, they ultimately are expected to make their own profession of faith. But until then, Christian parents are the representatives of their children in much the same way that God looks upon Christ the Second Adam as federal representative of the church. God has ordained that parents "stand in the room [stead] of infants . . . that what is in them shall be accepted as sufficiently countervailing the defects and hindrances that attend their infant state."[94]

It was Edwards's contention, a contention that ultimately cost him his pastoral position at Northampton, that only those who are church members ought to have the privilege of participating in the Lord's Supper.[95] He expected church membership in turn to require baptism, a public confession of faith, and consistent, visible evidence of the indwelling Holy Spirit and his gracious blessings.[96] The public confession was to include commitment to future obedience to Christ as Lord and King, for which the believer would forever be accountable before God and his fellow Christians.[97] For Edwards, such confession was actually a duty of believers, a solemn statement of their personally owning the covenant of grace and a "part of the public worship of God to be performed by all God's people."[98]

But any profession of faith in Christ, notably for membership in the Christian community, could be feigned; a person could deceive himself and others about the sincerity and validity of his profession. Since people cannot search one another's hearts, Edwards understood that

---

93. *WJE* 20, 75. At one time the word "room" meant "stead," "place," or "assigned position."

94. *WJE* 20, 77.

95. "Inquiry," 174. Edwards was either assistant (to his grandfather, Solomon Stoddard) or senior pastor of the congregational church in Northampton, Massachusetts, between 1727 and 1748. He was dismissed from that pulpit in 1748 because a majority of the church held that baptism was the *only* requirement for church membership. See Hall's "Editor's Introduction," *WJE* 12.

96. "Inquiry," 176–96.

97. "Inquiry," 206–10.

98. "Inquiry," 201; Edwards presents scriptural support for this position on 201–3.

hypocrites, false teachers, and liars may be admitted into congregations, just as they were in the apostolic church.[99] And because the Spirit's ways in the soul are often inscrutable, no confessor should be required to give a step-by-step account of his conversion or spiritual life.[100] Nevertheless, a profession should include an honest understanding of true piety, "some sort of belief of the being of a God, some sort of belief that the Scriptures are the Word of God, that there is a future state of rewards and punishments, and that Jesus is the Messiah."[101] "For persons to profess those things wherein the essence of Christianity lies, is the same thing as to profess that they experience those things," for only true Christians have that special sense of the heart and knowledge of divine matters.[102]

Edwards took great pains to emphasize that these external, public statements of devotion must be complemented and balanced by acts of righteousness, "which are of much greater importance in the sight of God than all the externals of his worship."[103] Attendance at Sunday services, even with the greatest apparent sincerity or fervency, is not a guarantee or substitute for true faith and genuine acts of piety. Like the Pharisees of Jesus' day or the "Sunday" or "holiday" Christians of today, some in Edwards's time thought that "if they are but baptized and go to church, and attend the public worship and ordinances of God, and do but keep to the outward forms, they shall undoubtedly go to heaven, without any scruple. They love to have an easy, smooth way to heaven."[104] But there is no such way because "a strict religious life is most contrary to corrupt nature."[105] Rather, true worship "is the creature's exercise and expression of respect to the Creator. But if there be no true respect or

---

99. "Inquiry," 226–28; 237–43; 321–24.

100. *WJE* 2, 416–18.

101. "Inquiry," 291. For detailed explanations of what constitutes an acceptable profession of faith, see *WJE* 2, 413–20; *WJE* 15, 556–61; "To the Reverend Peter Clark, May 7, 1750," *WJE* 16, 344–46; *WJE* 20, 112–15.

102. *WJE* 2, 416.

103. "Thoughts," 522.

104. "Future," 375. There is "a common unhappy shyness in great men with respect to religion, as though they were ashamed of it, or at least ashamed to do very much at it; whereby they dishonor and doubtless greatly provoke the King of kings, and very much wound religion among the common people" ("Thoughts," 513). See also the sermon "Unconverted," 357–70.

105. "Wicked Men's Slavery to Sin," *WJE* 10, 341.

love, then all his religion is but seeming religion, and there is no real religion in it, and therefore it is vain."[106]

The Role and Responsibilities of Pastors

Perhaps the greatest insight into the Puritan's thoughts about pastoral ministry comes from his own experience. Referring to his responsibilities at the church in Northampton, Edwards comments,

> It was implied in my ordination vows that I would study the Scriptures; that I would make the Word of God, and not the word of any man, my rule in teaching my people; and that I would do my utmost to know what was the counsel of God, and to declare it. This was implied in my covenant with God and the people at my settlement; and it was implied in their covenant with God and with me that, in my so doing, they would diligently and impartially hear and examine what I should offer to them as the counsel of God.[107]

Obviously, Edwards took his pastoral role and responsibility very seriously. He continues, "The laws of nature and the laws of Christ require me to love this people, to whom I have been so related, and to value their charity and esteem."[108] In obedience to God's design, ministers are to lead the congregations of Christ's church with integrity, being well-educated "pastors of worshiping societies, and their heads and guides in the affairs of public worship."[109] Following the example set by Christ and modeled by the apostles, pastors administer the sacraments, encourage prayer, and instruct those under their care "what Christ would have them to do, and . . . teach them" the meaning of true Christian faith and practice.[110] Because of this grave responsibility for souls, expectation of more severe divine judgment (Jas 3:1), and a pastor's need to be continually reliant upon God, "a man ought not to take upon him the work of the ministry, unless called to it in the providence of God; for a man has no right to take this honor to himself, unless called of God."[111]

106. "Charity," 137.
107. "Controversy," 565.
108. "Controversy," 570.
109. "Thoughts," 494.
110. *WJE* 13, 222.
111. "Inquiry," 296.

Though this point may seem obvious, every pastor needs to have genuine, vibrant faith in Jesus Christ.

> We that are ministers not only have need of some true experience of the saving influence of the Spirit of God upon our heart, but we need a double portion of the Spirit of God . . . to be as full of light as a glass is, that is held out in the sun; and with respect to love and zeal . . . to be like the angels, that are a flame of fire [Ps 104:4]. The state of the times extremely requires a fullness of the divine Spirit in ministers, and we ought to give ourselves no rest till we have obtained it.[112]

Because their greatest concern is to act for the benefit of the congregation they serve, the broader church, and public society, they must therefore live out a superior example of godliness.[113] Though pastors are subject to God's strict judgment, faithful ministers will be abundantly blessed. "Because he is both Christ's saint and ambassadorial co-laborer, the minister will have a special role in the marriage of the Lamb: the minister's position will be one of even 'higher privilege' and 'a much higher participation' than God's holy angels."[114]

So ministers are to propagate and reflect God's glory in exemplary fashion because they are "burning and shining lights, but then they don't shine by their own light, but only reflect the light of Christ."[115] The light of Christ shines particularly brightly when the Word of God is preached and the gospel proclaimed: "the glad tidings of a new way of acceptance with God, unto life, a way wherein sinners may come to be free from the guilt of sin, and obtain a title to eternal life."[116] Pastors are Christ's representatives, Christ incarnate so to speak, and possess God's authority only to the extent that their preaching reflects Scriptural teaching. "'Tis by the same faith whereby [believers] receive Christ and obey his word, that they receive and obey the instructions of ministers, for their

---

112. "Thoughts," 507.

113. "Inquiry," *WJE 12*, 179. For a discussion of how missionary David Brainerd provided a model for Christians and especially ministers, see *WJE 7*, 530–34.

114. Westra, "'Above All Others,'" 215, quoting Edwards from the sermon "The Church's Marriage to Her Sons, and to Her God," since published in *WJE 25*, 164–96.

115. *WJE 15*, 320. For more about the spiritual responsibilities of pastors, consult the sermon "Sons of Oil, Heavenly Lights" in *WJE 25*, 260–74.

116. "Justification," 240. To consider Edwards's methods regarding sermon production and preaching, consult Kimnach's introduction to *WJE 10*, 3–258.

instructions are no other than the word of Christ by them."[117] Preaching therefore should be heartfelt, clear, and vigorous, advocating and encouraging believers' holiness for the edification and expansion of the Kingdom of God.[118]

God's Word proclaimed is a means of grace used by the Holy Spirit to enlighten the soul, impress "divine things on the hearts and affections of men," and "stir up the pure minds of the saints, and quicken their affections, by often bringing the great things of religion to their remembrance."[119] "Our people don't so much need to have their heads stored, as to have their hearts touched; and they stand in the greatest need of that sort of preaching that has the greatest tendency to do this."[120] Stirring preaching must be biblically comprehensive, not only sharing the comforts the gospel affords to those who believe, but also boldly warning both adults and children of hell's horrors.[121] Until they become regenerate even baptized children are not innocent, "but are young vipers, and are infinitely more hateful than vipers, and are in a most miserable condition."[122] As Westra observes, "Faithful preaching is thus always consequential, even when it is ignored, for it is a divine power, either for salvation or for damnation, to those that hear it."[123]

Prayer and the Worldwide Church

Another paramount duty of ministers is to lead their congregations with an example of prayerfulness because prayer is a wonderfully unique practice by which the global church can be united.[124] It is indeed the "one great and principal means of carrying on the designs of Christ's kingdom in the world."[125] Prayer is "a principal part of the worship of

---

117. WJE 15, 583.
118. "Messiah," 278.
119. WJE 2, 115.
120. "Thoughts," 388.
121. "Marks," 247–48.
122. "Thoughts," 394. Edwards and his wife Sarah (Pierpont, 1710–58) had eleven children.
123. Westra, 210.
124. "Attempt," 435.
125. "Thoughts," 516. Edwards explains that prayers are not vain exercises in light of God's sovereign decrees and providence because both the decrees and the prayers are

the church of God, in the days of the gospel, when [Old Testament] sacrifices are abolished."[126] Rather than offering a lamb or dove, believers offer their hearts and seek "God's gracious presence, the blessed manifestations of him, union and intercourse with him; or, in short, God's manifestations and communications of himself by his Holy Spirit."[127] Prayer, both corporate and personal, is "the very breath of a spirit of piety."[128] God is honored when his children pray because prayer "is but a sensible acknowledgment of our dependence on him to his glory."[129] Through Christ's mediation, God readily hears Christian prayer and answers generously. He

> stands ready to shew mercy in answer to prayer. He that has done such great things, and has so wonderfully and speedily answered prayer for temporal mercies, will much more give the Holy Spirit if we ask him. He marvelously preserves us, and waits to be gracious to us, as though he chose to make us monuments of his grace, and not his vengeance, and waits only to have us open our mouths wide, that he may fill them.[130]

Given his context in the Great Awakening, Edwards was particularly concerned with prayers for the outpouring of the Holy Spirit during revivals of true Christian religion. He hoped that extraordinarily magnificent manifestations of grace might be revealed and enacted by God to reform both the church and society at large.[131] Edwards called

---

eternally present to him, and are part of one another in the harmony of his plan (*WJE* 13, 248). "When God is about to bestow some great blessing on his church," he orders "things in his providence as to shew his church their great need of it" and through the Spirit stirs them to pray for it ("Thoughts," 517).

126. "Attempt," 314.

127. "Attempt," 315.

128. *WJE* 9, 141. "Hence how rational is it to suppose, contrary to the principles of the deists, that God ought to be worshipped by prayer, confession, praise, and thanksgiving, and those duties in which we speak to God and have to do with [him] as a properly intelligent Being or one that perceives and knows what we say to him. . . . Never to go to God or to purpose to exhibit our thoughts to him or to direct any expression of any motion of our hearts to him as we naturally do to all properly intelligent beings with whom we are concerned certainly is not to treat him as a properly intelligent, voluntary being" (*WJE* 18, 397).

129. "Most High," 116.

130. "Attempt," 363.

131. "Calamity," 505. "There is no way that Christians in a private capacity can do so much to promote the work of God, and advance the kingdom of Christ, as by prayer"

for concerted prayer gatherings throughout the American colonies and Europe so "the union and agreement of God's people in his worship [is] the more visible, and puts the greater honor upon God, and would . . . assist and enliven the devotions of Christians."[132] Having large numbers of Christians praying simultaneously does not in itself influence God or earn his blessing. But it does increase his glory, bear witness to his presence and power, and encourage the faith of those who participate.[133]

Truly faithful prayers are not offered to acquire some gain but simply to please God. Prayer is the soul's intimate, honest conversation with its Creator, like a letter of adoration the soul writes to its Lord. Its intent is to worship and praise him by gratefully acknowledging his sovereign rule over all and eagerly consenting with other Christians toward his holy goals. As Edwards concludes, "I am persuaded that such an agreement of the people of God in different parts [of the world], to unite together, to pray for the Holy Spirit, is lovely in the eyes of Jesus Christ the glorious head of the church."[134]

To Edwards it was obvious that Christians should offer supplication to the Lord as an expression of their dependence on him. One way God may answer those prayers is through Christ's Body, the church. Edwards declares, "We are made for one another. We are not made for ourselves alone; we are made to be useful to society. Neither can we possibly subsist without the help of our fellow men. God in the creation designed men for society, that we might help each other and love each other."[135] But how *do* Christians help and love each other, practically speaking?

Edwards engages numerous far-ranging topics along this line, including how wealthy persons may contribute to the Kingdom of God in a unique way.[136] He addresses the important role Christian families have as the moral building blocks of greater society.[137] He describes the proper behavior of laypersons, especially in not assuming for themselves

---

because in prayer, even the weakest of the world may implore God's infinite power ("Thoughts," 518).

132. "Thoughts," 520; also "Attempt," especially 314–23, 427–34.
133. "Attempt," 374.
134. "Scotland," 183.
135. "Peaceably," 129.
136. "Thoughts," 514–15.
137. "Charity," 280.

the authority God has granted only to ordained ministers.[138] He explains that selfless love is essential for acting toward the common good of society and for pleasing God by "being at peace with our neighbors and brethren."[139] He also maintains that true religion is crucial to the propagation of the gospel for the conversion of souls, and the stability and happiness of society.[140] Though we do have these examples, in general Edwards's public concern was not preaching and writing about how to live out faith in practical ways, unlike most Christian authors and pastors today. No doubt practical suggestions for faith would have been part of his daily pastoral ministry. But we have to remember that our culture today highly values the individual and an individual's experience to an extent that would have astonished Edwards and his contemporaries. For him, individual faith was certainly important, but the "big picture" of Christ's cosmic church was far more compelling and significant.

When individual faith is healthy and vibrant, it looks outward to the needs of others. One such manifestation of this care lies in missions and evangelism, the sharing of the gospel with those who have not heard or heeded it. Though Edwards did not devote much time to writing a formal theology of missions, he did spend the latter part of his life ministering among Native Americans as his friend David Brainerd had for a lifetime.[141] Without a doubt, Edwards advocated the conversion of all peoples to faith in Jesus Christ and the global spread of the gospel by the church.[142] To him, non-Christian religions, including Roman Catholicism and Islam, were idolatrous, "invented" religions replete with superstitions, human traditions, and wickedness due to their distortions of natural and biblical revelation.[143] In fact, heathens were nothing more

---

138. "Thoughts," 427, 484–88.

139. "Peaceably," 132. "The gospel spirit is a catholic [universal] spirit, a noble and unconfined benevolence, like unto that of our Creator, not confined to any particular part of mankind exclusive of others; but the Christian's good will is general to all the seed of Adam" (121).

140. "Pleasantness," 114–15.

141. Beginning in 1750, Edwards pastored a church in Stockbridge, Massachusetts, while also serving as a missionary to the Housatonic people. He preached to the natives through an interpreter and defended them against whites who tried to take advantage of them.

142. "Apocalypse," 178.

143. *WJE* 9, 415.

than devil-worshippers.[144] But it is these same heathens, idolaters, and proponents of false religion who

> shall be enlightened with the truth, and there shall be a more extraordinary appearance of the power of godliness amongst those that profess it, when God's [S]pirit shall be poured out on old and young, and the knowledge of God shall cover the earth 'as the waters cover the seas' (Is. 11:9).[145]

Perhaps because Jonathan Edwards had such an obvious disdain for non-Christian religions and false "Christian" beliefs, he emphasized the importance of seeking the salvation of others' souls. Premier ways for Christians to accomplish this include sharing the gospel, living godly examples, and having reverence for holy ordinances such as the Sabbath, preaching, and the sacraments.[146] The power of the Holy Spirit to convert and transform souls is immeasurably stronger than the grip of false religion and idolatry. And the power of the Holy Spirit to draw forth Christ's elect into the Kingdom of God is immeasurably stronger than any person, institution, or army. We turn our attention next to the dramatic conversion of souls in times of spiritual and religious renewal, with an eye toward their eternal destiny on Judgment Day.

For Further Thought

1. What are the marks of the universal church and the people who comprise it? Could someone have been part of the church before Christ was born?

2. Explain the "mystical" dimension of the Body of Christ and how Christians "partake" of God. What are your impressions of Edwards's thoughts on these topics? How do his descriptions compare with your own religious experience? Read the Bible verses mentioned in footnotes 25–26 and 28–29 and examine how well they support Edwards's ideas.

3. How do Edwards's descriptions of the church and Christian behavior compare with your own experience of the church and Christians? If you profess to be a Christian, what are the strengths and weaknesses

---

144. *WJE 9*, 472.
145. "Value," 335.
146. "Value," 335.

of your Christian lifestyle? What are the strengths and weaknesses of the congregation with whom you worship?

4. Why is the Jewish church important for both positive and negative reasons? What impact did the event of Pentecost have on the Jewish church and the church overall?

5. Do you agree or disagree with Edwards's views of baptism and the Lord's Supper? Why? What do the sacraments mean to you, if anything? Do you believe there are more than two sacraments? Why?

6. Edwards believed that extraordinary gifts of the Holy Spirit ended. When did they end, and why to him is it important that they *did* end? Do you think that unusual spiritual gifts are active today? Why?

7. Summarize in your own words the role and responsibilities of ministers. Do you think Edwards's ideas still apply today? Why? If his standards for pastors were applied to modern churches, do you think they would make an impact? Why?

8. What is worship? Why should Christians do it? Who or what do you worship, and why? What kinds of worship do you take part in?

9. For Edwards, what is the importance of prayer to God, to the church, and to individual congregations? How do his thoughts about prayer compare with yours?

10. What are your reflections about how Edwards viewed hypocrites, heathens, other religions, and Roman Catholicism? From what you know of his thought, how would he justify seeing them as "non-Christian"? In what ways do you agree or disagree with him on this topic?

11. Review a bit the previous chapters. What so far has impressed you about Edwards's theology? What elements do you disagree with? Has his view of God changed your own at all? List your answers for future reference.

For Further Reading

Breckus, Catherine A. "Remembering Jonathan Edwards's Ministry to Children." In *Jonathan Edwards at Home and Abroad*, edited by David W. Kling and Douglas A. Sweeney. Columbia: University of South Carolina Press, 2003.

Caldwell, Robert W., III. "'Call the Sabbath a Delight': Jonathan Edwards on The Lord's Day." *Southwestern Journal of Theology* 47 (2005) 191–205.

Craig, Philip A. "'And Prophecy Shall Cease': Jonathan Edwards on the Cessation of the Gift of Prophecy." *Westminster Theological Journal* 64 (2002) 163–84.

Davies, Ronald E. "Missionary Benefactor and Strange Bedfellow: Isaac Hollis, Jonathan Edwards' English Correspondent." *Baptist Quarterly* 41 (2006) 263–80.

Gilbert, Greg D. "The Nations Will Worship: Jonathan Edwards and the Salvation of the Heathen." *Trinity Journal* 23 (2002) 53–76.

Hambrick-Stowe, Charles E. "All Things Were New and Astonishing: Edwardsian Piety, the New Divinity, and Race." In *Jonathan Edwards at Home and Abroad*, edited by David W. Kling and Douglas A. Sweeney. Columbia: University of South Carolina Press, 2003.

Hannah, John D. "Jonathan Edwards, the Toronto Blessing, and the Spiritual Gifts: Are the Extraordinary Ones Actually the Ordinary Ones?" *Trinity Journal* 17 (1996) 167–89.

Lucas, Sean Michael. "'A Man Just Like Us': Jonathan Edwards and Spiritual Formation for Ministerial Candidates." *Presbyterion* 30 (2004) 1–10.

Marsden, George M. "Jonathan Edwards, the Missionary." *Journal of Presbyterian History* 81 (2003) 5–17.

McDermott, Gerald R. *Jonathan Edwards Confronts the Gods: Christian Theology, Enlightenment Religion, and Non-Christian Faiths*. New York: Oxford University Press, 2000.

———. "Poverty, Patriotism, and National Covenant: Jonathan Edwards and Public Life." *Journal of Religious Ethics* 31 (2003) 229–51.

Nichols, Stephen J. *An Absolute Sort of Certainty: The Holy Spirit and the Apologetics of Jonathan Edwards*. Phillipsburg, NJ: P&R, 2003.

Piggin, Stuart. "The Expanding Knowledge of God: Jonathan Edwards's Influence on Missionary Thinking and Promotion." In *Jonathan Edwards at Home and Abroad*, edited by David W. Kling and Douglas A. Sweeney. Columbia: University of South Carolina Press, 2003.

Rightmire, R. David. "The Sacramental Theology of Jonathan Edwards in the Context of Controversy." *Fides et Historia* 21 (1989) 50–60.

Smith, Robert Doyle. "John Wesley and Jonathan Edwards on Religious Experience: A Comparative Analysis." *Wesley Theological Journal* 25 (1990) 130–46.

Stahle, Rachel S. "Jonathan Edwards on Pastoral Ministry." *Pittsburgh Theological Journal* (May, 2009).

Stout, Harry S. "The Puritans and Edwards: The American Vision of a Covenant People." *Christian History* 4 (1985) 23–25.

Waanders, David W. "Pastoral Sense of Jonathan Edwards." *Reformed Review* 29 (1976) 124–32.

Walls, Andrew F. "Missions and Historical Memory: Jonathan Edwards and David Brainerd." In *Jonathan Edwards at Home and Abroad*, edited by David W. Kling and Douglas A. Sweeney. Columbia: University of South Carolina Press, 2003.

Weddle, David L. "The Melancholy Saint: Jonathan Edwards' Interpretation of David Brainerd as a Model of Evangelical Spirituality." *Harvard Theological Review* 81 (1988) 297–318.

Westra, Helen Petter. "'Above All Others': Jonathan Edwards and the Gospel Ministry." *American Presbyterians* 67 (1989) 209–19.

Wheeler, Rachel M. "'Friends to Your Souls': Jonathan Edwards' Indian Pastorate and the Doctrine of Original Sin." *Church History* 72 (2003) 736–65.

Yarbrough, Stephen R., and John C. Adams. *Delightful Conviction: Jonathan Edwards and the Rhetoric of Conversion*. Westport, CT: Greenwood, 1993.

Youngs, Frederick W. "The Place of Spiritual Union in Jonathan Edwards's Conception of the Church." *Fides et Historia* 28 (1996) 27–47.

Addendum

Not surprisingly, Edwards found numerous biblical and natural types for the church. In *WJE 11, Typological Writings*, we find the church typed by a growing child, 61; trees, 79; a comparison of Mt. Zion and Jerusalem, 153, 299–305, and 319; Noah's Ark, 222; Deborah's victory over the Canaanites, 247–49; Solomon and his wives, 294; and the return of Israel from Babylon, 294–98. In *WJE 13, The "Miscellanies,"* we see Joseph's governing Egypt compared to the church, 169.

And *WJE 15, Notes on Scripture*, presents these types for the church: Christ calming the seas, 51; construction of the temple, 63–64; a woman, 69; the tents of Kedar, 75; Hannah and Moses, 77; Jonah, 78; Ruth, 85; Sampson's mother Sarah, 90; the Song of Solomon, 92 and 610; Pharoah's daughter, 96 and 237; Jericho, 101; the Ark of the Covenant, 246; Mary and Martha, 266; Noah's Ark, 268 and 271; Abraham, 274; a red heifer, 279; Mary the mother of Jesus, 288; an eclipse, 291; the church as Christ's house, 301; the wedding at Cana, 358; temple showbread, 572; temple candlesticks, 573–74; and Old Testament terms for God's people, 578.

6

Spiritual Renewal of the Church

IN JONATHAN EDWARDS'S THEOLOGY, the concept of revival, or far-reaching spiritual renewal, has numerous facets that draw upon thoughts we have explored in previous chapters. Broadly speaking, revival reveals in dramatic fashion the increased activity of the Holy Spirit in sanctifying Christians, bringing about conversion to faith in Christ, and enabling heightened human perception of that activity. Of course, the Holy Spirit is always ministering throughout the universe. But in revivals of the church, the concentration of the Spirit's activity is extraordinary during a "special season of mercy."[1] The church worships and lives out her faith with an outstanding fervency and liveliness, spiritually dead hearts are regenerated in widespread conversions, society is radically and positively impacted by fruit the Spirit grows, and the wicked are shamed and vexed.[2] The gospel is energetically proclaimed, and all the while the God of history uses revival to accomplish the advancement of his Kingdom. Revival "is a work wherein God's hand is remarkably lifted up, and wherein he displays his majesty, and shows great favor and mercy to sinners, in the glorious opportunity he gives them; and by which he makes our land to become much more a land of uprightness."[3]

Revival is essentially God's eternal plan of redemption writ large in society—a bold statement that he desires to conquer sin and be glorified in it. This "event of setting up the kingdom of God, should be open and public in the sight of the whole world, with clear manifestation."[4] Revivals are types and forerunners of the heavenly state, "the beginning of that work which in the progress and issue of it would at last bring on

1. *WJE* 9, 143.
2. "Apocalypse," 195.
3. "Thoughts," 352.
4. "Marks," 235.

the church's latter-day glory."[5] Even more, revivals for Edwards prove that this living God is true, biblical, and real, and that "we live in an age, wherein divine wonders are to be expected."[6]

Edwards begins his theology of revival by assuming that the Bible records normative descriptions of what a genuine revival ought to be.[7] Though unmistakably prompted by a desire to defend the work of God during his lifetime, Edwards believed that a theology of revival based self-consciously and thoroughly upon Scripture would be valuable for all ages. His work on revival strove to be not only a portrait of what occurred during the First Great Awakening, but also a portrait of how God relates to his children throughout history when their faith is waning and their preparedness for his judgment is lacking.[8] Revival is a cosmic wake-up call for sleepy saints and spiritually dead sinners, and denying the reality, power, and efficacy of this call has eternal implications.

True Revival

As we begin to delineate the nature and criteria of true revival, we will immediately notice two related points: that revival is entirely a work of God in and through people, and that revival therefore cannot be the product of human method, emotion, or imagination. Edwards contends that from Scripture and history we can deduce general patterns of the Spirit's ministry in revival, just as we noted for individual conversion. But these patterns are a guide, not an absolute, and are not subject to human jurisdiction or exploitation. Just as God made the world in the beginning, and just as a man can no more save his own soul than make his own heart beat, so revival is a creation of God alone in which hu-

---

5. "McCulloch B," 136. This explains why the Kingdom of God is also called the Kingdom of Heaven in the Bible (*WJE* 9, 350). Edwards believed that the Great Awakening was a sign of the end times: "a far more pure extensive and glorious revival of religion is not far off, which will more properly be the beginning of that work which in its time shall overthrow the kingdom of Antichrist, and of Satan through the world" ("Attempt," 427). The end times will be addressed in the next chapter.

6. "Scotland," 197.

7. "Marks," 226.

8. For Lovelace, revival is "an outpouring of the Holy Spirit which restores the people of God to normal spiritual life after a period of corporate declension.... Periods of spiritual decline occur in history because the gravity of indwelling sin keeps pulling believers first into formal religion and then into open apostasy" (*Dynamics*, 40).

mans are the blessed recipients of redemptive grace. Any attempt to "stir up" revival by design or ardor produces temporary spiritual fruit at best, but more likely rejects or quenches the Holy Spirit and undermines true religion.[9]

Though revival's yield of new converts is certainly an exciting, dramatic facet of the work of God, Edwards points out that usually those who are revived *first* are spiritually lackadaisical and slumping Christians. Edwards observed that in his congregation in Northampton, "The good people that have been formerly converted in the town have many of them been wonderfully enlivened and increased."[10] When unconverted hearts witnessed the refreshed faith and godliness that abounded from established Christians, many were moved to desire the work of the Spirit in their own hearts.

Along with them, many who were unsure of their own conversions and "before had labored under difficulties about their own state, had now their doubts removed by more satisfying experience, and more clear discoveries of God's love."[11] These assurances and marks of enlivened holy behavior were not fleeting; a true revival consists of genuine conversions and obvious sanctification resulting in permanently transformed lives. Though Edwards knew that during the Great Awakening a few hypocritical goats may have passed for God's sheep in Northampton and beyond, he nevertheless contended that due to the evident presence of the Holy Spirit, "in the main, there has been a great and marvellous work of conversion and sanctification among the people here."[12]

During the revival, Edwards claimed that "through the greater part of New England, the Holy Bible is in much greater esteem and use than it used to be."[13] Among Northampton Christians "religion was with all sorts the great concern, and the world was a thing only by the bye. The only thing in their view was to get the kingdom of heaven, and everyone

---

9. "Marks," 288.

10. "Faithful," 107.

11. "Faithful," 152.

12. "Faithful," 209. Edwards's letter "Colman" describes the events of the Great Awakening up to that point (*WJE* 16, 48–58). It is historically important as the foundational essay for Edwards's *Faithful Narrative* and as a catalyst used by God to spark the British revivals of the era.

13. "Thoughts," 327. Revival causes "in men a greater regard to the Holy Scriptures, and establishes them more in their truth and divinity," which the Devil would never do ("Marks," 253).

appeared pressing into it."[14] But if the human heart is unsearchable and can be clearly seen only by the eyes of God, how could Edwards state so certainly that Northampton was being blessed by the Spirit? He muses, "Is it not strange that in a Christian, orthodox country, and such a land of light as this is, there should be many at a loss whose work this is, whether the work of God or the work of the devil?"[15] Edwards saw the Great Awakening as an obvious creation from the hand of God. But what exactly made him so sure, when some other ministers reacted negatively to the uproar?

Edwards found it deeply ironic that in the years prior to the revival, when to him immorality and social disintegration seemed to be at their worst, nearly all New England ministers prayed for spiritual renewal, an outpouring of the Holy Spirit, and moral reformation. Yet when the awakening arrived in the 1730s, many of these same ministers regarded it coldly and skeptically, or even publicly denounced it because it included sin and error. That spiritual renewal would involve some sin hardly surprised Edwards simply because any work of God occurs in the realm of depraved humanity. The great love of God may lead to great sin if people heartily do what they believe is pleasing to God, yet are mistaken.[16] While their souls may be redeemed or refreshed, believers at the same time may react unwisely to the influence of the incredible power of God and even sin in ways that are new to them.[17] With the occasionally painful spiritual maturation of the early church in mind, Edwards notes that periods of renewal can resemble the growth of a tree, "Of which tree this peculiar thing is observed, that the fruit of it, though it be very sweet and good when it is ripe, yet before it has had time to ripen, has a mixture of poison."[18]

The sinful content of any revival is precisely the basis for Edwards's admonition that revivals' validity be judged according to Scripture and not accepted or rejected uncritically. The early church was given inspired apostles to point out its poor decisions, superstition, and wild zeal after

---

14. "Faithful," 150.
15. "Thoughts," 330.
16. "Thoughts," *WJE* 4, 316. Errors in revival should be expected because when "daylight first appears, after a night of darkness, we must expect to have darkness mixed with light, for a while, and not to have perfect day, and the sun risen at once" ("Marks," 269).
17. "Marks," 271.
18. "Thoughts," 318.

Pentecost; so the church since then has had Spirit-inspired Scripture as her guide. In fact, God may allow human errors in an awakening to teach the church lessons he will later use for her benefit.[19] He may humble the church, "for by man's exceeding weakness appearing in the beginning of [revival], 'tis evident that God don't lay the foundation of it in man's strength or wisdom."[20] That the Great Awakening was far beyond any one person's comprehension and was a relative rarity in the Western church were not reasons to reject it out of hand or to affirm unquestioningly its genuineness. "It has all along been God's manner to open new scenes, and to bring forth to view things new and wonderful ... to the astonishment of heaven and earth, not only in the revelations he makes of his mind and will, but also in the works of his hands."[21] So God's own Word provides the only sure means of interpreting spiritual phenomena because the "prophecies of Scripture give us reason to think that God has still new things to accomplish."[22] With this in mind, Edwards strenuously warned those who would attribute God's work to human effort or demonic power. Doing so would amount to blasphemy against the Holy Spirit. Instead, "We ought not ... limit God where he has not limited himself."[23]

God's accomplishments in periods of awakening gloriously exhibit a fine craftsmanship that transforms needy, feeble people. He uses ardent preaching about "the terrors of God's holy law" and the reality of hell to turn their sin and weakness to holy strength, for their sanctification and his glory.[24] He employs the words and examples of godly people to spur others on to faith, just as he does so often in the pages of Scripture; indeed, the Word of God fashions good examples in the elect, making them effective and deemed worthy of imitation.[25] God strives in all of this to promote avid discussion of religion and doctrine in the

---

19. Regarding revivals, Edwards notes that "God has been pleased, in his holy and sovereign providence, to suffer [Satan] to succeed, oftentimes in a great measure, to overthrow that, which in its beginning appeared most hopeful and glorious" ("Thoughts," 385). The nature of the demonic will be detailed in the next chapter.

20. "Thoughts," 324.

21. "Thoughts," 306.

22. "Marks," 228.

23. "Marks," 229.

24. "Marks," 246.

25. "Marks," 240.

church and in society, convicting people of all ages about their need for redemption.[26]

But whatever God's means, contends Edwards, and whether in Northampton or Philadelphia, among the poor or wealthy, the young or elderly, the smith or farmer, revival is genuine if it brings forth love like that of Jesus Christ. "The love that appeared in that Lamb of God, was not only a love to friends, but to enemies, and a love attended with a meek and humble spirit."[27] Meekness is a trait which follows from being in awe of God or having a healthy fear or reverence for him, which to Edwards "was not an irrational hysteria, it was the effect of truth brought home powerfully to the conscience."[28] Christlike love and meekness—a sincere, unpretentious love toward God and others—are wholly sufficient proof that a revival is true, regardless of its excesses and corruptions. Only the Holy Spirit is capable of enabling people to have such profound love for Christ, the Scriptures, and others. And only the Spirit can effectively oppose those humans and demons who revel in spiritual decay and dryness. A true work of God operates "against the interest of Satan's kingdom, which lies in encouraging and establishing sin, and cherishing men's worldly lusts."[29]

Excess in Revival

During the Great Awakening, Edwards learned well that whether through Satan's influence or natural weakness, people may be subject to "affectionate," or imaginative and emotional, excesses. Instances of extravagances included faintings, groanings, outbursts of shouting and crying, uncontrolled zeal, and outlandish cases of indecency and sin among new believers.[30] But Edwards refused to dismiss all of these irregularities out of hand; he notes that for both the newly convicted and the mature Christian, it is "no wonder that the wrath of God when

---

26. "Marks," 234.
27. "Marks," 258.
28. Murray, *Jonathan Edwards*, 130.
29. "Marks," 250–51.
30. "Marks," 242–43. Because God is a God of order, some opposed the revival based on the confusion and upheaval it caused. But to Edwards, by bringing about redemption, God also brings about a more important, essential kind of order: the restoration of order in souls (267).

manifested but a little to the soul, overbears human strength.... 'Tis not at all strange that God should sometimes give his saints such foretastes of heaven, as to diminish their bodily strength."[31] While bodily effects may be sensational or distracting, "the nature of the operations and affections that persons' minds are under, are what are to be inquired into, and examined by the rule of God's Word."[32]

Considering the Apostle Peter's behavior in Galatia (Acts 10:9–11:18, 15:1–35; Gal 2–5) and the Corinthian church's schizophrenic experience of both great works of the Spirit and terrible depravity, Edwards asserts that human errors in judgment and action are not sufficient grounds for dismissing the possibility that God has a work in process.[33] He reminds us pointedly that God pours out his Spirit to make men holy "and not to make them politicians.... There are but few that know how to conduct [themselves] under vehement affections of any kind, whether they be of a temporal or spiritual nature."[34] Rather, "Our follies and sins that we mix, do in some respects manifest the glory of it: the glory of divine power and grace is set off with the greater luster by what appears at the same time of the weakness of the earthen vessel."[35]

Those shaken and profoundly distressed by the sight of their dark sins compared with the light of God's holiness may physically tremble with apprehension of the dreadful truth of God's just wrath.[36] So it is with people who are being recreated by the Holy Spirit. When God's grace is infused into hearts that must be weeded of their corruption and hatred, sin must be mortified, put to death, and this is a painful, shocking matter. Indeed, the church should be more concerned when such great "religious affections" are *not* present because neither then

---

31. "Marks," 232. When God manifests his glory, "not to be affected and animated, and to lie still, and refuse to follow God, will be resented as ... high contempt of him" ("Thoughts," 348).

32. "Marks," 234.

33. "Marks," 243–44. Though "the degree of the influence of the Spirit of God on particular persons, is by no means to be judged of by the degree of external appearances, because of the different constitution, tempers, and circumstances of men; yet if there be a very powerful influence of the Spirit of God on a mixed multitude, it will cause, some way or other, a great visible commotion" ("Thoughts," 400).

34. "Marks," 241.

35. "Thoughts," 347.

36. "Marks," 265. Unusual behavior may come from those "in great distress, in an apprehension of their sin and misery; or those that have been overcome with a sweet sense of the greatness, wonderfulness and excellency of divine things" (264).

is true religion present. "Spiritual things are so great, and of such vast and infinite concern, that there is great absurdity in men's being but moderately moved and affected by them."[37]

At the same time, the presence of "affectionate excesses" is not necessarily evidence of the work of the Spirit. Though Edwards attributed some eccentric displays to imitation, he was more likely to suppose the power of human imagination was involved. As described in chapter 4, imagination is a God-given capacity that enables us to conceive of invisible things, including God. But its creativity must not be confused with the indwelling of the Holy Spirit by labeling "every strong impulse or impression to be divine."[38] Edwards warns that rather than being a conduit of the Spirit, imagination is often Satan's door, "the devil's grand lurking place, the very nest of foul and delusive spirits."[39] Though Satan is not omniscient, omnipresent, or omnipotent, he is granted by God a degree of power, even over the imagination. The regenerate must choose to resist Satan's lies and half-truths with the Spirit's gracious assistance, in accordance with the Word of God.

Generally, the theologian was extremely wary of employing products of the imagination to determine valid religious experience. Impressions that may seem holy and scripturally consistent, and may even seem to provide assurance of salvation, may just as easily be deceptive and shallow products of natural creativity. "There are multitudes that are deluded with a counterfeit faith, from impressions on their imagination."[40] Rather than moving toward God, the deluded nonbeliever strays toward atheism by essentially denying God's biblical revelation, salvation in Jesus Christ, and the ministry of the Holy Spirit. Meanwhile, the deluded *believer* turns "Christ, or the divine nature in the soul, into a mere animal," nothing but an object of experience.[41] It's no wonder that Edwards viewed false religious affections as Satan's main tool to bastardize revival. Holy and true religious affections, on the other

---

37. "Marks," 234.

38. "Thoughts," 321. The Spirit enlightens "the mind to understand the precepts or propositions of the Word of God, and [to] know what is contained and revealed in them, and what consequences may justly be drawn from them, and to see how they are applicable to our case and circumstances; which is done without any new revelation, only by enabling the mind to understand and apply a revelation already made" (435).

39. *WJE* 2, 288.

40. *WJE* 2, 310.

41. *WJE* 2, 213.

hand, contribute to a lively, edified imagination that is disciplined and shaped by the Word of God.[42]

The Old Light/New Light Controversy

Edwards analyzed the role Satan may play in revival and contended that during the Great Awakening, God's handiwork unfortunately at times was mistaken for the Deceiver's.[43] While clearly not all of the error present in the revival could be attributed directly to the Devil, Edwards saw Satan's influence to be pronounced. He asserted that the extremes of rationalism and emotionalism to which some Christians went in response to the Great Awakening were at the suggestion of the Devil. "Old Light" rationalists in the line of Charles Chauncy doubted the Spirit's extraordinary ministries that tested the boundaries of human reason.[44] Radical "New Light" enthusiasts like James Davenport exploited the same unusual spiritual manifestations and approved all kinds of crazy behavior.[45] Neither side of the Old Light/New Light controversy likely intended to promote Satan's evil cause—probably quite the opposite. However, they failed to oppose Satan's activity by preserving unity in the church, defending true religion, and promoting faith in Christ. While Satan prefers Christians to be in a state of spiritual complacency, "when he can do that no longer, he often endeavors to drive them to extremes, and so to dishonor God, and wound religion that way."[46]

And wound religion they did. Edwards ultimately attributed to the Devil those fanatical extremes that eventually led to the revival's decline and then cessation. Edwards claimed that just one fanatic on either the rationalist or emotionalist side of a renewal debate could do more damage

---

42. *WJE* 2, 291.

43. *WJE* 2, 86–88.

44. Chauncy (1705–87) was born in Boston and ordained pastor of the First Congregational Church of Boston in 1727. He served in that pulpit until his death and with Edwards was among the most influential preachers of the day. Chauncy's criticisms of the revivals focused on its emotionalism, apparent hypocrisy, and disorderliness, and advocated the reliability of reason and common sense to lead one to salvation.

45. Davenport (1716–57?) was born in Stamford, Connecticut, and educated at Yale. He was ordained a Congregational minister but during the Awakening became an itinerant preacher. Sickly and known for bizarre behavior, he later returned to parish ministry but died young in Hopewell (now Pennington), New Jersey.

46. "Marks," 269.

for Satan than one hundred heathen opponents.[47] He tied initial revival errors to people's "previous deadness" as well as to inexperienced preachers who took advantage of their authority as clergy and their respected place in society. But later excesses and divisions particularly displayed the Deceiver's influence through their outright ugliness. The awakening subsided not because the Lord arbitrarily chose to withdraw his power. It waned and ended because in response to the emotionalist/rationalist controversy, people gave in to the temptation to doubt God's work, credited its wonders to the Devil, and turned away from the Holy Spirit.[48]

For Edwards, it was a great act of mercy in the first place for God to send his Spirit for renewal. Despite the "provocations and wickedness" of England, Scotland, and "the American plantations," the Spirit manifested himself strongly but was mistreated, "his mercy and grace despised, and bitterly opposed."[49] Yet in Edwards's eyes the rationalists and emotionalists (or "enthusiasts") were not entirely to blame. He believed that the revival winds also died due to "imprudent management in the friends of the work, and a corrupt mixture which Satan has found means to introduce, and our manifold sinful errors by which we have grieved and quenched the Spirit of God."[50] When referring to "friends of the work," Edwards included himself. He admitted that he was partly responsible for some of the revival's excesses due to his youth, lack of good judgment, and inexperience. He was guilty of "great and sinful deficiencies and offenses" and did not "oppose received notions and established customs, and . . . testify boldly against some glaring false appearances and counterfeits of religion, till it was too late." He confessed that he should have guarded people "better from Satan's devices, and prevented the spiritual calamity of many souls, and perhaps the eternal ruin of some of them."[51]

Nevertheless, the mixing of corrupt with pure religion did not invalidate the entire revival. In fact, Edwards believed that human and demonic opposition to the awakening was proof of its being a genuine work of God.[52] The Devil's challenge to goodness, and promotion of sin

47. "Thoughts," 410.
48. "Faithful," 162.
49. "McCulloch C," 220.
50. "To the Reverend James Robe of Kilsyth, Scotland," WJE 4, 536.
51. "Gillespie B," 565.
52. "Unpublished Letter, May 30, 1735," WJE 4, 110.

both in hearts and in communities, were together a "sure sign" that he was battling against the Lord's infiltration of his evil kingdom.[53] Edwards recalls the examples of Judas and the many false teachers in the New Testament whose infidelity should have been expected in that time of tremendous spiritual accomplishment for the Kingdom of God.[54] Judas's betrayal neither negated nor conquered Jesus' ministry of redemption, but instead was used by a sovereign God to bring about the holiest act of selflessness known to humankind. "Therefore the Devil's sowing such tares is no proof that a true work of the Spirit of God is not gloriously carried on."[55]

Virtue in Revival

If the Great Awakening occasioned extraordinary militancy on Satan's part as well as human opposition and extremism, it is no wonder that Edwards sought to elucidate the *proper* role of faithful Christians in times of revival. Once again, Edwards's ideas are not merely theoretical musings; rather, he taught for the practical benefit of the church because he believed that at no other time than revival is the unpardonable sin against the Holy Spirit committed with more frequency. The New Testament era, most likely the greatest time of spiritual awakening in history, was replete with those who called the work of Christ and his disciples evil and the Spirit's ministry "confusion and distraction."[56] During revivals there will always be those who reject Christ, for though he is "a foundation and a sanctuary for some, he is remarkably a stone of stumbling and a rock of offense, a gin and a snare to others."[57] In fact, "a work of God without stumbling blocks is never to be expected."[58] Edwards warns, "When a people oppose Christ in the work of his Holy

---

53. "Marks," 251.

54. Though there are times of greater purity in the church than in others, there will always be false religion and hypocrites until the Day of Judgment (*WJE* 2, 86). See also *WJE* 18, 251–61.

55. "Marks," 246.

56. "Marks," 271.

57. "Thoughts," 350; see 1 Cor 1:18–25. Edwards uses the now-dated term "gin" to refer to a trap.

58. "Marks," 273.

Spirit, it is because it touches 'em in something that is dear to their carnal minds."[59]

Christians therefore must not be like the Pharisees who rejected and condemned the work of God because their arrogant legalism did not comprehend it.[60] Edwards also warns those who *refrain* from affirming the validity of a revival, because in doing so they are refusing to acknowledge Christ and will not share in his blessings.[61] Revival reinforces the special responsibility Christians have to behave at all times in ways that are glorifying to God. Though awakenings are not begun or carried on by humans, God expects believers to endorse them and battle with him for the salvation of souls.[62] To promote the work of God, each must first "look into his own heart and see to it that he be a partaker of the benefits of the work himself, and that it be promoted in his own soul."[63] Then Christians must affirm biblical orthodoxy, abound in fasting and prayer,[64] engage faithfully and wholeheartedly in formal worship,[65] perform sincere acts of kindness and charity,[66] use earthly wealth and power well toward God's purposes,[67] be at peace with all,[68] and teach students more about biblical holiness than philosophy.[69] And all of this good must be done without spiritual pride, which is the great enemy of awakenings

---

59. "Thoughts," 381. Such are like the people at Gadarenes (Matt 8:28–34) who "loved their filthy swine better than Jesus Christ; and had rather have a legion of devils in their country, with their herd of swine, than Jesus Christ without them" (381).

60. "Marks," 271.

61. "Marks," 273–74.

62. "Thoughts," 384.

63. "Thoughts," 502.

64. "Thoughts," 515–20, *passim*.

65. "Thoughts," 522.

66. "Thoughts," 524. Doing good is an invaluable way to receive "temporal benefits but also spiritual blessings, the influences of God's Holy Spirit in the heart, in divine discoveries and spiritual consolations" (524).

67. "Thoughts," 514.

68. "Thoughts," 496.

69. "Thoughts," 511. On that page Edwards writes, "It seems to me to be a reproach to the land that ever it should be so with our colleges, that instead of being places of the greatest advantages for true piety, one can't send a child thither without great danger of his being infected as to his morals. . . . There is a great deal of pains taken to teach the scholars human learning; there ought to be as much, and more care, thoroughly to educate 'em in religion, and lead 'em to true and eminent holiness."

and "the worst viper that is in the heart."[70] When witnessing the glorious results that the Spirit creates in such marvelous times, Christians must guard against taking for themselves the credit due to the Holy Spirit. "When we have great discoveries of God made to our souls, we should not shine bright in our own eyes."[71]

Based on his observations, Edwards deduced that pride was at the root of the Great Awakening's schismatic Old Light/New Light controversy because it led some of those involved to an uncharitable judgmentalism about the spiritual state of others.[72] As we saw in chapter 4, one who is truly converted habitually manifests observable signs of redemptive grace in daily life. But Edwards also was aware of the limitations of human spiritual insight, commenting, "I once did not imagine that the heart of man had been so unsearchable as I find it is."[73] Turning to revival conversions, Edwards proceeds thereafter to walk a fine line, for he contends on the one hand that "Christian practice is the greatest sign of grace . . . by which Christians are to judge, both of their own and others' sincerity of godliness."[74] The criteria for true faith and practice are enumerated in 1 John 4, and if persons exhibit public piety, "it is the duty of the saints to receive them cordially into their charity, and to love them and rejoice in them, as their brethren in Christ Jesus."[75]

On the other hand, Edwards adds that even the best people may be deceived by themselves, others, or Satan about the condition of their souls. Ultimately, it is not a human responsibility to judge whether a soul is redeemed or whether it ever will be. Edwards states,

> In Scripture, that judging of hearts that is spoken of as God's prerogative, is not only the judging of the aims and disposition of men's hearts in particular actions, but chiefly a judging of the state of the hearts of the professors of religion, with regard to that profession.[76]

---

70. "Marks," 277. Regarding pride, "there is no one sin that does so much let in the Devil into the hearts of the saints, and expose them to his delusions" (278).
71. "Marks," 277.
72. "Thoughts," 322.
73. "Marks," 285.
74. *WJE* 2, 406.
75. *WJE* 2, 182.
76. "Marks," 283.

So those who make harsh judgments about the motives or spiritual condition of others are seriously in error, presumptuously taking God's authority for themselves. Edwards believed "the effects of grace to be ascertainable and visible. The Christian experience presupposes a goal to be reached, and this goal bears distinguishing signs."[77] But those who haughtily "think themselves sufficient to discern and determine the state of others' souls by a little conversation with them" actually show themselves to be lacking appropriate concern for their own state.[78] Their misguided labor of absolute spiritual determination, of "passing censures upon others that are professing Christians, as hypocrites and ignorant of anything of real religion," cannot be scripturally justified.[79]

As was mentioned in the last chapter, ministers have a special responsibility to evaluate the state of others' souls.[80] This is especially true during the blessed but stressful times of renewal. Servants of the Great Shepherd must know the spiritual health or illness of their parishioners, yet this knowledge must always be bounded by a humility that keeps ministerial finitude in mind. Preachers cannot know without a doubt whether any member is truly redeemed, but must make prayerful judgments based upon Scripture (especially 1 John 4) to preach and minister most effectively. Pastors may see in piety and good works a mature Christian, and would be remiss to treat that professing believer as a new Christian or a proselyte. Meanwhile, someone they assess to be a nonbeliever or a recent convert should not be expected to consume substantial, biblical meat when she is still having difficulty handling basic milk.

In these cautious judgments ministers are responsible not only for the faithfulness of their thoughts and actions to the Word of God, but are at the same time accountable for setting an example of patient wisdom coupled with compassion and sound teaching.[81] For this reason, revivals are especially great times of testing and strain for preachers. They require a double portion of grace from the Holy Spirit to guide their congregants about the nature of salvation in Jesus Christ and the scriptural foundations of true faith.[82]

77. Simonson, *Jonathan Edwards*, 59.
78. "Marks," 285.
79. "Marks," 283.
80. "Thoughts," 300.
81. "Thoughts," 322.
82. "Thoughts," 507.

With the heavy responsibilities of pastors in mind, Edwards was vehement about those ministers who resisted the revival and obstructed those seeking God's holy, redemptive light during the awakening. Edwards states, "A supine carelessness and a vain, carnal, worldly spirit in a minister of the Gospel, is the worst madness and distraction in the sight of God."[83] The colonial minister who did not welcome the revival as a genuine work of God pretended to be a shepherd, but instead caused "the infinite provocation of the most high God, and displeasure of his Lord and Master . . . by continuing a secret enemy to him in his heart."[84] Such preachers are no different than the Jews who refused to acknowledge Christ—whether their opposition is active and vocal or passive and silent, they "create a suspicion of all vital religion" and "effectually keep the sheep from their pasture, instead of doing the part of shepherds to them, by feeding them."[85] Edwards grimly concludes, "No sort of men in the world will be so low in hell as ungodly ministers."[86]

Throughout the Great Awakening, Edwards presupposed that whether judging others or themselves, people must remember that all are ultimately measured by the standards of God's justice. Their behavior should accordingly reflect the understanding that while they are sinners in the hands of a God who is angry at sin, revivals of true religion are offered to them as extraordinarily plain evidence for hope of forgiveness and salvation through Jesus Christ. As was explained previously, all are able to know definitely whether the Holy Spirit indwells their own hearts. Based on this fact, God justly judges both those for whom atonement has been made by Jesus Christ and those who are utterly without excuse. Therefore "[m]en that live in ways of sin, and yet flatter themselves that they shall go to heaven, or expect to be received hereafter as holy persons, without a holy life and practice, act as though they expected to make a fool of their Judge."[87]

---

83. "Thoughts," 296.
84. "Thoughts," 506.
85. "Thoughts," 376.
86. "Thoughts," 507; see also *WJE 18*, 335–39.
87. *WJE 2*, 428. "The Judge at the Day of Judgment, won't . . . go about to examine men, as to the method of their experiences, or set every man to tell his story of the manner of his conversion; but his works will be brought forth, as evidences of what he is, what he has done in darkness and in light" (*WJE 2*, 452).

For Jonathan Edwards, true religion is called "experimental" religion because it tries and scrutinizes affections, thoughts, intentions, and deeds to determine their faithfulness to Christ, and stretches weak affections to healthy strength. Revivals test the veracity of the broader church's "experimental" religion and its witness of that religion to society. "We cannot suppose that the church of God is already possessed of all that light, in things of this nature, that ever God intends to give it; nor that all Satan's lurking-places have already been found out."[88] Therefore, times of renewal are periods both of Spirit-filled encouragement for the elect, and of warnings about God's eternal wrath for those who shun his clear revelation and his love.

To the theologian, the failure to understand true religion was the primary obstacle to all revivals "since the beginning of the Reformation" and probably "in all ages of the Christian church from the beginning."[89] But once again the obstacle is not merely human but also demonic, for "'tis by the mixture of counterfeit religion with true, not discerned and distinguished, that the devil has had his greatest advantage against the cause and kingdom of Christ, all along, hitherto."[90] The failure of Christians to define and defend true religion bears eternal ramifications for every age of the church, especially when the people of God are in doubt or confused about faith and when false "religion, and heresy, and infidelity, and atheism greatly prevail."[91] That failure is precisely what every revival overcomes; by his grace, the Lord stirs a prodigal church to return home to his open arms, where he had been waiting all along. Even today, the church awaits a wonderful revival in the end times and ultimately in heavenly bliss. These are the matters we turn to next.

For Further Thought

1. What are your initial impressions about the idea of religious revival? Do you believe revivals of the kind Edwards describes can happen today? Why?

---

88. "Preface," 570.
89. "Preface," 569.
90. *WJE* 2, 86.
91. *WJE* 2, 89.

2. According to Edwards, what are the major pieces of evidence to look for to determine if a revival is authentic? Why does he believe that false revivals can happen?
3. What role does the Bible play in a revival? What role do ministers play? And what about the Devil?
4. How do your beliefs about the Devil and the demonic compare with Edwards's?
5. What was the nature of the Old Light/New Light controversy? How did they apparently hurt the revival? How did Edwards say that he himself hurt the revival?
6. How can a person tell if he or she is behaving in the proper Christian manner during a revival? Who are Edwards's bad examples of behavior during awakenings?
7. In general, what are the proper reasons and ways to judge others? What are the improper reasons and ways? According to Edwards, are we capable of judging our own religious experience? Do you agree with him on these issues?
8. What is "experimental" religion? Do you practice "experimental" religion yourself? Should you? Explain why.

For Further Reading

Aldridge, A. Owen. "Enlightenment and Awakening in Edwards and Franklin." In *Benjamin Franklin, Jonathan Edwards, and the Representation of American Culture*, edited by Barbara B. Oberg and Harry S. Stout. New York: Oxford University Press, 1993.

Conforti, Joseph. "Antebellum Evangelicals and the Cultural Revival of Jonathan Edwards." *American Presbyterian* 64 (1986) 227–41.

Crawford, Michael J. "New England and the Scottish Religious Revivals of 1742." *American Presbyterians* 69 (1991) 23–32.

Edwards, Jonathan. "Directions for Judging of Persons' Experiences" and "Signs of Godliness." In *The Works of Jonathan Edwards, Vol. 21: Writings on the Trinity, Grace, and Faith*, edited by Sang Hyun Lee. New Haven: Yale University Press, 2003.

Haykin, Michael A.G. *Jonathan Edwards: The Holy Spirit in Revival—The Lasting Influence of the Holy Spirit in the Heart of Man*. Darlington, UK; Webster, NY: Evangelical, 2005.

Jinkins, Michael. "The 'True Remedy': Jonathan Edwards' Soteriological Perspective as Observed in His Revival Treatises." *Scottish Journal of Theology* 48 (1995) 185–209.

Lang, Amy Schrager. "'A Flood of Errors': Chauncy and Edwards in the Great Awakening." In *Jonathan Edwards and the American Experience*, edited by Nathan O. Hatch and Harry S. Stout. New York: Oxford University Press, 1988.

Lloyd-Jones, D. Martyn. "Jonathan Edwards and the Critical Importance of Revival." In *Puritan Experiment in the New World*, edited by S. Brachlow et al. Huntingdon, UK: Westminster Conference, 1976.

McDermott, Gerald R. *Seeing God: Jonathan Edwards and Spiritual Discernment*. Vancouver, BC: Regent College, 2000.

Proudfoot, Wayne. "From Theology to a Science of Religions: Jonathan Edwards and William James on Religious Affections." *Harvard Theological Review* 82 (1989) 149–68.

Simonson, Harold P. "Jonathan Edwards and His Scottish Connections." *Journal of American Studies* 21 (1987) 353–76.

Winiarski, Douglas Leo. "Jonathan Edwards, Enthusiast? Radical Revivalism and the Great Awakening in the Connecticut Valley." *Church History* 74 (2005) 683–739.

7

The End of the World, and Beyond

"God's ways are all analogous, and his dispensations harmonize one with another."[1]

AS WE HAVE CONSIDERED, the harmony of God's inner being and the harmony of its communication in creation and history have the grand purpose of his glorification in the salvation of humans. In this cosmic design, there is no waste and no issue or event that is extraneous to the divine intention—God has always planned "to gather together in one all things in Christ in heaven and earth, i.e. all elect creatures."[2] We know that for Edwards, the Holy Spirit undergirds and maintains all of reality through continuous creation and carries it toward its consummation on an awesome and terrible Day of Judgment. The culmination of the entire history of redemption is nothing less than "the mystery of godliness," because "all the ancient mysteries, types, shadows, and prophecies relating to the kingdom and interest of godliness, have their fulfillment in it."[3] The final flourish of this mystery is the grand climax of God's intentions; with it the fog of sin will be lifted and the church will arrive at the "most perfect state, which the whole general assembly both in heaven and earth are designed for."[4]

When Edwards writes of the "latter days" or the "end times," he at times is referring to the period since Jesus Christ's birth that is divided into four "great, successive dispensations of providence."[5] These four

1. *WJE 18*, 240.
2. *WJE 9*, 124.
3. *WJE 15*, 313, based on 2 Thess 2:7.
4. *WJE 13*, 483.
5. *WJE 9*, 351. Edwards's eschatology, or his theology of the "end times," is self-consciously oriented around the Book of Revelation, which gives "an account of the main events of providence, with relation to the church of Christ to the world's end, and

periods are marked by Christ's physical presence on earth, the destruction of the heathen Roman Empire, the destruction of Antichrist, and the final judgment. Each period advances the church and begins a new era of the Kingdom of Heaven, and each is a type of its successor.[6]

But most often, Edwards refers to the "latter days" as immediately preceding the onset of the millennium, during which time the Kingdom of God permeates the globe.[7] This era involves a gradual process in which God progressively conquers elements of Satan's kingdom, manifests Christ's majesty more and more, and gathers "the elect from the [four winds] by God's angels."[8] Eventually, every part of the habitable world will be touched by the gospel and "possessed by the true religion."[9] And all this is accomplished, as we would expect, by the Holy Spirit, who will give measures of "freedom and riches of divine grace towards sinners" to an extent never before witnessed.[10]

In early 1743, Edwards believed that the revivals of the Great Awakening were part of the latter days, "the dawning, or at least a prelude" to the millennium, and that "there are many things that make it probable that this work will begin in America."[11] He wrote to Rev. William McCulloch on May 12, 1743, that though he expected the current revival to end, he thought God would resume "his work again before long, and that it will not wholly cease till it has subdued the whole earth."[12] But when writing to McCulloch on March 5, 1744, he clarified that he did not believe the millennium had yet begun nor that it had begun in Northampton in particular.[13] Rather, he expected the church to

---

especially to encourage the church with the hopes of that glorious event" ("Apocalypse," 183). To Edwards, the Book of Revelation should not be read literally because it uses "similitudes as we are capable of receiving, taken from such things as are found upon earth" ("Nothing," 138).

6. *WJE* 9, 353.

7. For a survey of Edwards's millennial views in relation to other Reformed and Puritan thinkers, see Wilson, "History, Redemption," 131–41.

8. *WJE* 9, 352, based on Matt 24:31.

9. "Attempt," 331.

10. "Thoughts," 361. The end times constitute the matchless season of redemption. "Before this the Spirit of God is given but very sparingly, and but few are saved" ("Attempt," 342). "The comparatively little saving good there is in the world, as the fruit of Christ's redemption . . . is as it were granted by way of anticipation" of the last days (344).

11. "Thoughts," 353; the argument proceeds through 356.

12. "McCulloch A," 540.

13. "McCulloch B," 134.

endure many trials before the millennium was initiated.[14] In *A History of Redemption*, written for the most part between 1750 and 1757, he states that the European settlement of North America and the spread of the gospel there is a way "by which divine providence is preparing the way for the future glorious times of the church when Satan's kingdom shall be overthrown . . . throughout the whole habitable globe."[15] We must consequently deduce that for Edwards, America (not the United States as a nation) would play an important role in the millennium, but that he did not expect to see its fruition in his own lifetime. He envisioned that an amazing work of God would occur to bring the millennium to pass by the year 2000.[16]

In essence, the millennium will involve a worldwide revival on a grand scale that features prayer as the main human endeavor. "It is the revealed will of God, that he should be inquired of by his people, by extraordinary prayer, concerning this great mercy, to do it for them, before it is fulfilled."[17] Their having a desire to pray for this sweeping spiritual event actually is evidence of the Spirit's work in them and of God's intention to bring it to pass.[18] And these saints cannot presume that the latter days are far off, because God has not revealed when exactly the end of time will occur. In sum, in her desire to have ultimate fellowship with God it is the duty of the church to pray that the end will come speedily,

> and not only to be praying for it, but to be seeking of it, in the use of proper means; endeavoring that religion may now revive everywhere, and Satan's kingdom be overthrown; and always to be waiting for it, being in a constant preparation for it.[19]

The onset of the millennium manifests the "last and greatest outpouring of his Spirit" and the "time of Christ's reign: the reign of Satan as god of this world lasts till then."[20] But the ascended Christ does not reign physically on earth in Edwards's eschatological scheme, as he does

---

14. "McCulloch B," 136.
15. *WJE* 9, 434.
16. "Attempt," 410.
17. "Attempt," 396.
18. "Attempt," 353.
19. "Attempt," 395-96.
20. "Thoughts," 358. For a discussion of Old Testament references to the millennium, see *WJE* 15, 264. To understand why Edwards believed that the millennium would likely be a literal term of one thousand years, see "Saints Dwell Alone," *WJE* 25, 50-52.

in many other postmillennial perspectives. "Christ's reigning on earth by his Spirit is more glorious and happy for his church than his human presence would be."[21] Through the power of the Spirit, the struggles the church has always faced during times of persecution and of spiritual dryness will greatly subside. During the millennium, goodwill and peace will increase to the greatest level known to humanity apart from the idyllic, original condition of Adam and Eve. Though unregenerate sinners will still dwell on the earth, civility and learning will prevail, despotism and slavery will end, and the saints will focus more than ever on "contemplative and spiritual employments."[22] Academics will then properly be "a handmaid to religion" and "subservient to understanding the Scriptures and [to] a clear explaining and glorious defending the doctrines of Christianity."[23] Just as when Israel returned to the land of Canaan, the church will dwell in a "state of glorious rest, plenty, prosperity, and spiritual joy, and delights, in the latter days."[24] All in all, "the distant extremes of the world shall shake hands together and all nations shall be acquainted, and they shall all join the forces of their minds in exploring the glories of the Creator, their hearts in loving and adoring him."[25]

When true religion has largely prevailed in the world, the enemies of Christ and the church will arise for a final battle "just before the utter destruction of Antichrist and of the visible kingdom of Satan upon earth."[26] This war is of a spiritual nature over the state of souls and does not involve physical or military conflict. It arises through the opposition of Satan and sinners to the church's "prosperity in a great revival, and restoration from her long continued, captivated, desolate state under Antichrist," that is, the Roman Catholic Church.[27] There will be "the greatest and most extensive convulsions and commotions that ever were upon the face of the earth, wherein doubtless many particular Christians

---

21. *WJE* 18, 537.

22. *WJE* 13, 369; also "Apocalypse," 136, based on Rev 16:19. For his analysis of the vials or bowls in Rev 16 and their historical fulfillment at the end of time, see "Attempt," 412–26.

23. *WJE* 9, 441.

24. *WJE* 15, 469.

25. *WJE* 13, 213.

26. *WJE* 15, 514, based on Ezek 38–39 and Rev 16:13–21; 19:17–21.

27. *WJE* 15, 515. For a detailed account of the oppression of the church by Antichrist and Satan, see "Attempt," 378–90.

will suffer."[28] In this last battle, the church "may suffer extreme oppression" but will not be defeated.[29]

Edwards joined many in the Reformed tradition in labeling the Roman Catholic Church as Antichrist, which he defines as the most eminently sinful "opponent or adversary of Christ" and the "masterpiece of all the contrivances of the devil" against God's holy Kingdom.[30] In this view, the Church of Rome professes Christ yet denies him in its teachings.[31] This spiritual Babylon has also been an awful persecutor of true saints, nearly driving genuine faith prior to the Reformation to extinction "in the depth of the darkness of popery."[32] This "mystery of iniquity" has swayed countless people to apostasy because its pope pretends "to be vested with the power of God himself, as head of the church."[33] What's more, priests are "instruments of the devil" who "work by his power" and have "deceived all nations."[34] So Edwards rejoices that Antichrist will be destroyed by the preaching of the Word of God, "the clear light of the gospel," according to God's plan.[35]

Similarly, the rest of Satan's kingdom will be subdued "by means of the blowing the trumpet of the gospel and preaching the Word of God."[36] While "some great parts of Satan's visible kingdom shall have a very sudden fall, yet all will not be accomplished at once, as by some great miracle, as the resurrection of the dead at the end of the world will

---

28. "McCulloch B," 136.

29. "Apocalypse," 216.

30. *WJE* 9, 411. "Popery is the deepest contrivance that ever Satan was the author of to uphold his kingdom" ("Apocalypse," 119).

31. *WJE* 13, 186. Egypt and Pharoah are types of the Antichristian church and the pope, based on Isa 51:9 (*WJE* 15, 205). The apostate Jewish church serves in this capacity as well, based on Matt 21:12–16 (313).

32. "McCulloch B," 137. "Thus did the devil, and his great minister Antichrist, rage with such violence and cruelty against the church of Christ; and thus did the whore of Babylon make herself drunk with the blood of the saints and martyrs of Jesus; and thus by these persecutions the Protestant church has been much diminished" (*WJE* 9, 429). The Reformation "was the beginning of the church's revival, after it had for many ages been almost in a state of death," and was the beginning of Antichrist's decline" ("Apocalypse," 207).

33. *WJE* 9, 450.

34. "Apocalypse," 122.

35. "Apocalypse," 118.

36. "Apocalypse," 130.

be all at once."[37] Heresies, infidelity, superstition, Antichrist, and "the Mohammedan [Muslim] kingdom of Satan" will eventually be totally destroyed.[38] At the same time, the redeeming power of the Holy Spirit will be felt in a breathtaking degree comparable to Pentecost.[39] There will be mass conversions of Jews who "shall flow together to the blessed Jesus, penitently, humbly, and joyfully owning him as their glorious king and only savior."[40] Satan's dominion over heathens will cease and many of them will be converted. In response to all of this, the "church on earth and the church in heaven shall both gloriously rejoice and praise God as with one heart."[41]

The ensuing lengthy dispensation, which is unique to Edwards's thought, provides for another period of peace and prosperity for the church, "a time of great light and knowledge" prior to the final judgment.[42] During this time, the Kingdom of Heaven is manifest more strongly than ever. The Holy Spirit sheds greater light on Christian doctrines and Scripture passages that had before been misunderstood in the church. Wickedness is less evident, and true religion is increasingly valued around the world. Once again, all of the world's nations will be at peace, Christian virtues will flourish, and temporal prosperity will abound through "the remarkable blessing of heaven."[43]

Finally, right before the end of the world as we now know it, there will occur a terrible and widespread apostasy of the "most aggravated wickedness" as Satan is loosed for the final time before being banished to hell by God.[44] Many professing Christians will reject God and prove themselves to be hypocrites, resembling the devils who "apostasized and turned enemies to Christ, though they enjoyed the light of heaven."[45] Despite the prevailing depravity, God will preserve the elect and prepare

37. *WJE* 9, 458.

38. *WJE* 9, 467–69; also "Apocalypse," 107, regarding Rev 11–12. Satan's kingdom on earth is supported by the three powers of heathenism, hypocrisy, and false prophecy, and is manifest in three kingdoms: the Antichristian/false Christian kingdom, the "Mahometan" (Muslim) kingdom, and the heathen kingdom ("Apocalypse," 173).

39. *WJE* 15, 358.
40. *WJE* 9, 469, based on Rom 11.
41. *WJE* 9, 477.
42. *WJE* 9, 480.
43. *WJE* 9, 484, based on Isa 65:21.
44. *WJE* 9, 489.
45. *WJE* 9, 490.

them for the imminent return of Christ and the ultimate judgment of all. In this era, no more souls will be converted, the mystical Body of Christ will be complete, and "in this respect the Work of Redemption will be now finished."[46]

The Day of Judgment

Before we continue this examination of Edwards's eschatology, it is necessary to pause to remind ourselves that unless a reader agrees with Edwards's fundamental presuppositions about the authority of Scripture, the Trinity, and the purposes of creation and history, the end of the story of redemption may seem bizarre or unbelievable.[47] We remind ourselves also that history and biblical typology are so intertwined for Edwards that time's consummation is absolutely required for the sake of God's revealed purposes for humanity and for his own glorification.[48] A modern Western audience may find talk of a utopian millennium for the church or a single day of reckoning foreign or preposterous. But given Edwards's assumptions, history *must* end because it is in essence a divine myth that is also a true story, and its truth is to be proved by its actuality and completion.[49] For Edwards, anyone who doubts the impending reality of the Day of Judgment is basically one who has not trusted the veracity of the story in the Word of God, believed in Christ and his victorious

---

46. *WJE* 9, 492.

47. According to Lee, "The possibility and indeed the inevitability of the historical millennium is grounded in Edwards's doctrine of God's creative activity, and thus his self-enlargement, within the very fabric of time and space" (*Philosophical Theology*, 218).

48. For Edwards, there *must* be a future state according to Scripture and reason. First, the reality of this state is instilled by God into the human conscience ("Warnings," 208; "Impending," 217). But second, the eternality of the soul demands it (*WJE* 20, 106). "The end of making man, therefore, must be the glorifying of God and the enjoyment of him, which ends are not to any effect obtained if men's souls are turned to nothing at death" ("Future," 359). In fact, the "whole of religion depends on it. If there be no future state of rewards and punishments in the other world, then the whole of religion is immediately thrown up and destroyed" (362). Since the reality of a future state in fellowship with God validates the entire plan of redemption, if it does not exist, God may not exist either, which for Edwards is impossible.

49. As Wilson comments, "Edwards was deeply committed to understanding the human saga as the production of a play that God had authored. His interest, moreover, was very much in the play's text as well as in its production" ("Editor's Introduction," *WJE* 9, 74).

conquest over Satan and sin, and stood in awe of the design of nature and history—all shaped by a God who desires eternal, perfect fellowship with his creatures.

Blazing the light of God's righteousness and glory, the purpose of the Day of Judgment is "to *manifest* what men are, to their own consciences, and to the world."[50] Many erroneously assume that Edwards's God dangles sinners over the eternal fire, torturing them until he viciously thrusts them into brimstone.[51] But Edwards asserts instead that "God has no pleasure in the destruction or calamity of persons or people; he had rather they should turn and continue in peace. . . . He is a God that delights in mercy, and judgment is his strange work."[52] Nevertheless, for the sake of his own paramount glory the "honor of God's justice won't suffer sin to go unpunished. 'Tis a dispute whether God's absolute justice obliges him to punish sin; but his *rectoral* justice . . . as judge and governor of the world, requires it, and as it belongs to him to see the order of it."[53] When people die prior to the Day of Judgment, they are judged immediately in God's presence, sent to heaven or hell, and then wait until the end of time for public judgment.[54] On that awesome and horrific day, all in heaven and earth will face their Creator. The ungodly will be shamed and disgraced, while the saints will be publicly honored with their God.[55]

The Day of Judgment, which includes the triumphant Second Coming of Jesus Christ, is "what all that God has made, and all that Christ has done and suffered, and all the events of providence from the beginning of the world, and all that he has foretold, ultimately terminates in."[56] Since it was Christ who bound Satan through his death

---

50. *WJE* 3, 419. Though all people have knowledge of God's justice, the "general judgment is not a doctrine that is sufficiently discoverable by the light of nature. . . . 'Tis one of the peculiar [unique] doctrines of divine revelation and a doctrine of the gospel of Jesus" ("Judgment," 513, based on Ps 96:13 and Eccl 12:14).

51. "Sinners," 404–18.

52. "Impending," 221.

53. "None Saved," 336. In this quote "absolute justice" refers to the holiness at the heart of God's character. Certainly "the righteous Judge of all the earth won't bring death on thousands of millions, not only that are not worthy of death, but are worthy of no punishment at all" (*WJE* 3, 209).

54. "Future," 363.

55. "Judgment," 517.

56. *WJE* 15, 343, commenting on Jude 14.

and resurrection and purchased the salvation of the elect, it is naturally Christ the God-Man who returns to declare final victory over evil.[57] As God incarnate and King of the church, it falls to Christ to be the Judge, the one who completes the eternal plan of redemption.[58] Both saints and sinners will be judged according to their works, which will be evident to all. But the ungodly will be judged by both Christ and the saints, and convicted of their rejection of him and his gospel.[59]

On this literal Day of Judgment, "Christ Jesus will in a most magnificent manner descend from heaven with all the holy angels" and heaven for this time will be deserted of its inhabitants."[60] Explaining how this event can be possible both globally and simultaneously, Edwards asserts that Christ's sudden, surprising descent will happen "at such a distance from the surface of the earth that everyone, when gathered together, shall see him."[61] "Christ shall probably first appear at a great distance as a star, though a star of inconceivable brightness and glory, as the bright morning star [Rev. 22:16], and as he approaches near he will appear as the Sun of Righteousness in full glory."[62] All of the dead will rise, but sinners will not have the chance to accept "the benefits of the death of Christ offered to 'em again."[63] Rather, the Holy Spirit will cease his work in sinners and they will predictably refuse again to repent. "[T]heir wickedness will then be brought to perfection, and wicked men ... accordingly will be sent away as cursed into everlasting fire prepared for the devil and his angels."[64] Destined for hell, the reprobate will suffer "the misery and darkness of eternal death."[65]

57. "Christ," 581–82. "And 'tis the greatest manifestation of his high judicial authority to judge and condemn this grand rebel, and head and leader of all the rebellion in the universe, and to execute vengeance upon him" (*WJE 15*, 591).

58. "Judgment," 517–20, *passim*.

59. "Judgment," 521; also 527–29, based on Mark 16:16 and Rom 2:16.

60. "Judgment," 522.

61. "Judgment," 523, based on Mark 13:35–6 and Rev 1:7. As far as I know, Edwards unfortunately does not account for the rotation of the earth preventing all people to see Christ at once.

62. *WJE 20*, 206.

63. "Future," 355. With God's power, a body can still be resurrected even if its original atoms are spread all over the universe (*WJE 13*, 180).

64. "Virtue," 598.

65. *WJE 3*, 324. Hell will be addressed below. For the full meaning of death, see *WJE 3*, 239–41; and "Concerning the Endless Punishment of Those Who Die Impenitent," *BT 2*, 515–25.

The saints, on the other hand, will "now appear clothed with the glorious robe of Christ's righteousness," their holiness exhibited for all to see.[66] The elect will experience a change in their resurrected bodies, which will be made to resemble Christ's glorified body: "the transformation and glorification of their whole man both soul and body shall be at once all together."[67] They will be granted the eternal life that was always their hope and was forever in the designs of God for them.[68] Christ and his completed, perfected church will then ascend into heaven in a manner similar to his own ascension, and he will

> present them before the Father without spot or {blemish}, having given them that perfect beauty and crowned them with that glory and honor and happiness which was stipulated in the covenant of redemption before the world was, and which he died to procure for them.[69]

After the ascent of Christ and the church, "the world shall be set on fire, and be turned into a great furnace, wherein all the enemies of Christ and his church shall be tormented forever and ever."[70] In fact, all of reality apart from heaven will suffer a great conflagration to purify it of any depravity.[71] The universe as we know it will end, leaving only heaven and hell and the being of God.[72]

Edwards has thus brought us full circle, from the pre-creation state in which the eternal plan of redemption was forged within the Godhead, through its manifestation in time and space, to its fulfillment by the mediation of Christ and the ministry of his Holy Spirit. For Edwards, based upon biblical testimony, the holiness and nature of God, and God's idealism expressed in providence, there could be no other way.[73] From

---

66. *WJE* 9, 503.

67. *WJE* 20, 462. "[I]t shall be the beams of Christ's glory, the light of life shining on the dead, that shall raise them. . . . The first beams of his light . . . will change their bodies and also change their souls to a conformity to Christ's glorified body and soul, and shall drive away all sin. And as Christ draws nearer and nearer his glory will appear brighter and brighter, and more and more transporting and ravishing to the saints, 'till they shall be as it were drawn up by it off from the ground to meet the Lord in the air" (206–7).

68. *WJE* 3, 325.

69. "Judgment," 531; see Luke 24:50–53, and Acts 1:1–11.

70. *WJE* 9, 505, based on 2 Pet 3:7.

71. *WJE* 23, 64–68.

72. "Apocalypse," 142.

73. "All revolutions from the beginning of the world to the end, are doubtless but

the divine perspective, there are never surprises. From our perspective, due to divine revelation there should be no surprises about the human need for salvation in Christ and the reality of heaven and hell.

Satan and Hell

In our analysis of the fall of humanity in chapter 3, we learned that for Edwards Satan had a significant role in tempting Adam to rebel against God while Adam retained his responsibility for disobeying divine law. Edwards had no substantial explanation for why Adam would make such a choice, except that God withheld the influence of the Holy Spirit and allowed him to fall into depravity and judgment. As we consider Satan, we find that Edwards still lacks an answer for the origin of evil. Why did Satan choose to rebel against God? Given Edwards's silence, we may assume that God withheld his grace as he did with Adam. But ultimately for Edwards, the unsearchable wisdom of God is the only explanation possible.

Edwards speculates that *before* the creation of the universe, God made a covenant with the angels asking that they obey him by being the servants of humanity.[74] The terms of the covenant were actually a trial of angelic obedience. According to God's plan

> it was fit that some should be suffered to fail in the trial. Otherwise, the rest would not have been duly sensible of the possibility of failing in a trial, and so would not be sensible of the trial, nor of the need of care and watchfulness, nor sensible of the goodness of God in their preservation. . . .[75]

---

various parts of one scheme, all conspiring for the bringing to pass the great event which is ultimately in view. . . . The world, it is most evident, is not an everlasting thing; it will have an end, and God's end in making and governing the world will not be fully obtained, nor his scheme be finished, till the end of the world comes" (*WJE 18*, 93–94).

74. *WJE 20*, 198. Edwards writes that there were traditions "from the fathers of the ancient church of God that was after the flood, concerning the fall of the angels, or the war between the devil and God the Father, and the Son, and the holy angels" (*WJE 15*, 406). Further, "God's people under the Old Testament were sensible that there was an evil and malignant spirit, or invisible agent, that sought the ruin of man, as even the heathen nations had a notion of evil demons" (272, based on Ps 17:4). Apparently, Edwards believed that the reality of the demonic was part of general revelation, obvious to anyone but confirmed by special revelation and traditions.

75. *WJE 18*, 203.

Satan (or Lucifer) was created as the chief of all the angels, and before his own fall was the greatest in strength, wisdom, honor, and dignity, existing sinlessly and happily in the presence of God.[76] His excellency and dominion were types of Christ's impending rule over the world.[77] But due to envy and pride, Lucifer refused to submit to the terms of the covenant and rebelled against God.[78] He refused to serve humanity on behalf of Christ and sought to have himself be worshipped as lord of the earth.[79]

The Devil and the lesser angels who decided to follow him in his rebellion against Christ were cast out of heaven to earth, where their powers are divinely restrained but still succeed in spreading misery.[80] It was only due to God's grace that not all of the angels fell.[81] And it was, of course, part of God's plan that Lucifer should fall at all, showing the vanity of even the greatest of creatures in comparison with himself. "God's design was first to show the creature's emptiness in itself, and then to fill it with himself in eternal, unalterable fullness and glory."[82]

Still motivated by envy and pride, Satan and his demons sought to ruin humanity.

> 'Twas the dignity of our nature that was greatly envied by Satan; and that which particularly galled him [was] that man, who was of an earthly [origin], should be advanced to such honors when he, who was of [an] heavenly [origin], and of so great strength and knowledge, should be cast down to such dishonor.[83]

---

76. *WJE* 13, 401–2. For a sampling of types related to Satan, see "Images" (54, 75); "Messiah" (240–41); *WJE* 13, 440; *WJE* 15, 237, 532; and *WJE* 20, 190–95.

77. *WJE* 20, 191. We must deduce that the world was created after the angelic covenant but before Satan's rebellion. Edwards does not clarify this as far as I know.

78. *WJE* 13, 382–83: "Then the question is, how came the devil by [sin], seeing he had no tempter? I answer, 'tis probable some extraordinary manifestation of God's sovereignty was his temptation, the occasion of his sin and rebellion."

79. "Thoughts," 416. "[A]lthough the devil be exceeding crafty and subtle, yet he is one of the greatest fools and blockheads in the world, as the subtlest of wicked men are. Sin is of such a nature that it strangely infatuates and bewitches" (*WJE* 13, 227).

80. *WJE* 15, 336, based on Exod 12:35–36; *WJE* 20, 194. "When the angels sinned, their punishment was immediately executed in a degree: but their full punishment is not till the end of the world" (*WJE* 3, 259). God allows Satan's power to reach only to the boundary of the earth's atmosphere; the rest of the universe is directly ruled by God (*WJE* 15, 299).

81. *WJE* 20, 195.

82. *WJE* 20, 192.

83. *WJE* 13, 304.

His purposes "in tempting mankind were, to deprive of holiness and happiness, and to bring into sin and misery," with the higher end of "injury to God."[84] Taking the form of a serpent, he seduced Adam and Eve to be devoted to him rather than the Creator, and continued thereafter to tempt humans to worship him.[85] Satan accomplished his goal of devastating the happy state of Eden, and thereby fulfilled a part of the plan of redemption that paved the way for salvation by Christ.[86]

Satan and his devils still continue to harass all people, especially Christ's saints, by eagerly and continuously seeking to have them give in to temptation and striving to overthrow "all Christian meekness and gentleness."[87] Satan tries to deceive everyone, mimicking the work of the Holy Spirit for some while prejudicing others against God.[88] He charms people to act as he does, with envy, pride, and hatred toward God and others.[89] They vainly pursue the shadows of riches and pleasures "that the devil represents to them instead of the substance" of the wealth of God's Kingdom.[90]

Affecting souls through both the body and the power of imagination, the Devil actively opposes true religion in human hearts by working to prevent its establishment and laboring to see it undone once built.[91] Until a person is regenerated and welcomed into the Kingdom of God, he dwells in Satan's kingdom of sin and cannot escape, nor does he want

---

84. *WJE* 13, 307–8.

85. *WJE* 15, 202, based on Gen 3:1. "Christ tells us that Satan is a liar, and the father of lies [John 8:44]; and his kingdom is a kingdom of darkness. 'Tis upheld and promoted only by darkness and error: Satan has all his power and dominion by darkness.... And devils are called the 'rulers of the darkness of this world' [Eph. 6:12]" ("Marks," 255).

86. "Charity," 224. Through the human kingdoms of the Babylonians, Persians, Greeks, and Romans, "God suffered Satan's kingdom to rise to so great a height of power and magnificence before his Son came to overthrow it, to prepare the way for the more glorious triumph of his Son" (*WJE* 9, 248).

87. "Thoughts," 419. When God dispersed the nations from Babel (Gen 11), they inhabited the area surrounding Canaan to suit God's "design of propagating the gospel among them.... The devil afterwards led many nations unto remote parts of the world to that end to get 'em out of the way of the gospel, led 'em unto America. Others were led unto northern cold regions that are almost inaccessible" (*WJE* 9, 155).

88. "Apocalypse," 218, based on Rev 16:13–14.

89. "Charity," 230.

90. "Job," 408.

91. *WJE* 2, 288–89. The Devil strives against the Bible and those who would read it ("Marks," 254).

to.⁹² Sinners are, in fact, participants in Satan's war against God.⁹³ "The devil loves to have to do with such souls [as] are a caviling and quarreling with God: he sets them on and helps forward their carnal reasonings, and God suffers [allows] him so to do."⁹⁴

Though powerful and wicked, Satan remains under God's ultimate control and does not know who is elect.⁹⁵ Like their leader, devils "can do nothing at all but by divine permission, and as subject to the disposal of Divine Providence."⁹⁶ At Satan's whim, they work evil in and through men by taking "advantage of bodily distemper and disorder of the brain," or occasionally in an extraordinary fashion by possessing someone.⁹⁷ Demons resemble unregenerate people in that while they have a natural sense of God's greatness, they do not value his excellency and are thus doomed to eternal punishment.⁹⁸ But God never offered redemption to devils because their sin was blasphemy against the Holy Spirit in "downright spiteful rebellion and a direct malicious war against God."⁹⁹ Sinners and devils will congregate in hell forever; when "a wicked man dies, the soul is immediately seized on by devils."¹⁰⁰

While Edwards clearly viewed our world as wicked due to the corruptions of sin, hell is unimaginably worse, a "world of hatred, a world of the wrath of God, and cruelty and malice of devils and damned spirits."¹⁰¹ The temporal suffering and death we experience and observe all around us is only a shadow, a type, of the dreadfulness of perpetually

---

92. "Future," 366.
93. *WJE* 15, 405.
94. "Reasonable," 196.
95. *WJE* 15, 360. For a description of God's sovereignty over Satan shown in Israel's deliverance out of Egypt, see *WJE* 9, 175ff.; during the Roman Empire and during Constantine's era, see *WJE* 9, 390–98 and 405–10, *passim*.
96. "Most High," 115; see, for example, Job 1.
97. *WJE* 15, 72, based on Matt 17:21.
98. *WJE* 13, 366. "The devils and damned spirits see a great deal of God's greatness, his omnipotence and the like. God makes them sensible of it by what they feel of the[ir] sufferings. . . . But they have no humility nor ever will have, because though they see God's awful greatness, yet they see nothing of his loveliness. The saints and angels in heaven see both" ("Charity," 237).
99. *WJE* 13, 385.
100. "Warnings," 209.
101. "Charity," 394.

being filled to one's capacity with misery.[102] Eternal death, a process of continually dying, involves an utter lack of any goodness; even instinct will be absent.[103] But what is not absent is God's detestation of depravity, which permeates hell even as grace permeates heaven. "All things in the whole universe which are hateful shall be gathered together in hell, as in a grand receptacle provided on purpose, that the universe which God has made may be cleansed of its filthiness by casting it all into this great sink."[104]

Recalling that sin is an infinite offense because it offends an *infinite* Being, Edwards asserts that the justice of God will never be satisfied by the eternal damnation of sinners because they are *finite* creatures.[105] Though some may find the concept of hell to be in conflict with the love of God, divine honor and justice require that God defend and vindicate the holiness of his name and the requirements of his Law.[106] Consequently, the wicked in hell will always be conscious of the eternality of their condition and will grow only in the knowledge of evil and their own odiousness.[107] Upon death, souls of the wicked have no further opportunity to hear the gospel and respond to it; their punishment essentially is to be deprived of God's presence, a deprivation that they sinfully desired all along.[108] Left with no pleasures whatsoever, the damned will be inflamed

102. "Images," 51.
103. *WJE* 3, 324.
104. "Charity," 390.
105. *WJE* 13, 225–26.
106. "End," 498; and "The Justice of God in the Damnation of Sinners," *WJE 19*, 339–76. "Eternal death is not only the wages but the proper fruit and natural produce of sin; that is, sin brings the soul into such a condition, so destroys and ruins the nature, so corrupts and poisons the heart, that the soul can never recover itself.... And the health and life of the soul being forever ruined, it necessarily becomes everlastingly miserable. God is the fountain of happiness, and to be separated from him is the greatest misery. But by sin man has drove away God from the soul, and therefore must be miserable forever if God returns not" ("Reasonable," 187).
107. *WJE 13*, 276. The wicked in hell, where hatred is perfected, will always recall their refusal of Christ and will see everywhere "the footsteps of God's wrath and hatred" (348).
108. "Future," 367. Edwards advises sinners to find God or face hell, where "your being will be entirely lost to you, and you will wish that you had never been born, or that you might but be turned to nothing" ("Fragment," *WJE 10*, 385). He clearly does not adhere to annihilationism, the theological view that sees sinners suffering in hell in accordance with their offenses but evaporating into nothing when their just time of punishment is completed.

to hate God even more, meriting for themselves even more punishment and compounding the eternality of their sentence.[109] Their bodies will be prisons that burn eternally, in every part "excruciated with intolerable pain."[110] "After the soul and body have roasted millions of ages in hellfire, it will not be at all nearer the end of its misery, and this the soul shall know and be assured of."[111]

Angels and Heaven

Just as Adam would have remained perfectly holy forever had he not sinned, so those angels who did not fall and who obeyed the terms of their covenant with God remained the morally excellent ministers to humanity they were created to be: God permanently preserved them from sin.[112] From the Scriptures Edwards deduces that angels are finite creatures, have intelligence and understanding, exist in an ordered hierarchy, and are assigned assorted spheres of responsibility in service to humanity.[113] In this service angels can influence reality "beyond the established laws of matter" because their existence itself is grounded upon *spiritual* laws; humans are not capable of comprehending and are not subject to these laws.[114] As they assist God in the fulfillment the work of redemption, angels celebrate their own election and sinless perfection, and persevere in aiding all humans but especially those who are also elect.[115]

As already mentioned, God never undertook an effort to redeem fallen angels, nor did he take on their nature in the way that Christ took

---

109. "Value," 320.

110. *WJE* 13, 263.

111. "Value," 321; "Wicked," 125–29.

112. *WJE* 2, 257. "The angels, we know, were especially then given to Christ God-man, when he ascended. Then it was, that he was made the head of all principality and power; and the great congruity of it confirms me, that when they once were given to Christ God-man, then they were in [a] confirmed state and incapable of perishing. For 'tis most congruous, that there should be no possibility of any such thing as perishing or death in his hands who is the prince of life, and the end of whose very being in such a constitution of his person, was life and salvation" (*WJE 18*, 129).

113. *WJE 20*, 195. Because angels and men both have understanding and reason, the "soul of man, were it not depraved, would be [like] an angel incarnate" ("Nothing," 149).

114. *WJE 13*, 326.

115. *WJE 9*, 301. Angels carry the souls of the saints to heaven when they die (*WJE 9*, 139; *WJE 15*, 298). Contrary to popular belief today, people do not become angels when they die; the two are different kinds of creatures.

on human nature. Thus though the "angelical nature is the highest and most exalted created nature," only humans have been blessed with the special unity with God the incarnation of Christ merited.[116] Indeed, the "angels are as his ministers and servants, but believers his bride (Rev. 19:7)."[117] Angels may forever excel the saints in strength and wisdom because of their nature and role in the Kingdom of God, but they cannot surpass perfected humans "in grace and sweet holiness and love to God."[118] Thankfully, the Kingdom of God is not a competition: "angels and saints make up but one family, though members of a different character. . . . [S]aints and angels are united in Christ, and have communion in him."[119]

Of course, the fellowship of the saints and angels occurs in heaven, a place that is beautiful and holy because it is filled with the beautiful holiness of God.[120] Heaven's existence is the Holy Spirit's continuous creation *par excellence,* increasing in glory as God himself does.[121] In heaven is the "glorious presence of God the Father; the glorified Lamb of God; and the heavenly Dove, spirit of all grace and [origin] of all holiness."[122] Through the power of Christ's incarnation, the elect in heaven have the ability to see God and others "with their bodily eyes as well as by an intellectual view."[123] Heaven is for Edwards everything

---

116. *WJE 18,* 241. "So it can truly be said of the angels that they have eternal life by sovereign grace through Christ in a way of self-emptiness, self-diffidence, and humble dependence on him" (*WJE 20,* 196).

117. "Nothing," 155.

118. *WJE 13,* 271.

119. *WJE 13,* 284, based on Eph 1:10; also, 285, based on Col 1:15–22. Edwards contends that the saints and angels in heaven communicate with one another, though we cannot know exactly how (*WJE 2,* 288).

120. *WJE 2,* 258. Pauw writes, "In heaven, as on earth, religious experience in its highest form is a practical, communal affair. In neither realm is the individual the primary locus of spiritual discernment. Even the heavenly vision of God was for Edwards not an inward, private rapture but a cooperative social effort" ("Heaven Is a World of Love," 396).

121. *WJE 20,* 193. In "'Heaven Is a World of Love,'" Pauw also points out that Edwards's notion of divine glory and the saints' holiness progressively increasing in heaven is unique in the Reformed and Puritan tradition (399).

122. "Holiness," 471; also *WJE 15,* 221, based on Exod 33:18–19.

123. *WJE 13,* 501. It follows from Edwards's thought that in heaven, the physical and spiritual have no bifurcation whatsoever. "And it is out of doubt with me, that there will [be] immediate intellectual views of minds, one of another and of the supreme mind, more immediate, clear and sensible than our views of bodily things with bodily eyes" (*WJE 13,* 329).

of earthly good, magnified and expanded to the utmost degree in "unknown and inconceivable happiness."[124] He writes that it "is a garden of love, the Paradise of God, where everything has a cast of holy love, and everything conspires to promote and stir up love, and nothing to interrupt its exercises."[125] "What beauteous and fragrant flowers will these be, reflecting all the sweetnesses of the Son of God! How will Christ delight to walk in this garden, among these beds of spices, to feed in the gardens and to gather lilies!"[126]

While the incarnation of Christ is the ultimate physical manifestation of an idea in God's mind, heaven is next in prominence because it consists of human existence immediately and intimately in God's very presence. Edwards did not conceive of "the new heavens and the new earth" (Isa 65:17, 66:22) as being literal, geographic places in the sense we are currently aware of. Rather, this "new state of things in the spiritual world" is a numinous, mystical condition with some indeterminate kind of material-temporal property.[127] There, the mysteries about God that the elect encountered on earth will be unveiled as the Holy Spirit shares knowledge of the Godhead to lovely humans no longer corrupted and hindered by sin.[128] Heaven is truly a place of lush fertility, where the holiness of the saints always grows and "by length of time things become more and more youthful, that is, more vigorous, active, tender and beautiful."[129]

Prior to the Day of Judgment, when the saints in heaven have not yet been united with new bodies, they observe the fulfillment of the plan of redemption on earth from heaven.[130] Christ's redemptive work merited

124. "Nothing," 143.

125. "Charity," 385.

126. *WJE 13*, 281.

127. "Apocalypse," 166. Lee notes that for Edwards, "eternal life is not a realm of timelessness. Eternity transcends and perfects time and space *but also includes them*. Eternity is neither timelessness nor mere unending duration (i.e., duration without a qualitative perfection of time)" (*Philosophical Theology*, 237, original italics).

128. "Apocalypse," 172.

129. *WJE 13*, 341. Glorified saints will grow in holiness and happiness for eternity because they will build upon memories retrieved from earthly life and their ideas will grow in number ceaselessly (275).

130. *WJE 13*, 478; "True Saints, When Absent from the Body, Are Present with the Lord," *WJE 25*, 225–59. There are miraculous exceptions to this, however. Referring to the girl whom Christ raised from the dead in Matt 9:24, Edwards observes that "her soul was not finally separated from her body, so as to enter into the spiritual and eternal

for the saints the privilege of reigning with him, so he does not keep them ignorant of earth's history and they with their glorified souls pray actively for the redemption of the elect.[131] In fact,

> the affairs of the church in heaven have some way or other a dependence on God's providence towards his church on earth, and ... their progress is dependent on the progress of things in God's providence towards his church here. For heaven and earth are both framed together.[132]

Believers thus have eternal life and its perfect holiness immediately upon their deaths but do not have it in its "highest completion"; as we have explored, that occurs only after the Day of Judgment.[133]

A common Sunday school question for children and adults is, "What do people *do* in heaven?" No doubt Edwards must have encountered this query himself. His answer? "We know not particularly how the saints in heaven shall be employed; but in general we know they are employed in praising and serving God."[134] Essentially, the business of heaven is true religion in "its utmost purity and perfection."[135] The saints assist each other in contemplating God's glory in creation and providence, praising him with music and "going from one part of heaven to another, to behold the glories of God shining in the various parts of it."[136] The continuous healthiness of their bodies, filled with sensual pleasures, will only add to their spiritual delight as they discover more and more beauty in themselves, each other, and their heavenly union in Christ.[137] This spiritual and physical beauty of glorified bodies comprises the light

---

world; nor had there that transformation passed upon her soul from a middle state to perfect holiness or misery. And her soul was kept in a state of insensibility, as in a sound sleep, that her resurrection might not be inconvenient" (*WJE 15*, 67). This also occurred in John 11:11 with Lazarus, whose "state was only intermitted" (67).

131. *WJE 18*, 71–73, 99–100; also *WJE 13*, 481–84.

132. *WJE 15*, 385. The church in heaven observes and rejoices in "the progressive wonderful doings of God with respect to his church here in this world.... The church in heaven and the church on earth are more one people, one city, and one family than generally is imagined" (*WJE 13*, 478).

133. *WJE 3*, 259.

134. "Charity," 384.

135. *WJE 2*, 113.

136. *WJE 13*, 296.

137. *WJE 13*, 328–29. Though heaven is a new *spiritual* state, it does have some kind of matter beyond our present comprehension of which bodies are composed.

of heaven; the "light of the bodies of the saints shall be some way or other a communication of the light of Christ . . . as the light which is reflected from a lily is the same light but less bright than the sun."[138]

The saints all enjoy God's immediate presence. But Edwards believed that just as there are degrees of punishment in hell depending on the egregiousness of a person's wickedness, there are also varying levels of glorification and giftedness in heaven. The most exalted are those who most faithfully imitated the greatest servant, Jesus Christ.[139] All revel in the unity of holiness and happiness, but the most virtuous have greater insight into the "divine perfections" and "penetrate further into the vast and infinite distance that is between them and God, and their delight of annihilating themselves, that God may be all, shall be greater."[140] Indeed, every Christian there is so "lost in the will of God, that he had rather have it according to God's will than any way in the world."[141] And there is no envy in heaven: the holiest of saints are celebrated and adored by the lesser, whose reflections do not dwell on themselves or their remembered failures while on earth, but on having "the more admiring and joyful sense of God's grace in pardoning them."[142]

Compared with the saints on earth, the inhabitants of heaven are more aware of "what great love it manifested in Christ, that he should lay down his life for them. Then Christ will open to their view the great fountain of love in his heart far beyond what they ever before saw."[143] The love of Christ through the ministry of the Holy Spirit flows to every saint and angel, "and they all with one heart and one soul, without any schism in the body, love their common Redeemer."[144] An unchanging,

---

138. WJE 13, 370. The beauty of the saints' bodies in heaven will not just be due to external features, "but much in the manifestation of the excellence of their mind; which exceeding readily will appear in their bodies, the bodies being more easily and naturally susceptive and manifestative of the affections and dispositions of the mind, than here" (301).

139. WJE 18, 240. Consult Matt 20:25–8 and Luke 9:48, for example.

140. WJE 13, 202. Edwards uses the word "annihilating" here to mean a setting aside of self-focus in order to glorify God with one's complete attention and energy. It does *not* mean to kill oneself or lose one's identity, both of which clearly contradict God's good purpose for believers. In fact, the self is more complete the more it is devoted to its Creator.

141. WJE 13, 184.

142. WJE 13, 482; also "Charity," 374–77, *passim*.

143. "Charity," 377.

144. "Charity," 374.

unflagging love abounds consisting of perfect mutual consent, harmonious and in "due proportion."[145] The saints are not merely related to one another as children of God; they belong to each other and to God "as one family in their heavenly Father's house."[146] Fulfilling the plan of redemption, the saints through the grace of the Spirit "all are united with one mind to breathe forth their whole souls in love to their eternal Father, and to Jesus Christ, their common head."[147]

In heaven "Christ will most freely and intimately converse with them as friends and brethren."[148] Beholding his glory, the beatific vision of God in the face of Christ, the elect will celebrate his redemptive work always "and they shall forever feed on him, as the food of eternal life."[149] In sum, they will "see the man Christ Jesus, and even Jehovah himself, the Eternal Three in One, and shall be intimately united to him, and this happiness of theirs shall endure as long as God endures."[150]

Thus, we come to the end of a cosmic salvation story that is really only the beginning for the elect in the heavenly presence of their eternal God. These saints are now "one society, one family; that the church should be as it were admitted into the society of the blessed Trinity."[151] But because the saints are finite, their union with infinite God will perpetually improve, increase, and never really be final: "there never will come the moment, when it can be said, that now this infinitely valuable good has been actually bestowed."[152] Due to the incarnation, the eternal union between God and creature will more and more resemble the eternal union between the Father and the Son, "who are so united, that their interest is perfectly one."[153]

And the eternal union in the Trinity itself then returns to its full rule over reality, as it was before the Son was given viceregency over the earth and command of the Holy Spirit in order to complete his covenant with the Father. Proceeding from the harmonious Godhead to the saints

---

145. "Charity," 377.
146. "Charity," 380.
147. "Charity," 374.
148. *WJE 18*, 107.
149. "Job," 407.
150. "Value," 325.
151. "Christ," 594.
152. "End," 536.
153. "End," 533.

and back again, holy love flows forth: "There in heaven this fountain of love, this eternal three in one, is set open without any obstacle to hinder access to it."[154] So the saints, angels, and God "will live and thus they will reign in love, and in that godlike joy which is the blessed fruit of it, such as eye hath not seen, nor ear heard, nor hath ever entered into the heart of any in this world to conceive [cf. 1 Cor 2:9]. And thus they will live and reign forever and ever."[155]

For Further Thought

1. Read footnote 26 and look up the Bible passages mentioned there. How do your impressions of those Bible passages compare with Edwards's ideas?

2. Do you believe that our world will come to an end? How do your thoughts compare with Edwards's?

3. Consider Edwards's theology about the "end times" just prior to the Day of Judgment. Do you find his description of that scenario plausible? If you were alive to experience that scenario, what do you suppose your reactions would be?

4. According to Edwards, what are the joys and responsibilities of Christians during the "last days" and the millennium? How do these joys and responsibilities differ from those of Christians in other eras?

5. What was Edwards's rationale for denoting the Roman Catholic Church "Antichrist"? What do you think the flaws and strengths of this rationale are? Would you define "Antichrist" differently than he does?

6. What are the major phases and events that comprise the millennium? And the Day of Judgment? What are your impressions of this part of his theology? Does he raise for you any issues you had not considered before?

7. What are the major differences between the lives of those in heaven and those in hell? Do you believe these places exist? Why?

8. Do you believe that angels and demons exist? Why? How do your ideas compare with Edwards's?

---

154. "Charity," 370.
155. "Charity," 386.

9. Supposing that Edwards is correct in his thoughts about heaven and hell, in which place do you expect to spend eternity? Why?

10. In what ways does the Day of Judgment "wrap up" God's eternal plan of redemption? Can you think of any "loose ends" that are not resolved in Edwards's eschatology?

11. In reflecting upon this book, how has reading about Jonathan Edwards's thought changed your views? Are there any ways in which you will live your life differently as a result?

For Further Reading

Colwell, John E. "The Glory of God's Justice and the Glory of God's Grace: Contemporary Reflections on the Doctrine of Hell in the Teaching of Jonathan Edwards." *Evangelical Quarterly* 67 (1995) 291–308.

Davidson, Bruce W. "Reasonable Damnation: How Jonathan Edwards Argued for the Rationality of Hell." *Journal of the Evangelical Theological Society* 38 (1995) 47–56.

Erickson, Millard J., editor. *A Basic Guide to Eschatology: Making Sense of the Millennium*, rev. ed. Grand Rapids: Baker, 1998.

Gregg, Steve, editor. *Revelation: Four Views: A Parallel Commentary*. Nashville: Thomas Nelson, 1997.

Grenz, Stanley. *The Millennial Maze: Sorting Out Evangelical Options*. Downers Grove, IL: InterVarsity, 1992.

Jang, Kyoung-Chul. "The Logic of Glorification: The Destiny of the Saints in the Eschatology of Jonathan Edwards." PhD diss., Princeton Theological Seminary, 1995.

Lowance, Mason I., Jr. "Typology and Millennial Eschatology in Early New England." In *Literary Uses of Typology*, edited by Earl Miner. Princeton: Princeton University Press, 1977.

Pahl, Jon. "Jonathan Edwards and the Aristocracy of Grace." *Fides et Historia* 25 (1993) 62–72.

Pauw, Amy Plantinga. "'Heaven Is a World of Love': Edwards on Heaven and the Trinity." *Calvin Theological Journal* 30 (1995) 392–400.

Stein, Stephen J. "Providence and the Apocalypse in the Early Writings of Jonathan Edwards." *Early American Literature* 13 (1978–79) 250–67.

Westbrook, Robert B. "Social Criticism and the Heavenly City of Jonathan Edwards." *Soundings* 59 (1976) 396–412.

Withrow, Brandon G. "A Future of Hope: Jonathan Edwards and Millennial Expectations." *Trinity Journal* 22 (2001) 75–98.

8

Sinners in the Hands of an Angry God?

MOST PEOPLE WHO HAVE heard of Jonathan Edwards came to know of him through reading his 1741 sermon "Sinners in the Hands of an Angry God." In a sense, any knowledge of a man who is among the greatest American theologians and thinkers is a good thing. But in another sense to "know" Edwards through this sermon alone is deeply unfortunate because it hardly represents the breadth of his work and his view of the Trinitarian God. It is at best unwise and at worst intellectually dishonest to evaluate a person's contributions based on just one example, especially for a voluminous writer such as Edwards.

What has driven this project for me is the great need for us all to understand the broad contours of Edwards's theology not for its own sake, but for its value for us today and for generations to come. I have pursued this project with the belief that anyone who expounds biblical truth expounds truth that is crucial for life in any age, under any circumstance, simply because the Bible itself is crucial for life in any age, under any circumstance. Though you may not agree with that presupposition, one that I share with Edwards, I would be astonished to learn that you have found nothing whatsoever to take from him to enhance your life. Integrity requires that we seek to learn from others, even if we disagree in the end.

Since the word "Puritanical" has strongly negative associations in the West these days, I have to think that many people have either come to read Edwards with a bias against him, or have avoided him altogether. Those with a negative bias may well have that reinforced by the "Sinners" sermon due to its heavy, intense descriptions of human sinfulness, divine judgment, and eternal hell. But in this final chapter I would like to examine the extent to which the sermon's contents are representative

172 THE GREAT WORK OF PROVIDENCE

of the theology we have discussed to this point, and then consider how Edwards's insights may be helpful for us in the twenty-first century.[1]

The Trinitarian God, Through Edwards's Eyes

The Bible verse Edwards chose to base this sermon upon is Deut 32:35: "Their foot shall slide in due time."[2] While our first impression may be that his focus is upon the precarious position of sinners as they stand on the brink of hell, his underlying assumption is that God is sovereign over time and human lives. God does keep sinners from falling into hell, but is never obliged to do so and has the power to release his grip on their lives at any moment. Given that God's Law has already condemned them, divine justice requires that sinners be punished. God is not like us as we tolerate or even make light of sin in our lives; he is righteously angry, deeply offended, and wrathful not just against sin *in general*, but the sinners who are guilty of it. God doesn't just hate the sin, he hates the sinners—in fact, he "abhors" them because they "are ten thousand times so abominable in his eyes as the most hateful venomous serpent is in ours."[3]

From these comments we see that God is utterly holy and just, and yet also supremely merciful, compassionate, and loving. How is he loving? Even though God detests sinners, he still cares for them by extending their lives and thus their opportunities to profess faith in Jesus Christ to receive forgiveness and new life. As we read this sermon our focus can easily be that God seems malicious in holding the unregenerate "over the pit of hell, much as one holds a spider, or some loathsome insect, over the fire."[4] But the preacher's point is that God does not need to hold sinners there, because their sinfulness merits them being *in* the pit of hell. We sinners *are* loathsome and puny, especially in the hands of a pure, holy God.

Particularly when compared with God, our lives are incredibly fragile and can end at any instant, regardless of our best efforts and our

---

1. If you have not recently read this fairly brief sermon, I encourage to you to seek it online, particularly at the site for the Jonathan Edwards Center at Yale University, www.Edwards.yale.edu.

2. "Sinners," 404; Edwards also refers here to Ps 73:18–19 and 1 Thess 5:3.

3. "Sinners," 411.

4. "Sinners," 411. The mascot of Yale's Jonathan Edwards College is the spider.

perceptions of security. The Lord gives life and takes it away, but he is still to be blessed and adored (Job 1:21). Recall that God's sovereignty is one of the attributes Edwards esteemed most, and its proper comprehension will lead a sinner to humility, or "evangelical humiliation." God doesn't need us at all and has no reason to tolerate our sinful existence—apart from the covenant of grace. Those who have not been born again have no interest in this covenant, its promises, or its Mediator, so God is not required even for a second to keep them from eternal destruction.[5]

The fact that God is so merciful and compassionate only heightens his provocation against those who continue to persist in rejecting Christ as their Savior. Not only that, but they offend the Lord by deluding themselves about their future state and flattering themselves by thinking that somehow they will avoid hell and trump God's justice. Referring either to those who are already in hell or those who seem to be on their way there, Edwards states that God is fierce in his fury against them; as the infinite, great, almighty Creator and King of kings, he inflicts punishment on sinners in hell without any pity, compassion, moderation, or mercy.[6] Because "God hath had it on his heart to show to angels and men, both how excellent his love is, and also how terrible his wrath is," he manifests contempt, hatred, and indignation to such a degree that he even mocks sinners.[7] Why such apparently harsh descriptions of God's imposition of eternal misery? Just one sin is an infinite offense against an infinite God. "[T]he great God is also willing to show *his wrath*, and magnify his awful majesty and mighty power in the extreme sufferings of his enemies."[8]

Just above I quoted Edwards's contention that God desires to demonstrate both his excellent love and his terrible wrath. Though this sermon leans quite heavily towards the description of the latter, I think I have demonstrated in previous chapters that Edwards's God is fundamentally a God of love. One of the reasons that God is so fierce toward hell's inhabitants is *because* God showered them with love, compassion, and mercy during their earthly lives. Clearly Edwards saw preaching as a divine blessing through which people may come to see that their lives really are in the Lord's hands, totally subject to his will and power—and

---

5. "Sinners," 409.
6. "Sinners," 413, based on Ezek 8:18.
7. "Sinners," 414, based on Prov 1:25–32.
8. "Sinners," 414, original italics, referring to Daniel 1–3 and Rom 9:22.

in this realization, they may humble themselves and express faith rather than deceiving themselves by believing that they have no need for God. Edwards emphasizes that even as his congregants hear this powerful message, a change of heart through the ministry of the Holy Spirit is still available to them.[9] The sermon's closing section tells us of the God who through Scripture and providence still gives them an "extraordinary opportunity" to become new creations: "Christ has flung the door of mercy wide open, and stands in the door calling and crying with a loud voice to poor sinners."[10] Edwards counsels, "Therefore, let everyone that is out of Christ, now awake and fly from the wrath to come."[11]

Creation and the Eternal Plan of Redemption

As we continue to assess the extent to which "Sinners" represents the whole of Edwards's theology, we are reminded that his preaching assumes that God, creation, and the eternal plan of redemption are intertwined. We saw in prior chapters that people are sinners due to Adam's Fall and they exist in God's time according to his plan and mercy. In the sermon's first paragraph, Edwards compares some in his congregational audience with the unbelieving Israelites who lived wickedly under means of grace and falsely presumed themselves to be God's people. Even though people in Northampton would have been well accustomed to Edwards's preaching style, this manner of beginning a sermon seems as tactful as hitting someone over the head with a club. But Edwards states his purpose in preaching clearly: "The *Use* may be of *Awakening* to unconverted persons in this congregation."[12] In other words, he calls the falsely religious in his congregation to genuine redemption in Christ.

While the plan of redemption can be read between the lines in every part of "Sinners," the pastor does explicitly refer to its chief elements with some frequency. Edwards highlights the covenant of grace, its promises, and its Mediator, noting that those who reject these are not truly children of the covenant.[13] "Thus are all you that never passed

9. "Sinners," 411.
10. "Sinners," 416.
11. "Sinners," 418.
12. "Sinners," 409.
13. "Sinners," 409.

under a great change of heart, by the mighty power of the Spirit of God upon your souls. . . ."[14] Nevertheless, through the plan of redemption, "Now God stands ready to pity you; this is a day of mercy; you may cry now with some encouragement of obtaining mercy," but do so before it is too late![15] Not only that, but God is working to bring the plan of redemption to its culmination and they may well come to see an outpouring of the Holy Spirit comparable to Pentecost.[16]

> [M]any are flocking to him, and pressing into the kingdom of God; many are daily coming from the east, west, north and south; many that were very lately in the same miserable condition that you are in, are in now an happy state, with their hearts filled with love to him that has loved them and washed them from their sins in his own blood, and rejoicing in hope of the glory of God.[17]

He even points out that people in the neighboring town of Suffield "are flocking day to day to Christ."[18] So in essence, "Why not join them? Why not be like them in heeding the Word of God preached to you today? What are you waiting for?"

Consistent with his thoughts on creation, divine revelation, and the plan of redemption, Edwards also often uses prophetic passages from the Bible to emphasize God's sovereign activity in salvation and damnation. His mention of such passages (Isa 33:12–14; 63:3; 66:15, 23–24; Ezek 8:18; Rev 19:15) hammers home the expectation that God will punish sinners in a manner that "'tis inexpressible and inconceivable."[19] But what these Bible passages also have in common is imagery that graphically depicts the destruction sinners will face. Burning in fire is the major theme by far, in addition to being slashed by the sword of divine justice, devoured by a pit, pounced upon by devils who are like greedy, hungry lions, and trampled by God until their blood splatters his garments. While such imagery makes for interesting and impressive preaching, it is Edwards's theology that leads him to use the physical to describe the spiritual, for in reality the two are never separated.

---

14. "Sinners," 411.
15. "Sinners," 413–14.
16. "Sinners," 418.
17. "Sinners," 416–17.
18. "Sinners," 417.
19. "Sinners," 416.

This point is especially obvious when the preacher construes the recoil creation is experiencing due to humanity's Fall. Should someone sin and fall, apart from God's kind pleasure the earth would not bear him any more "than a spider's web would . . . stop a falling rock"; in fact it would spew him out with repugnance. Edwards goes on to explain that creation groans because of the burden of humanity's sin.

> [T]he sun don't willingly shine upon you to give you light to serve sin and Satan; the earth don't willingly yield her increasing to satisfy your lusts; nor is it willingly a stage for your wickedness to be acted upon; the air don't willingly serve you . . . while you spend your life in the service of God's enemies.[20]

Instead, God's creatures are good and given to humanity for use in his service, but groan when "abused to purposes so directly contrary to their nature and end."[21]

Similarly, Edwards uses illustrations from creation to paint in his listener's imaginations the reality of the doom they face apart from Christ. Sinners bring forth bitter and poisonous fruit; teeter on a slippery slope; are like chaff before a whirlwind and on a summer threshing floor; are poor, feeble, despicable worms and despised grasshoppers; and are foolish children of the devil. Meanwhile, God's wrath is far worse than any human king has ever exerted; like black clouds with thunder and rough wind; great waters that are presently dammed but always increase with power and might; fiery floods rushing forth; arrows shot from a bow to be made drunk with blood; a fierce winepress; and quick like a thief. Edwards does not explicitly mention typology in this sermon, but his use of images such as these is definitely consistent with his thoughts about the interfusion of divine will, the plan of redemption, and creation. To what end? To warn vividly that "as it was in the days of John the Baptist, the ax is in an extraordinary manner laid at the root of the trees, that every tree that brings not forth good fruit, may be hewn down, and cast into the fire."[22]

---

20. "Sinners," 410.
21. "Sinners," 410.
22. "Sinners," 418, referring to Matt 3:10.

Religious Affections, Damnation, and Glory

While it's clear that "Sinners" is heavily laden with emphasis upon sin, judgment, and God's wrath, the preacher does offer the gospel of Christ in clear terms and with passion. I use the word "passion" because we need to keep in mind that delivering a sermon of this kind, even in the Puritanical days of 1741, was a mission of love and courage. Even though the people of Northampton had known Edwards since he was a boy and had heard him preach countless times, no one likes to hear words such as these or consider the unpleasant possibility that he or she may be at dire risk of damnation. While some mature Christians would have appreciated his attempt to preach the gospel and call people to repentance and faith, there would have been a lot of coughing, sniffing, shifting in seats, angry eyes, and tears. It took backbone for Edwards to speak these words, risking criticism, censure, and even the loss of his pulpit.

"Passion" is also an appropriate word because the sermon conveys an unmistakable sense of urgency and severity blended with sincere love—he truly wants Northampton to join him in heaven and not suffer endless agony apart from the goodness and presence of God. In his appeal Edwards discusses in several instances the spiritual perspective of those who foolishly ignore the gospel. "Hellish principles" reign in the souls of the wicked—and by the way, the "wicked" are not only the murderers and thieves of the world, but *anyone* who rejects Christ as their Savior. These corrupt principles are active, powerful, exceedingly violent seeds of hell fire.[23] But interestingly, the misery sinners experience in hell is at least in part comprised of sin itself: their souls are their own furnaces of ruin, a fire pent up in their hearts that is bursting at the seams while they live on earth.

Edwards also highlights the psychology and reasoning of every person as we go about our daily business, never thinking that the next moment could be the last before we face God's judgment. Even if we take good care of our health and use every means to feel secure, we are always subject to accidents and unknown illnesses that can be used by God to take us out of the world. When we go to sleep we can't even know for certain that we will rise in the morning; it is only God's care and mercy that gets us through the night. Some may plan to heed the gospel later in life, while others convince themselves that they uniquely have figured

---

23. "Sinners," 407.

out a way to avoid damnation. Others remain unconvinced about the reality of hell, but Edwards assures them that either through faith or damnation, some day they will be persuaded.

This discussion of common human experiences to emphasize the fragility of life and our dependence on God is especially effective when Edwards projects them onto people who can speak to us from hell about their misery. The sermon quotes those who thought their schemes to avoid judgment were all set to succeed. We hear others tell us of their foolishness and self-flattery because none of them really expected to end up in hell. So what do they say it is like to be in hell? Agony, compounded by the constant awareness that the agony *will never end*. We experience pain in this life, even for extended periods of time. But the worst pain here is nothing compared to this "exquisite horrible misery" in a "boundless duration . . . which will swallow up your thoughts, and amaze your soul," and never be complete even after "millions and millions of ages."[24]

The boldest section of "Sinners" addresses religious affections and false religion, obviously Edwards's greatest concerns for his congregants. "'[T]is plain and manifest that whatever pains a natural man takes in religion, whatever prayers he makes, till he believes in Christ, God is under no manner of obligation to keep him a *moment* from eternal destruction."[25] Edwards asks them to remember those in the congregation who have died and where they used to sit. Despite their presence at one time, only God now knows for sure whether they are in heaven or hell, and only God knows who will be gone tomorrow, next week, or a year from now. To those who have not been born again and experienced "light and life," he counsels that

> however you may have reformed your life in many things, and may have had religious affections, and may keep up a form of religion in your families and closets [for prayer], and in the house of God, and may be strict in it . . . you are thus in the hands of an angry God.[26]

How awful it will be to be left behind when others are turning to Christ! "To see so many others feasting, while you are pining and perishing! To

---

24. "Sinners," 415.
25. "Sinners," 409.
26. "Sinners," 411.

see so many rejoicing and singing for joy of heart, while you . . . mourn for sorrow of heart, and howl for vexation of spirit! How can you rest one moment in such a condition?"[27]

Finally Edwards pointedly preaches to particular age groups in the gathering while noting that this message for conversion applies to everyone, male and female, young and old. "There is reason to think, that there are many in this congregation now hearing this discourse, that will actually be the subjects of this very misery to all eternity." They may even be "at ease, and hear these things without much disturbance, and are now flattering themselves that they are not the persons, promising themselves that they shall escape."[28]

After reminding all of them that they should wonder why they are not at that very moment in hell, Edwards focuses on the elderly congregants. Having spent their lives storing up wrath against themselves, they are in an especially dangerous place with great guilt and hardness of heart. They have had the most time to repent and believe in Christ; they have a dire need to examine themselves and wake from their sleep. Edwards then warns the young men and women not to be like the older unregenerate, not to pass up this extraordinary opportunity and precious season. Why would they pass it up, when so many others of their age were "renouncing all youthful vanities, and flocking to Christ?" Otherwise they will whittle away their "precious days of youth in sin" and end up spiritually blind and hardened. And to the children: "Don't you know that you are going down to hell, to bear the dreadful wrath of that God that is now angry with you every day, and every night? Will you be content to be the children of the devil when so many other children . . . are become the holy and happy children of the King of kings?"[29]

Edwards doesn't mince words. He has already reminded the unconverted that their being in the congregation provokes God's pure eyes because of their "sinful wicked manner of attending his solemn worship. . . ."[30] But he does so toward this end: that in his sharing the reality of hell they will avoid being "tormented in the presence of the holy angels, and in the presence of the Lamb." Rather they will join heaven's inhabitants in witnessing the "carcasses" of those who are suf-

---

27. "Sinners," 417.
28. "Sinners," 416.
29. "Sinners," 417.
30. "Sinners," 412.

fering God's wrath, "and when they have seen it, they will fall down and adore that great power and majesty."[31]

In the midst of their reverie of worship and praise, they will agree with Edwards that God is love—pure, holy love beyond our full comprehension. Again, this is why "Sinners" frequently contrasts those who lack saving faith with those who profess Christ as their Savior. To the unregenerate the preacher pleads, "Now God stands ready to pity you; this is a day of mercy; you may cry now with some encouragement of obtaining mercy. . . ."[32] Such individuals need to abandon their ideas of religiosity and self-sufficiency, and instead throw themselves upon God's mercy *today*. "The wrath of almighty God is now undoubtedly hanging over great part of this congregation: let everyone fly out of Sodom. Haste and escape for your lives, look not behind you, escape to the mountain, lest you be consumed."[33]

To modern sensibilities, this sermon's repeated illustrations and references to God's terrible wrath and horrible human suffering in hell may seem excessive and may lead one to wonder whether God is really like this. Like Edwards, there are people today all over the globe who respond, "Yes, God is really like this"—not because they delight in the idea of the wicked agonizing forever, but because they are convinced that the Bible is the Word of God and these are the Bible's conclusions. Like Edwards, those who earnestly hold these convictions face challenges daily where faith in Jesus Christ intersects with life. We now turn our attention to just some of the practical questions Edwards's theology lays before us.

Questions Edwards Raises for Us Today

Michael J. McClymond has observed that for Edwards "Christianity should be defended not by isolating individual elements and seeking to establish them one by one but rather by recounting the entire biblical narrative in such a way that its human relevance and explanatory power become fully evident."[34] Thus he "interpreted the world as a thorough-

---

31. "Sinners," 415.
32. "Sinners," 413–14.
33. "Sinners," 418, referring to Gen 19:17, in which Lot's wife was turned to a pillar of salt for looking back toward Sodom.
34. McClymond, *Encounters*, 101.

going unity in which God functioned as the unifying principle" and "sought to use every conceivable form of reasoning—metaphysical, moral, experiential, and historical—in a many-sided effort to establish the centrality and supremacy of God."[35] As we have seen, Edwards's entire theology is deliberately grounded upon a biblical, Trinitarian view of a God who is intimately involved in every aspect of reality and particularly human life, a grand, eternal plan of redemption unfolding in history. Having said that, what is the apologetic for Edwards himself? Is there contemporary relevance for his perspective, which some view as being antiquated, prudish, or even cruel?

Edwards offers numerous challenges to ideas in the modern West, largely due to the sharp contrast between his theological orientation and those prevalent today. One of the most fundamental implications of Edwards's view of God is that despite what some scientists and philosophers, our senses, or our confusion and despair in daily life may tell us, there is in fact meaning in reality. That divinely-endowed meaning is there to console us and to be celebrated by us. It is there not only for those with the faith to believe that that meaning is continuously created by the Spirit of Christ, though for Edwards the saints have far deeper insight into its divine origins. Rather, life's inherent meaning and value is a divine gift for everyone through general revelation. Edwards's theology ultimately leaves no room for nihilism or chaos. God is so utterly real that his beautiful, excellent, holy presence is typologically attested by everything; each moment is his creation and each breath taken by a creature is one granted by him in loving fashion. Contrary to Samuel Beckett's *Waiting for Godot*, there is no need to wait for God to arrive when he is already there, and in fact never left. And there is no need to be threatened by the fact of God's involvement in each detail of existence, because existence itself is a loving, divine provision that opposes the very chaos and purposelessness many today fear.

Life has incredible meaning that is rooted in God's own Being; death does as well, as an example from recent history illustrates. In November, 1998, Dr. Jack Kevorkian was charged in Michigan with the murder of Thomas Youk, 52, who suffered from Lou Gehrig's disease.[36] Kevorkian

---

35. McClymond, *Encounters*, 85.

36. On March 26, 1999, Jack "Dr. Death" Kevorkian (b. 1928) was convicted of second-degree murder by a Michigan jury and sentenced to 10–25 years in prison. He was released on June 1, 2007, for good behavior. Since then he has had several speaking

had videotaped the euthanasia incident early in that month and the tape was aired a few weeks later on the CBS news program "60 Minutes." Kevorkian's intention was to challenge the courts, once and for all, to prove the illegality of his practice of euthanasia. Kevorkian announced that if found guilty, he would starve himself to death in jail. There is no doubt that Edwards would condemn Kevorkian's act as murder, criticize Youk's consent, and view both men as those who assumed upon themselves God's role as the giver and taker of life.

But in often-publicized, Kevorkian-like euthanasia cases there is rare mention in the media of the meaning of such deaths. There may be vague references to a relief of suffering that allows patients to be released to a "better place." But what is that place? Or there may be the sentiment that putting a person out of his misery is far better than allowing him to continue in a pathetic state, below any standard of human dignity. Edwards's theology challenges us to define the meaning of dignified personhood from God's perspective; the tie between body and soul; whether the soul is eternal; and if so, what its destiny may be beyond our meaningful lives.

Edwards's ideas about heaven may seem unbelievably utopian to some and his views of hell unbelievably cruel. But the broader question remains, as with the rest of his theology: Are those ideas *true*? And further, how do we know whether they are true? Edwards may be criticized for blindly relying on biblical evidence, trusting implicitly a book many today see as being of restricted moral and historical value. But he challenges us again: If the Bible will not be our ultimate foundation for knowledge of God, and thus knowledge of what is true, then what will be? And so, is it possible to have a truly meaningful death, if there is no eternal meaningfulness for life? Or are life and death merely biological?

Of course Edwards saw morality as a component of the image of God in humans. As such, it is the foundation for a civil society in which believers and non-believers can co-exist despite their differing ideas about who God is, and what human relationship to God and others ought to be. If a society cannot agree upon a core set of values (based on general revelation), not only does it fracture its moral foundation but it also rejects God and the image he creates in the souls of its constituents. Further, when a society undertakes to formulate its own code for morality,

---

engagements. Though terminally ill with hepatitis C, in 2008 he ran unsuccessfully for U.S. Congress to represent Michigan's Ninth District.

it assumes for itself a role that belongs only to God. Ultimately, Edwards did not see the American colonies to be equivalent with the Kingdom of God. He knew that even within his own community there were those who disagreed with his valuation and interpretation of the Scriptures. Nevertheless, because God does create reality with that instilled meaningfulness, Edwards did expect that society as a whole reflect some concern for common truths. If a society does not share that concern for common truths, consenting to those truths as each member of society consents to other members, Edwards's theology predicts its social, spiritual, and material decay.

But morality is a tricky subject in modern times, partly because it presupposes *immorality*. Depravity is not a popular topic even among some Christians who shy away from considering its ugliness and its temporal and eternal consequences. If many sympathize with Kevorkian's motives in relieving the pain of someone suffering so apparently needlessly and meaninglessly, ought the law of society condemn him as a murderer, a sinner? Edwards asks us to consider the grounds upon which our laws define moral offense, whether those grounds be popular opinion, a standard of common morality, and/or a traditional interpretation of biblical justice. Though Kevorkian was convicted of second-degree murder, some might still be mortified to think that upon death Kevorkian may join some of his euthanasia patients in eternal hell due to God's judgment of them and their sins. Still, Edwards insists that we ask ourselves about the nature and grounds of human justice. Is that justice grounded upon a divinely-given knowledge of the cosmic God and his justice?

The answer to that question is actually an urgent matter of life and death. If a woman and her unborn child are either murdered or killed accidentally, our laws seek justice for two deaths. If that woman would have aborted the very same child, she would face no punishment whatsoever; in fact, the law allows her to murder this child. An infant who is born five months premature is intensively nursed in a neonatal unit at great cost, even though the same child could have been legally aborted. Jack Kevorkian is brought up on charges for euthanizing a terminally ill man, but millions of children are aborted every year—some on the basis of presumed illnesses. In these examples our society's conflict over morality glares at us and belies a monumental failure that costs lives every single day. What exactly is justice?

And what of God's justice? There is clearly a sense of injustice that Kevorkian's patient had to suffer so, for no obvious reason. Some may contend that Kevorkian is even more merciful than God in euthanizing Youk; no loving God would allow such suffering in the first place, much less let it continue for years. Was it just to sentence Kevorkian to prison for exercising "mercy"? Though Edwards does not fully address the suffering of the "innocent," or those who undergo trials that are not direct consequences of their own sins, his basic answer is that such suffering is part of the price of original sin. Ultimately none of us is truly "innocent." By faith someone suffering from a terrible disease may glorify God in the same manner as other Christians who are tossed into jail or worse for claiming the name of Christ. What kind of faith landed Kevorkian in jail?

Even devout Christians today will find Edwards's answer about "innocence" troubling or inadequate. We recall that Edwards does not adequately explain the origin of evil. Though God may not be the author of evil, in Edwards's system he must be its Creator in some sense. Like all products of evil, suffering must be an idea in God's mind, and he must be its sovereign disposer. For Edwards, God certainly uses our trials for his own glory and his own good ends. But should we still object that God must consequently be seen as one who toys with his creatures' lives for his own satisfaction, irrespective of their pain or concerns? Is Jack Kevorkian really the "good guy" and God the "bad guy"?

I think Edwards would respond that God's glory ought to be the ultimate human concern regardless of the circumstance, and that Christ's redemptive work has purchased eternal bliss in stark contrast to any pain encountered on earth. In this, even though modern people may point out his theological weakness and disagree with his conclusions, Edwards nevertheless asks us to recount the nature of faith. It is faith that carries the sufferer, and that faith is unshakable if grounded in election and endowed and sustained by the Spirit of Christ. Only God and Thomas Youk know of his spiritual state just prior to his being euthanized by Kevorkian. But his suffering really only takes on its proper meaning when understood against the backdrop of God's universal perspective, and when there is trust that God himself is good, loving, and faithful. For Edwards, suffering may not seem fair or just, and may stretch its bearers to the breaking point. But it retains its meaning in the plan of God, who must be trusted by faith to carry out his plan of redemption as he sees fit. Christ surely did not enjoy his suffering, but submitted to it in light of the larger, eternal goals upon which the Trinity had agreed from eternity. Christ's suffering greatly enhances the reality that our suffering is real, important, and meaningful regardless of whether we ever understand the "whys" and "hows."

When Edwards asks us to consider the nature and scope of faith, he also asks us to explore what exactly human nature is: its components and the extent of its moral dimension. Does humanity have a built-in moral dimension, and is it good? What is the ultimate origin of morality? How do the will, the intellect, the imagination, and the emotive capacity interact, particularly in relation to morality? And if Edwards is correct that there is false morality and false religiosity, what is the cause of such falsehood? Edwards asserts that religiosity and the capacity for its exercise are reliant upon the condition of the image of God, notably whether it has been regenerated. Edwards challenges us to evaluate whether the image of God is as he describes; if it is, every human bears a heavy responsibility not only for morality but for holiness before this excellent God.

Is there a proper relation that human nature ought to have with the Divine? Edwards describes an intensely personal relationship between humanity and God, one that reaches from the core of God's being to the core of human identity and back again through the indwelling of the Holy Spirit. Genuine religious experience is not only personal but communal, among people and into the reality of the Trinity. But what of the religious experience of Hindus, New Age adherents, or Confucians? Is it enough to say with Edwards that their religious experience is real but basically false, falling short of the ideal of experience granted by the Holy Spirit?

There is little question that Edwards would have been out of place in modern ecumenical discussions and inter-faith dialogue given his regard for Roman Catholics, Muslims, Jews, and those he generically refers to as heathens and pagans. In Edwards's thought, the idea of consent in community is important. But as evidenced by these views and the conflicts during his ministry at Northampton, that consent is qualified by an overarching concern for what is biblically true. Remember that Edwards was as a pastor, not a politician. Because for him the Protestant position is the only one that properly regards the Bible and its God, it *has* to be superior simply because its regard for Christ is superior; rejection of Christ and of the Godhead is not to be taken lightly. Neither is the value of religious experience, that human need for spiritual interaction with God and others that is redemptively mediated only by Christ.

So the religious experience of adherents to other faiths is real but false, still needing the remedy of the Christ's gospel, sanctification, and genuine Christian community. There is a certain amount of respect that Edwards nevertheless extends to those of other faiths; if they are devout, at least they are seeking after God, who may use their religiosity as a tool for conversion by the Holy Spirit. At least they are striving towards Edwards's ideal of a theocentric life, though they are mistaken in the manner of their pursuit. Even if the doctrine of election appalls modern democratic sensibilities, and even if Edwards's brand of ecumenism seems outdated and narrow-minded, he challenges us to define for ourselves whether God is one whose love, truth, and justice provides salvation for all and allows thoroughly valid experience of the Divine for all.

Questions about the nature of the spiritual dimension follow from this. Edwards clearly believed in the reality and power of both angels and demons, though his thought about them is somewhat speculative due to the paucity of biblical references. We can grant that if there is a spirit God, there certainly can be spiritual beings of which we may be little aware, beings who are superior to us in some ways and can influence earthly affairs. Given the popularity of neo-paganism and the paranormal, there is ample evidence that many today seek meaning in another dimension. Both Edwards and the psychic hotlines challenge us to consider the nature of that spiritual dimension, the extent and manner in which humans are involved in it, and its relation to goodness and truth. Further, we are pressed to consider God's relationship to that spiritual dimension, and his purpose for it if he is indeed sovereign. In Edwards's thought, God always looms large and always demands that we examine every issue in relation to him—his is, after all, a theocentric theology.

As we noted in the "Sinners" sermon, Edwards's thought offers its brashest challenge to those who would dare to call themselves "Christian." Is Edwards correct in his requirements for professions of faith and church membership? Are there particular doctrinal, eschatological, ecclesiological, sacramental, and behavioral expectations for one who bears the name of Christ? And given the importance of consent and harmony in the Body of Christ, what should proper relations be among denominations that disagree about matters of faith? Obviously, Edwards did not have to deal with modern denominational squabbling and schism, but he certainly advocated Protestant unity in the proclamation of the gospel. In his view, that unity was especially crucial in the context of revival because it winsomely witnesses truth and love as the message of salvation is proclaimed.

But the more crucial issue, indeed the most important one for Edwards's religious anthropology, is that unity in the Church both fosters and confirms personal and corporate holiness. Every aspect of life, as we have observed repeatedly, involves God and his holiness. Edwards challenges us to consider holiness as seriously as he did, to define its nature and scope, and to appreciate its import for eternity. To him, the meaning of life is subsumed by this single concept simply because God's holiness provides life's meaning. There is a dynamic interplay between divine and human holiness, an interplay that God intends to expand into ever-increasing glory in heavenly bliss.

We cannot know of Thomas Youk's personal holiness. But we can know how well he was cared for by those who call themselves Christians, and how well they demonstrated to him the holiness for which they profess to strive. For Edwards, Youk in some respects might represent the orphan, the poor, the widow, the outcast, or even the stricken stranger lying by the side of the road. If Christians look at the church and themselves and see a consistent failure to reach out to and care for the suffering, they will also see a failure to imitate God, who revels in reaching out from "within" the Godhead to grant and nurture life.

Edwards challenges us in the end to pursue knowledge of God, a truth that is transtemporal because it is founded in a holy God who never changes or falters. In knowing God, Christians and the church can succeed, however feebly, in imitating him and magnifying his glory through humble service to others. Through the mediation of Christ and the ministry of the Holy Spirit, the plan of God is incarnated and effected through lowly, sinful creatures who will one day perfectly remanate God's holiness in the eternal state. Edwards was blessed to see many come to faith through his labors; generations to come will judge how well Christians in our day have taken up the gospel's mantle.

How Should We Then Live?

When I was a graduate student a professor once asked me how much I agreed with Edwards's worldview. I replied that I held to most of his beliefs because I saw them to be consistent with the Scriptures, and my areas of disagreement with him were over fairly minor theological points. He mused that someone in our time could function with such an archaic worldview, though he realized that I was not the only one. He asked, "How can you live that way, day to day?" Though I don't recall my exact words, I do recall thinking, "Quite easily, thanks be to God." The bigger question that many Christians join me in asking is, "How can anyone live any other way?"

One reason for this second question is the reality that the Christian life is hard, but its difficulties pale in comparison to the struggles and strife faced by those who have no ultimate hope. The Christian life is difficult because there is an inherent opposition between "the world" and God. Further, Christian spiritual life is highly demanding when a believer is serious about the pursuit of holiness. There is painful longing to see God, painful prayer for others who are suffering, painful angst as we wrangle and wrestle with our own sin, painful humiliation when we fail the Lord, painful breaches when we are rejected for our beliefs. As Dietrich Bonhoeffer asserted, there is a "cost" to discipleship when Christians take their name and their calling seriously. But the cost and pain are nothing compared to the glory and love of God we know now, and the glory and love of God we will perfectly know someday soon, forever and ever.

The title of this book, *Jonathan Edwards for Life Today*, was intended to bear a double entendre. First, my hope was that reading Edwards's theology and being exposed to its biblical foundations would, in effect, *give life*: give substance in reflection, give pause, give hope, give conviction, give inspiration, give courage to change and to believe. If the Lord uses these pages to bring you to faith or to bring your faith new life, nothing would please me more. But it is also crystal clear to me that Edwards's theology is immensely practical and really can be *lived today*. This practical value is not primarily due to the theologian's brilliance, though that is a factor. Rather, its practical value is squarely based upon its faithfulness to the Scriptures, and the Scriptures themselves are *in truth* always supremely practical and valuable. God makes them so.

Much of what you have read of Edwards's theology is held in common by Christians around the world and across denominations, languages, and ages. These basic beliefs are essential to any Christian who professes that the Bible is God's Word, inspired without error. With this basic assumption, Christians can agree that God is Trinitarian; that the Father, Son, and Holy Spirit are the Triune Persons; that God somehow created the universe and everything in it; that God is living and active, and intimately involved today in literally everything that is occurring. And so we can confidently affirm the Apostle's Creed and joyfully pray the Lord's Prayer together with one voice, without reservation. Together we look to Christ's Second Coming with expectation and wonder, and are certain of our place in the Kingdom of Heaven. No one should wonder how a person can live in modern times with such a worldview, because the basics of this worldview transcend time and place—they originate in God's revelation of himself, and he is utterly trustworthy, faithful, and true.

The sticking point lies in the fact that while Christians are living out a biblical worldview that in its essentials has never changed, not all agree upon the definition and significance of the "non-essentials." Even solidly biblical theologians come to different conclusions when thinking about the meaning of the sacraments, election, the place of good works in redemption, how God's sovereignty interplays with human will, and eschatology, just to name a few. The crux is that some Christians simply do not love other Christians who disagree with them about such topics. Then there are some Christians who are biblically illiterate and do not know enough theology to disagree, but also do not know enough to grow consistently in faith or share their faith with others. On the heels of these issues comes the reality that not all Christians live as faithfully as one might hope or expect. Edwards expected Christians to disagree because we are finite people, still sinning even while we strive to be obedient. But then, sometimes Christians cannot even agree on what it means to be obedient. Though many Christians accomplish much for the Lord, there unfortunately remains no shortage of arguments, dissension, and gossip that they carry on, instead of loving each other as they ought. How much time, energy, and money is wasted in this manner, when it should be spent sharing the gospel, feeding the hungry, and caring for orphans and widows?

So I have told you that the Christian life is marvelous and most difficult. I have confirmed what you probably already know: that Christians can be terrible witnesses of the love of God, that Christians are at times especially vicious toward other Christians, and that all of this rancor leads a good many people to ask, "Why would anyone *want* to be a

Christian?" Or, adding another dimension to my professor's question, "Why would anyone *want* to live that way?"

With Edwards in mind, we recall that nobody really wants to be a Christian! Submitting ourselves to God, professing faith in Christ, worshipping and studying the Bible—sinners do not want to undertake these activities. We sinners do not want to live God's way, or do anything God's way. But when we are blessed with salvation through faith in Jesus Christ and the Holy Spirit indwells us, the difference should be night and day.

The difference starts with being enabled by the Holy Spirit to love God truly, deeply, honestly, with everything we are and ever will be. Remember just some of the words Edwards uses to describe God: living, active, holy, creative, omnipotent, joyful, loving, glorious, wise, excellent, great, beautiful, lovely, vibrant, effulgent, harmonious, dynamic, perfect, communicative, radiant, self-loving, consenting, happy, self-sufficient, eternal, omniscient, good, worthy, merciful, omnipresent, faithful, immutable, and all of this beyond our comprehension. A Christian's heart sings at each of these words because they attempt to capture who God is: a God who loves us more than we will ever understand, has rescued us from eternal death, made us new creations, sustained us, blessed us, and promised us eternal glory in his presence. But if an unregenerate person or a sleepy, lazy Christian reads these words, he will be turned off, bored, in a hurry to skip over them, unimpressed, and may feel no guilt for this apathy or disgust.

Another dimension to this difference between night and day lies in loving God more than we love ourselves, others, or anything else—especially the busyness and materialism that are common idols today. The Holy Spirit indwells believers and therefore provides the "fuel" for us to be earnest and ardent in our devotion to the Lord. While this love for God does include emotions, there is more to it than mere emotions, as Edwards touches on regarding "religious affections." This love requires thoughtfulness about life, how life relates to the Bible, what God teaches us from day to day, who God has made us to be, and how our actions and words are to demonstrate that we belong to God. It also involves action, putting into gestures what the Spirit builds and shapes in our souls. And this love encompasses praising God, defending God, speaking about God, spending time with God in conversation (prayer), knowing God better and better, imploring God, and pouring our lives out before God.

This kind of love is all-consuming because Christ is the Lord of *all* of our lives, in every respect. God comes first in our lives, always, to the best of our abilities. Sinners don't want this kind of a life . . . but sinners who have been redeemed grow and mature in faith to want nothing else.

When Christians are loving and worshipping God as they ought, when living is Christ and dying is gain, when all else is dung compared to the phenomenal gift and privilege of knowing and loving Jesus Christ (Phil 1:21; 3:7–11), the difference is night and day. In some Christian congregations today there is a vibrant, striking, wonder-filled resemblance with the early Church described in Acts 2:42–47. This kind of loving, selfless fellowship is so unlike any other gathering, be it at a sports event, a bar, a pizza joint, a bowling alley . . . and miles from the lonely, solitary existence many people today bear. In its prime, the church *is* a family of God's children who have been bonded eternally through the power of the Holy Spirit. And what Edwards correctly describes as the church's ideals are lived out—not perfectly—but joyfully lived out to God's glory. But it does not stop there.

When Christians are loving God as they ought, they love fellow believers deeply but also refuse to dam up or hoard that love. They speak of God publicly, not to force-feed people with the Bible but to remind them of their *spiritual emergency*. Those apart from Christ are "dead people walking," dead in their sins and transgressions just as all Christians once were. Believers share the good news about salvation through faith in Christ and do so regardless of their own shyness or insecurities. Talking about their Savior is as natural to them as discussing a dearly loved one who's come to live with them. And like Edwards they genuinely care about those who do not yet believe. They pray fervently to see their friends, family members, coworkers, and acquaintances turn to Christ forever.

As Edwards shows us, God deserves and requires nothing less than our complete selves in loving obedience. Because we humans are too sinful and feeble to meet these requirements, we *need* Jesus Christ. If there is one thing that Edwards's "Sinners" sermon is representative of in his entire theology, it is his tangible sense of urgency in pleading with sinners to repent of their sinfulness, turn to Christ, and believe. Edwards knew that apart from Christ a soul is in a constant state of emergency, first because our lives are fragile and precarious, and second because apart from God's mercy and grace we ultimately can do only harm to ourselves and others. Edwards did expect mature Christians to share in this sense of urgency, and his preaching and teaching led many to do just that. And he prayed that many would respond to the Holy Spirit by re-dedicating themselves to greater faithfulness or confessing faith in Jesus Christ for the first time. During the Great Awakening, tens of thousands in America and Europe did just that.

So what will you do?

Bibliography

Alexis, Gerhard T. "Jonathan Edwards and the Theocratic Ideal." *Church History* 35 (1966) 328–43.
Carse, James. *Jonathan Edwards and the Visibility of God.* New York: Scribner, 1967.
Cherry, C. Conrad. "Symbols of Spiritual Truth: Jonathan Edwards as Biblical Interpreter." *Interpretation* 39 (1985) 263–71.
Daniel, Stephen. *The Philosophy of Jonathan Edwards: A Study in Divine Semiotics.* Bloomington: Indiana University Press, 1994.
Donne, John. *Devotions upon Emergent Occasions.* Edited by John Sparrow. Cambridge: Cambridge University Press, 1923. Meditation 17.
Edwards, Jonathan. *The Works of Jonathan Edwards.* Vol. 2. Edinburgh: Banner of Truth Trust, 1974.
———. *The Works of Jonathan Edwards, Vol. 1: Freedom of the Will.* Edited by Paul Ramsey. New Haven: Yale University Press, 1957.
———. *The Works of Jonathan Edwards, Vol. 2: Religious Affections.* Edited by John E. Smith. New Haven: Yale University Press, 1959.
———. *The Works of Jonathan Edwards, Vol. 3: Original Sin.* Edited by Clyde A. Holbrook. New Haven: Yale University Press, 1970.
———. *The Works of Jonathan Edwards, Vol. 4: The Great Awakening.* Edited by C. C. Goen. New Haven: Yale University Press, 1972.
———. *The Works of Jonathan Edwards, Vol. 5: Apocalyptic Writings.* Edited by Stephen J. Stein. New Haven: Yale University Press, 1977.
———. *The Works of Jonathan Edwards, Vol. 6: Scientific and Philosophical Writings.* Edited by Wallace E. Anderson. New Haven: Yale University Press, 1980.
———. *The Works of Jonathan Edwards, Vol. 7: The Life of David Brainerd.* Edited by Norman Pettit. New Haven: Yale University Press, 1985.
———. *The Works of Jonathan Edwards, Vol. 8: Ethical Writings.* Edited by Paul Ramsey. New Haven: Yale University Press, 1989.
———. *The Works of Jonathan Edwards, Vol. 9: A History of the Work of Redemption.* Edited by John F. Wilson. New Haven: Yale University Press, 1989.
———. *The Works of Jonathan Edwards, Vol. 10: Sermons and Discourses 1720–1723.* Edited by Wilson H. Kimnach. New Haven: Yale University Press, 1992.
———. *The Works of Jonathan Edwards, Vol. 11: Typological Writings.* Edited by Wallace E. Anderson and Mason I. Lowance Jr., with David Watters. New Haven: Yale University Press, 1993.
———. *The Works of Jonathan Edwards, Vol. 12: Ecclesiastical Writings.* Edited by David D. Hall. New Haven: Yale University Press, 1994.

———. *The Works of Jonathan Edwards, Vol. 13: The "Miscellanies," a–500.* Edited by Thomas A. Schafer. New Haven: Yale University Press, 1994.

———. *The Works of Jonathan Edwards, Vol. 14: Sermons and Discourses, 1723–1729.* Edited by Kenneth P. Minkema. New Haven: Yale University Press, 1997.

———. *The Works of Jonathan Edwards, Vol. 15: Notes on Scripture.* Edited by Stephen J. Stein. New Haven: Yale University Press, 1998.

———. *The Works of Jonathan Edwards, Vol. 16: Letters and Personal Writings.* Edited by George S. Claghorn. New Haven: Yale University Press, 1998.

———. *The Works of Jonathan Edwards, Vol. 17: Sermons and Discourses, 1730–1733.* Edited by Mark Valeri. New Haven: Yale University Press, 1999.

———. *The Works of Jonathan Edwards, Vol. 18: The "Miscellanies," Entry Nos. 501–832.* Edited by Ava Chamberlain. New Haven: Yale University Press, 2000.

———. *The Works of Jonathan Edwards, Vol. 19: Sermons and Discourses, 1734–1738.* Edited by M. X. Lesser. New Haven: Yale University Press, 2001.

———. *The Works of Jonathan Edwards, Vol. 20: The "Miscellanies," Entry Nos. 833–1152.* Edited by Amy Plantinga Pauw. New Haven: Yale University Press, 2002.

———. *The Works of Jonathan Edwards, Vol. 21: Writings on the Trinity, Grace, and Faith.* Edited by Sang Hyun Lee. New Haven: Yale University Press, 2003.

———. *The Works of Jonathan Edwards, Vol. 22: Sermons and Discourses, 1739–1742.* Edited by Harry S. Stout and Nathan O. Hatch, with Kyle P. Farley. New Haven: Yale University Press, 2003.

———. *The Works of Jonathan Edwards, Vol. 23: The "Miscellanies," Entry Nos. 1153–1360.* Edited by Douglas A. Sweeney. New Haven: Yale University Press, 2004.

———. *The Works of Jonathan Edwards, Vol. 24, Pts. 1 & 2: The "Blank Bible."* Edited by Stephen J. Stein. New Haven: Yale University Press, 2006.

———. *The Works of Jonathan Edwards, Vol. 25: Sermons and Discourses, 1743–1758.* Edited by Wilson H. Kimnach. New Haven: Yale University Press, 2006.

Jenson, Robert W. *America's Theologian: A Recommendation of Jonathan Edwards.* New York: Oxford University Press, 1988.

Jinkins, Michael. "'The Being of Beings': Jonathan Edwards' Understanding of God as Reflected in His Final Treatises." *Scottish Journal of Theology* 46 (1993) 161–90.

Lee, Sang Hyun. *The Philosophical Theology of Jonathan Edwards.* Princeton: Princeton University Press, 1988.

———. "Jonathan Edwards on Nature." In *Faithful Imagining: Essays in Honor of Richard R. Niebuhr,* edited by Lee et al., 39–59. Atlanta: Scholars, 1995.

Logan, Samuel T. "The Doctrine of Justification in the Theology of Jonathan Edwards." *Westminster Theological Journal* 46 (1984) 26–52.

Lovelace, Richard. *Dynamics of Spiritual Life: An Evangelical Theology of Renewal.* Downers Grove, IL: InterVarsity, 1979.

Mavrodes, George I. "Is the Past Unpreventable?" *Faith and Philosophy* 1 (1984) 131–46.

McClymond, Michael J. *Encounters with God: An Approach to the Theology of Jonathan Edwards.* New York: Oxford University Press, 1998.

Minkema, Kenneth P. "The Other Unfinished 'Great Work'": Jonathan Edwards, Messianic Prophecy, and 'The Harmony of the Old and New Testament.'" In *Jonathan Edwards's Writings,* edited by Stephen J. Stein, 52–65. Bloomington: Indiana University Press, 1996.

Murray, Ian. *Jonathan Edwards: A New Biography.* Edinburgh: Banner of Truth, 1987.

Pauw, Amy Plantinga. "'Heaven Is a World of Love': Edwards on Heaven and the Trinity." *Calvin Theological Journal* 30 (1995) 392–400.

Plantinga, Alvin. "On Ockham's Way Out." *Faith and Philosophy* 3 (July 1986) 235–69.

Schafer, Thomas. "Jonathan Edwards' Conception of the Church." *Church History* 24 (1955) 51–66.

Simonson, Harold P. *Jonathan Edwards: Theologian of the Heart*. Grand Rapids: Eerdmans, 1974.

Stahle, Rachel. "The Trinitarian Spirit of Jonathan Edwards' Theology." PhD diss., Boston University, 1999.

———. "Jonathan Edwards on Pastoral Ministry." *Pittsburgh Theological Journal* (May 2009).

Storms, C. Samuel. *Tragedy in Eden: Original Sin in the Theology of Jonathan Edwards*. Lanham, MD: University Press of America, 1985.

Strauss, James D. "A Puritan in a Post-Puritan World—Jonathan Edwards." In *Grace Unlimited*, edited by Clark H. Pinnock. Minneapolis: Bethany Fellowship, 1975; reprint, Wipf & Stock, 1999.

Westra, Helen Petter. "'Above All Others': Jonathan Edwards and the Gospel Ministry." *American Presbyterians* 67 (1989) 209–19.

Wilson, John F. "History, Redemption, and the Millennium." In *Jonathan Edwards and the American Experience*, edited by Nathan O. Hatch and Harry S. Stout, 131–41. New York: Oxford University Press, 1988.

Wilson-Kastner, Patricia. *Coherence in a Fragmented World: Jonathan Edwards' Theology of the Holy Spirit*. Washington, DC: University Press of America, 1978.

Index

Adam, 27, 39, 51–52, 56, 59–71, 95, 109–10, 125, 151, 158, 160, 163
Angels, 13, 25, 28, 33–34, 55, 67, 92, 121, 149, 156, 158–59, 161n98, 163–69, 173, 179, 186
Animals, 3, 4, 28, 74, 96, 137
Antichrist, 131n5, 149, 151–53
Antitypes, 45, 53–54, 73
Assurance of Salvation, 92–93, 132, 137
Atonement, 54–56, 70, 100, 144
Attributes, Divine, 9–11, 16, 26–28, 30, 46, 173
Authority, Pastoral, 121, 125, 139
Authority, Divine, 18, 34–35, 55, 64, 143, 156n57
Authority, Scriptural, 6, 60, 154

Baptism, 58–59, 85, 115, 117–18
Beauty, 9, 15–16, 21, 28–33, 44, 69, 78, 82, 85, 86n67, 88, 89n83, 90, 101, 106–9, 157, 166, 167n138
Bellamy, Joseph, 68n95
Bible, 6, 12n52, 36, 45–47, 60–62, 66, 71–75, 85, 88, 90, 95, 98, 111, 113, 122, 125, 129, 131–32, 137, 141, 154, 157, 160n91, 171–72, 175, 180–83, 185–86, 188–91
Body, of Christ, 51, 58, 104, 106, 109, 114–15, 124, 154, 167, 186
Body, Human, 28, 41, 60, 69, 77–79, 85, 88, 98, 106, 115, 156n63, 157, 160, 163, 165–67, 182
Brainerd, David, 36n70, 84n53, 121n113, 125

Cause, God as, 6–9, 15, 28, 40, 65, 89
Charity, 88–89, 92, 93n116, 120, 141–42
Chauncy, Charles, 138
Children, 20, 69n104, 88n80, 91n99, 99, 117–18, 122, 129, 141, 179, 183
Children of the Devil, 176, 179
Children of God, 56, 93, 107–8, 123, 131, 168, 174, 179, 191
Colman, Benjamin, 81n37, 132n12
Community, Divine, 17, 40, 58n48, 104, 114
Community, Divine-Human, 21, 29–30, 58n48, 59, 86n67, 106, 107n21, 108, 110, 116, 164
Community, Human, 40, 104, 106, 114–15, 118, 164, 183, 185–86
Conscience, 39–40, 79, 135, 154n48, 155
Consent, 15–21, 29, 31–32, 34, 40, 44, 62–3, 70, 79, 84–85, 96, 98, 109, 115, 124, 168, 183, 185–86
Contingency, 6, 7, 37
Continuous Creation, 36, 40–42, 46, 53, 58, 73n124, 87n73, 87n74, 88n78, 90, 105, 148, 162, 164, 181
Conversion, 80–86, 89, 91–92, 94, 96–98, 100, 104, 113, 119, 125–26, 130–32, 142, 144n87, 153, 179, 186
Covenant of Grace, 52, 84, 106n17, 110, 116–18, 173–74
Covenant of Redemption, 18–21, 24, 49, 52, 84, 157
Covenant of Works, 51–52, 54, 63, 68n97

197

Creation, 6–8, 10–11, 17–21, 24–48, 53–57, 60, 62, 67, 70, 78, 82, 85–86, 96, 105, 107, 124, 131, 133, 148, 154, 157–58, 164, 166, 174–76, 181, 190

Damnation, 27, 69, 84n54, 122, 162, 175, 177–78
Davenport, James, 138
Deism, 40, 61, 111, 123n128
Demons, 25, 67, 87, 98, 101, 112, 113n64, 134–35, 139, 141n59, 145, 153, 158n74, 159–61, 186
The Devil, 64, 67n93, 115n73, 126, 132n13, 133, 137–40, 142n70, 145, 152, 156, 158n74, 159–61, 176, 179
Devils, 141n59, 153, 160–61, 175
Donne, John, 104
Dudley, Paul, 3

Edwards, Jonathan, Jr., 68n95
Edwards, Sarah Pierpont, 122n122
Effulgence, 10, 57, 190
The Elect, 21, 51, 53–59, 62, 66, 68n96, 70, 74, 79, 84, 87, 92, 96, 101, 106, 134, 145, 149, 153, 156–57, 164–66, 168
Election, 50–52, 55, 71, 92–3, 105, 114, 163, 184, 186, 189
Emanation, 11, 46, 74
End Times, 53, 57, 131n5, 148–69
Error in Revival, 133–34, 136, 138–39, 143, 160n85
Erskine, John, 81n36
Essence, Divine, 6, 8, 9n29, 12–14, 16–18, 20, 41–42, 87–88, 107
Eternal Life, 50–51, 55, 57, 63, 70, 71n114, 85, 114, 121, 157, 164n116, 165n127, 166, 168
Eternal Plan of Redemption, 33–40, 44, 57, 59, 64, 71–72, 104, 109, 114, 130, 156–57, 174, 181
Eternity, 12, 14, 18, 25, 31, 50, 52, 64, 74, 90, 105, 165n127, 179, 185

Evangelical Humiliation, 81–82, 96, 101, 173, 188
Eve, 27, 63, 68–69, 95, 151, 160
Evil, 7, 9, 40, 62–8, 70, 78, 98, 138, 140, 156, 158, 161–62, 184
Excellence, 7, 9–11, 14–16, 18, 25, 26n13, 27–32, 37, 65, 80, 85, 87n71, 89–90, 98, 101, 106, 108, 113n67, 114, 136n36, 159, 161, 163–64, 167n138, 173, 181
Excess in Revival, 135–39
Experience, Religious, 91, 93, 98, 104–26, 137, 164n120, 185–86
Extraordinary Gifts of the Holy Spirit, 20, 59, 112–14

Faith, 20, 36, 44, 50, 52, 61, 69n104, 71, 80, 83, 89, 96–101, 109, 111–21, 124–25, 130–32, 134, 137–38, 142–45, 152, 172, 174, 177–78, 180–81, 184–92
The Fall, 18, 29n29, 62–69, 84, 85n61, 95, 158
Federal Theology, 56, 62–63, 106, 118
First Great Awakening, 81n36, 82n40, 112, 113n64, 123, 131–35, 138–40, 144, 149
Foreknowledge, Divine, 37–38, 50, 52, 95
Free Will, 67, 92–97, 189
Fruits of the Holy Spirit, 37, 80, 83, 89–90, 92, 93n116, 98, 104, 108, 112, 115, 130, 132, 149
The Future, 28, 57, 72, 119, 150, 154n48, 173

Glorification of God, 12–13, 17–18, 24, 44, 50, 77, 97, 154
Glorification of the Saints, 59, 90n97, 157, 167
Glory of God, 10–15, 20, 24, 25n4, 26n13, 28n20, 29–35, 37, 42, 45–47, 53, 54n23, 55, 57, 64, 74, 81–86, 88, 91, 94, 97, 100, 102, 105, 107, 109–10, 115, 121, 123–24, 134,

136, 155–57, 159, 164, 166, 168, 175, 184, 187–88, 190–91
The Godhead, 11–16, 18, 20–21, 24–26, 31–32, 37, 54–55, 58, 87–88, 104, 108–9, 114, 157, 165, 168, 185, 187
Grace, 20, 37–38, 51n10, 52, 55, 63, 65, 67, 70, 80–81, 83–84, 88, 89n91, 90n96, 91–94, 99–102, 105–6, 108, 110–11, 114, 122–23, 132, 136, 139, 142–43, 145, 149, 158–59, 162, 164, 167–68, 174, 191

Habits, 39, 40n101, 70, 84, 89, 90n96, 94–95, 142
Harmony, 15, 31–33, 37, 44, 46, 53n20, 62, 114, 123n125, 148, 168, 186
Heaven, 20, 24, 45n123, 51, 53–54, 57, 65–66, 73, 84, 91n100, 102, 106, 114, 119, 131n5, 132, 134, 136, 144, 148-9, 153, 155–59, 161n98, 162–69, 177–78, 182, 189
Hell, 53, 134, 144, 153, 155–63, 167, 171–73, 177–80, 182–83
History, 18, 21, 27, 36n70, 42–43, 45n123, 45n125, 47, 51–57, 59–62, 67n94, 72–73, 86, 96, 110, 111n54, 131, 148, 154–55, 181
Holiness, Divine, 7, 9–11, 14–16, 18, 26, 28–29, 34, 37, 39, 55, 58, 60, 63–64, 66n92, 67, 69, 101, 113, 136, 155n53, 162, 164, 187
Holiness, Human, 21, 28–29, 51, 55–56, 63, 83n51, 84–93, 97–98, 106, 113–14, 117, 122, 141, 157, 160, 164–65, 167, 185, 187–88
Hope, 46, 89, 117, 144, 149n5, 157, 175, 188
Hopkins, Samuel, 68n95
Human Nature, 54, 57n45, 58, 95, 164, 185
Hypocrites, 80, 100–101, 119, 132, 138n44, 140n54, 143, 153

Idealism, 11–15, 16n71, 29n30, 42–44, 49, 53, 62, 67, 77, 108, 157, 165, 184
Illumination, Divine, 74, 87n74, 88, 97
Image of God, in Christ, 19, 59, 71, 84
Image of God, Human, 8n23, 28–30, 40–41, 43, 59, 70, 80, 84, 87, 90n97, 114, 182, 185
Imagination, 86–87, 92, 112, 131, 135, 137–38, 160, 185
Imputation, 56, 68, 70, 97
Incarnation of Christ, 19, 46, 53–55, 57n45, 58, 60–61, 72, 110, 121, 156, 164–65, 168
Indwelling by the Holy Spirit, 20–21, 36, 58–61, 74, 79, 86–88, 90, 92–93, 99, 101, 107, 112, 118, 137, 144, 185, 190
Inspiration, Divine, 45, 60, 71–73, 112, 133–34, 188
Instinct, 39n96, 162
Intelligent Beings, 4, 25, 28–30, 33–36, 42, 63, 87, 123n128, 163
Islam, 111, 125, 153, 185

Jews, 109–14, 144, 152n31, 153, 185
Joy, 9–11, 13, 15, 19, 21, 24, 26, 28–29, 31, 51, 63, 74, 78, 86n67, 88, 90n97, 92, 96, 101, 106–9, 112, 151, 153, 154n48, 167, 169, 179, 185, 191
Judgment Day, 61, 116, 117n91, 126, 140n54, 144n87, 148, 154–58, 165–66
Justice, Divine, 27, 34n57, 51, 53n22, 58, 64, 66n92, 81, 110, 144, 155, 162, 172–73, 175, 183–84, 186
Justification, 56, 70–71, 85, 97

Kevorkian, Jack, 181–84
Kingdom of Antichrist/Satan, 131n5, 135, 140, 149–53, 160
Kingdom of God, 24, 72, 84n57, 102, 105, 108–9, 114, 122, 123n131, 124, 126, 130, 131n5, 132, 140, 145, 148–49, 152–53, 160, 164, 175, 183, 189

Knowledge, Divine, 10–12
Knowledge, Human, 4–6, 10, 20, 29–30, 39, 68, 74, 81, 86, 88–90, 91n99, 119, 126, 153, 155n50, 162, 165, 182–83, 187

Light, 10, 46, 87, 89–90, 101, 121, 133, 136, 144–45, 152–53, 155, 157n67, 166–67, 176, 178
Locke, John, 9n30
Logic, 6, 8, 14, 18, 38n89, 50, 67, 95
Lord's Supper, 115–16, 118
Lucifer, 159

Membership, Church, 51, 58, 118, 143, 186
The Millennium, 117n91, 149–54
Mind, Divine, 6, 29, 42, 44, 67–68, 95, 112, 113n67, 134, 164n123, 165, 184
Mind, Human, 6, 13, 25n4, 29, 34, 38n89, 42–44, 65, 67, 68n96, 74, 77, 79, 81, 87–88, 90, 94–95, 107, 137n38, 164n123, 167–68
Ministers, 120–22, 125, 133, 139, 143–44
Missions, 36n70, 81n37, 93n115, 105, 121n113, 125
Mystical Dimension, 53n21, 58, 85, 106, 154, 165

Old Light/New Light Controversy, 138–40, 142
Order, 4, 6, 28n18, 32–36, 44, 49, 53n20, 53n22, 54, 67, 72, 74, 81, 96, 115, 123n125, 135n30, 155, 163–69, 181
Ordinary Gifts of the Holy Spirit, 112–14
Original Sin, 40, 61, 69–70, 94, 184
Outpouring of the Holy Spirit, 109, 113, 123, 126, 131n8, 133, 136, 150, 175

Partaking of God, 20–21, 59, 78, 86n67, 88, 107–9, 141

Participation in God, 30, 86n67, 106, 108, 121
Pastors, 83n50, 93, 118, 120–22, 125, 143–44, 185
Peace, 58, 70, 108, 116, 125, 141, 151, 153, 155
Pentecost, 109, 112–13, 134, 153, 175
Pepperrell, Mary, 17
Persons of the Trinity, 11–21, 24, 26, 29, 32, 43, 55, 189
Piety, 100, 119, 123, 141n69, 142–43
Prayer, 55, 74, 90n96, 98–99, 114, 120, 122–26, 141, 143, 150, 178, 188–90
Preaching, 36, 38, 71n116, 74, 98, 112, 114, 121–22, 125–26, 134, 139, 143–44, 152, 172–75, 177, 179
Prophecy, 72, 73n126, 112–14, 134, 148, 153n38, 175
Providence, 34–39, 40n103, 49, 67n94, 72, 86, 95, 110n43, 120, 122n125, 134n19, 148, 150, 155, 157, 166, 174

Reality, 3–4, 6, 8, 21n99, 24–26, 28, 31–33, 38, 40–45, 49, 53n20, 54, 73, 104, 148, 157, 163, 168, 175, 181, 183
Reason, 11, 16n71, 28n23, 29–30, 35–36, 39, 61, 79, 94–95, 138, 154n48, 161, 163n113, 177, 181
Redemption, 17–27, 33–40, 44, 49–72, 84, 86, 92, 96–97, 104, 107, 109–17, 130, 135, 148, 149n10, 154, 156–57, 160–63, 165–68, 174–76, 181, 184, 189
Regeneration, 82, 84–85, 91, 97, 105
Religion, False, 80, 92, 98–102, 111, 126, 137, 139–40, 145, 153, 174, 178, 185–86
Religion, True, 54, 98, 101, 106, 112, 116, 125, 132, 137–38, 144–45, 149, 151, 153, 160, 166
Religious Affections, 79, 97–102, 122, 135–37, 145, 167n138, 177–78, 190
Renewal, 113, 126, 130–45

Repentance, 80, 84, 91, 100, 156, 177, 179, 191
Reprobation, 51n10, 53, 68n96, 156
Resurrection of Christ, 54, 56–57, 70–71, 156
Resurrection of the Dead, 85, 152, 156n63, 157, 166n130
Revelation, 4–6, 12, 24, 30, 35–36, 42, 44–45, 54–55, 60–62, 69, 71–75, 86, 88, 90, 104–5, 111–13, 125, 134, 137, 145, 155n50, 158, 175, 181–82, 189
Revival, 112, 113n64, 123, 130–45, 149–51, 152n32, 187
Roman Catholicism, 125, 151–52, 185

Sacraments, 98, 115–17, 120, 126, 186, 189
The Saints, 13, 21, 34, 54, 57, 60, 62, 80n32, 86, 92, 94, 99–101, 105–11, 121–22, 131, 136, 142, 150–52, 155–57, 160–61, 163
Salvation, 4, 6, 19–20, 35–36, 49, 50n7, 51–53, 56, 62, 70–74, 82–84, 89, 91–94, 97, 101, 104, 108, 111, 114, 116–17, 122, 126, 137, 138n44, 141, 143–44, 160, 163n112, 168, 175, 186–87, 190–91
Sanctification, 58–59, 61, 85n61, 90n97, 91–92, 97, 104–5, 108, 113, 116, 117n91, 132, 134, 186
Satan, 64, 79, 82, 92, 100–101, 105, 131n5, 134n19, 135, 137–40, 142, 145, 149–55, 158–63, 176
Scripture, 4–6, 10n40, 11, 14n62, 16–17, 24n1, 36, 45, 50n4, 53, 56, 60–62, 66, 71–74, 83–86, 90, 100, 108, 115n77, 116, 119–20, 131–35, 142–43, 151, 153–54, 163, 174, 183, 188
Second Adam, 56, 59, 68n96, 118
Sense of the Heart, 88–90, 97, 119
Sewall, Samuel, 17
Sin, 18–19, 24, 29n29, 33–36, 39–40, 45, 49–75, 78–81, 83–87, 91–94, 97, 100–101, 113n64, 114, 121, 130, 131n8, 133–36, 139–40, 142n70, 144, 148, 155, 157n67, 159n78, 159n79, 160–63, 165, 172–73, 176–79, 184, 188
The Soul, 8n25, 25, 28, 29n29, 41, 43, 46, 59–60, 65, 69–70, 77–79, 81–82, 84–92, 96–98, 100, 105–6, 108, 113, 115, 119, 122, 136–37, 141–42, 154n48, 157, 161, 162n106, 163, 165n130, 167, 178, 182, 191
Sovereignty of God, 18, 34–38, 40–44, 50, 64, 66–67, 70, 78, 81n37, 82, 84, 122n125, 124, 134n19, 140, 159n78, 161n95, 164n116, 172–73, 175, 184, 186, 189
Spiritual Conviction, 80–82, 100, 135, 156
Stoddard, Solomon, 118n95

Time, 17–18, 28n24, 36n70, 38, 40–44, 45n125, 46–47, 49, 60, 62, 96, 104–5, 109, 114, 172, 174
The Trinity, 5–21, 24–47, 49, 54–55, 57–60, 80n28, 86, 106, 109, 114–15, 154, 168, 171–72, 181, 185, 189
Truth, 5, 10, 21n99, 33, 43–45, 60–62, 73–74, 80, 85, 88, 100–101, 126, 132n13, 135, 171, 183, 186–88
Types, 33–6, 53, 72–73, 85n64, 91n99, 110–11, 116, 129–30, 148–49, 152n31, 154, 159, 161, 176, 181

Unity, Christian, 70n109, 105–6, 109, 124, 138, 166–67, 187
Unity, Divine-Human, 29, 34, 56, 58, 77–78, 86n67, 88, 106–8, 123, 164, 166, 168
Unity, Trinitarian, 15, 18, 168
The Unregenerate, 80, 90, 92, 100–101, 151, 161, 172, 179–80, 190

Watts, Isaac, 115n77
Will, Divine, 9, 29n26, 72, 95, 112, 150, 167

Wisdom, 7, 10, 12, 27–28, 32, 35, 38, 40–41, 57n45, 61, 67, 68n96, 86, 89–90
Word of God, 62, 71, 73–74, 98, 116, 119–21, 134, 137–38, 143, 152, 154, 175, 180
Works, 30, 50n7, 51–52, 92, 97–100, 104, 108, 112, 136, 143, 144n87, 156, 189
Worship, 5, 6, 34, 61n65, 105, 110, 112, 114–20, 122, 123n128, 124, 130, 141, 179–80, 190–91

Youk, Thomas, 181–87

www.ingramcontent.com/pod-product-compliance
Lightning Source LLC
Chambersburg PA
CBHW031816220426
43662CB00007B/673